Rethinking Reference for Academic Libraries

Rethinking Reference for Academic Libraries

Innovative Developments and Future Trends

Edited by
Carrie Forbes
Jennifer Bowers

ROWMAN & LITTLEFIELD
Lanham • Boulder • New York • London

Published by Rowman & Littlefield
A wholly owned subsidiary of The Rowman & Littlefield Publishing Group, Inc.
4501 Forbes Boulevard, Suite 200, Lanham, Maryland 20706
www.rowman.com

16 Carlisle Street, London W1D 3BT, United Kingdom

British Library Cataloguing in Publication Information Available

Library of Congress Cataloging-in-Publication Data

Rethinking reference for academic libraries : innovative developments and future trends / edited by Carrie Forbes, Jennifer Bowers.
p. cm.
Includes bibliographical references and index.
ISBN 978-1-4422-4451-1 (cloth : alk. paper) – ISBN 978-1-4422-4452-8 (pbk. : alk. paper) – ISBN 978-1-4422-4453-5 (ebook)
1. Academic libraries–Reference services. 2. Academic librarians–Effect of technological innovations on. 3. Libraries–Special collections–Electronic information resources. 4. Academic libraries–United States–Case studies. I. Forbes, Carrie, 1975– editor. II. Bowers, Jennifer, 1962– editor.
Z675.U5R4567 2015
025.5'2777–dc23
2014031996

Printed in the United States of America

Contents

Acknowledgments

We would like to thank Martin Dillon, our editor at Rowman & Littlefield, for his encouragement, insightful recommendations, and thoughtful guidance throughout this project. We would also like to thank our colleagues Michael Levine-Clark and Peggy Keeran for their wise counsel and Martin Garner for his timely suggestions, as well as recognizing our colleagues in the Reference Department at the University of Denver for their support and enthusiasm for embracing innovative reference services. Finally, we wish to acknowledge our contributors' hard work, dedication, and valuable expertise, which made editing this volume a pleasure.

Introduction

Reimagining Reference and Research Services for the Twenty-First-Century Academic Library

Jennifer Bowers and Carrie Forbes

The current literature on postsecondary education indicates that the system of higher education is at a tipping point, and that it will soon look nothing like it does today. At a time when college revenues and cash reserves are down, many institutions are facing bigger debts and ever-increasing expenses. Furthermore, too many students now must borrow heavily just to keep pace with tuition increases. Institutions of all types are struggling to meet the realities of today's economy as they grapple with shrinking resources, increasing demand, and calls for accountability.[1]

At the same time, higher education is challenged to meet the needs of a new generation of college students. Data show that our institutions of higher learning currently serve only about a third of students well. More and more students are from low-income families, or they are older, juggling life, jobs, and family as they pursue their educations. They are often first-generation college-goers who lack the support and guidance crucial to navigating the thicket that is higher education. These students need highly personalized coaching, mentoring, and other supports tailored to their individual needs and goals.[2] Emerging technologies and partnerships with communities and corporations hold promise for making this kind of personalization possible by enabling colleges to effectively target these diverse student needs while reducing costs.[3]

All of these trends in higher education have impacted academic libraries and continue to shape reference and research services. In particular, collaboration with campus partners, diverse student populations, technological innovations, the need for assessment, and new professional competencies present new challenges and opportunities for creating a twenty-first-century learning environment. In order to reimagine reference service, librarians must not only understand, but also embrace these emerging reference practices. This edited volume, containing five sections and fourteen chapters, reviews the current state of reference services in academic libraries with an emphasis on innovative developments and future trends. The main theme that runs through the book is the urgent need for inventive, imaginative, and responsive reference and research services. Through literature reviews and case studies, this book provides professionals with a convenient compilation of timely issues and models at comparable institutions. As academic libraries shift from functioning primarily as collections repositories to serving as key players in discovery and knowledge creation, value-added services, such as reference, are even more central to libraries' and universities' changing missions.

COLLABORATION: PARTNERSHIPS FOR LIFELONG LEARNING

Collaboration is a common refrain that runs throughout the recent Association of College and Research Libraries (ACRL) *Environmental Scan 2013* report. Designed to be a guide for future planning, the report identifies key trends and factors that will influence the direction academic libraries take as they strive to meet the needs of their communities and adapt to the changing higher education landscape.[4] The report outlines opportunities for collaboration and partnerships to support ongoing and emerging forms of scholarship, including digital humanities projects, data curation, and online publishing; central to these efforts will be the imperative to take a more active role in the research process. In addition, building on a shared goal of fostering student learning through effective practices, libraries can partner with campus stakeholders to assess and analyze student learning and outcomes. The report also calls for libraries to work with other groups and departments on campus to create shared spaces for innovation and collaboration, such as those represented by Digital Scholarship Centers, as well as to consider radical collaborative endeavors to merge technical services and collections with external institutions. Efforts to integrate the library more fully into the academic enterprise will underscore the value of libraries' contributions to their institutions' educational mission.

Although the ACRL report discusses collaborative opportunities for libraries in general, a survey of the professional literature demonstrates that many reference departments, in particular, are already actively pursuing opportunities to partner with faculty and other affiliated groups on campus. Reference librarians have an established tradition of working together with faculty to support student learning through library workshops, curriculum-integrated instruction, and online educational tools. Building on this foundation, reference librarians are exploring multiple ways to further enhance students' development into lifelong learners, such as collaborative teaching with faculty[5] and partnerships with Writing Centers and student organizations. In addition to supporting student learning, librarians are collaborating with faculty and other campus entities to establish centers for digital humanities projects and data-management services,[6] among other endeavors. Successful efforts have been grounded in creating communities of practice with shared goals,[7] recognizing the critical role of communication,[8] and shifting away from a service culture to forming genuine partnerships.[9]

The first section in this volume, "Collaboration," addresses the trend in expanding reference services beyond traditional boundaries. Michael Courtney and Angela Courtney's chapter, "Step Away from the Desk: Re-casting the Reference Librarian as Academic Partner," shows us that collaboration is not a new idea but that proactive partnerships will be key to the vitality and future of reference services. The authors offer a review of reference partnerships, from teaching endeavors to research activities, with a specific emphasis on digital scholarship projects. Encouraging librarians not to abandon but to build on their traditional strengths while also acquiring new skills to meet changing needs, Courtney and Courtney see this transformative time as an opportunity for reference librarians to reimagine their role "as partners in the vibrant academic life of their institutions." Merinda Kaye Hensley provides a working model for new collaborative enterprises with her chapter, "The Scholarly Commons: Emerging Research Services for Graduate Students and Faculty." This case study at the University of Illinois at Urbana-Champaign presents a suite of research services that range in areas of specialization from data services to digital humanities and from scholarly communication and copyright to online publishing, among other areas. Hensley identifies each partner, describes its contribution to the Scholarly Commons, and concludes with assessment and plans for future collaboration. Through building strategic partnerships, the Scholarly Commons serves to inspire practitioners and lead the way in innovative reference.

DIVERSITY: MEETING THE INFORMATION NEEDS OF A CHANGING DEMOGRAPHIC

The changing demographics of higher education are significantly impacting the communities served by academic reference services. The ACRL *Environmental Scan* states quite directly that the "assumption of an 18–24-year-old age group as the traditional student will soon be a thing of the past."[10] Not only is the academy seeing an increase in a wider age range of students as veterans and professionals return to seek new educational opportunities, but growing numbers of Hispanics and African Americans, some of them first generation students, will also alter academic communities. With these changes come concerns about how libraries can position themselves to meet the needs of these students and best contribute to their recruitment and retention. Outreach to and partnerships with academic programs, such as the Ronald E. McNairs Scholars program, minority student affairs programs, and multicultural student centers on campus illustrate some of the ways that libraries are proactively working to attract and support a diverse clientele. [11]

The globalization of education through the popularity of distance education, online learning, and MOOCs, in particular, has led to a more geographically dispersed and diverse student body. [12] Students from other countries are an integral part of the American on-campus community as well, with their own unique information and research needs, [13] which could be partly served through offering library workshops and resources in foreign languages. [14] Published in 2012, the ACRL *Diversity Standards: Cultural Competency for Academic Libraries* has prompted reference librarians to focus attention on cultural issues of library use, linguistically diverse populations, and critical information literacy, among other diversity-related issues, and to consider how these can transform existing or initiate new reference services. Diversity, in the literature and in practice, is being defined in increasingly expansive terms to include not only racial and ethnic minorities, but also "any student who differs from the typical college student with regard to abilities, age, gender/sexuality, nationality or ethnicity, and locale." [15] In turn, librarians are assessing these students' needs and responding with tailored programs, services, and recommendations for best practices. [16]

The chapters in this section engage with their diverse communities through innovative reference and outreach. Matthew P. Ciszek's chapter, "The Rainbow Connection: Reference Services for the LGBT Community in Academic Libraries," is packed with good advice about creating a supportive reference environment for this increasingly visible population. He recommends easily implemented and effective practices, from creating top-level LGBT research guides to integrating LGBT topics and resources into instruction and reference consultations, as just some examples, and encourages librarians to become both knowledgeable and proactive about serving the LGBT community at their institutions. Valeria E. Molteni and Eileen K. Bosch describe their experience providing reference services in Spanish to meet the information needs of heritage language learners, immigrants, and international students. Their chapter, "Reference Services in a Shifting World: Other Languages, Other Services," offers two case studies from California State University, Long Beach, and San José State University, which both have highly diverse populations and a significant number of Latino students. Bilingual proficiency will become even more central to reference services and they remind us that to "serve the influx of library patrons with different cultural and language backgrounds, academic librarians need to rethink the English-only paradigm." Also concerned with a shifting student population, Li Fu's chapter, "As Needs Change, So Must We: A Case Study of Innovative Outreach to Changing Demographics" illustrates how the imperative to become a "changemaking campus" at the University of San Diego initiated major transformations in their reference services. Outreach and reference librarians at USD joined together to partner with academic and non-academic units for wide-ranging and targeted outreach to the underserved, including international students, disabled students, staff, and community members, among others.

TECHNOLOGY: REFERENCE SERVICE BEYOND THE LIBRARY WALLS

The *NMC Horizon Report: 2014 Higher Education Edition*, written in collaboration by the New Media Consortium and the EDUCAUSE Learning Initiative, details the following technology trends as having the most impact on higher education within the next five years: "the growing ubiquity of social media, the integration of online, hybrid, and collaborative learning, the rise of data-driven learning and assessment, and the shift from students as consumers to students as creators."[17] These evolving technological changes continue to push the boundaries of reference services, both literally and figuratively. Reference increasingly can happen anywhere and anytime, whether through Skype, chat, IM, or e-mail as students are served both on and off campus through these services as well as traditional means.[18] In the chapter "Roving Reference: Taking the Library to Its Users," Zara Wilkinson urges librarians to reconsider the benefits of roving reference, a traditional model of service that is seeing a rebirth due to the proliferation of tablets and mobile devices. She considers roving reference to be an important form of outreach to today's millennial students, noting, "Roving reference is a way to combat what might be called the library *catch 22*: the only patrons who come to the reference desk for help are those patrons who already know to come to the reference desk for help."

Technology developments also impact both the ways in which librarians communicate with their communities and the discovery tools and databases that are the foundation of their work.[19] In "Connecting Questions with Answers," Ellie Dworak and Carrie Moore provide a case study on the robust development of Frequently Asked Questions as a method of improving communications with students. Their chapter details the successful implementation and evaluation of LibAnswers, a Springshare reference product, at Boise State University to "bridge" the information gap between librarians and students. In the *Horizon Report*, the authors stress the intelligent use of technology: "Simply capitalizing on new technology is not enough; the new models must use these tools and services to engage students on a deeper level."[20] Likewise, reference librarians need to be creative about how best to integrate new technologies in order to effectively serve the library's and institution's goals.

ASSESSMENT: DOES REFERENCE MAKE A DIFFERENCE?

In order to remain relevant in today's digital age, reference librarians need to rethink traditional methods of reference evaluation. Current assessments of reference services still mostly focus on the quantity of reference interactions, rather than the quality. In *Value of Academic Libraries: A Comprehensive Research Review and Report*, prepared for the ACRL, Megan Oakleaf states, "Internal, service quality, and satisfaction measures are of great utility to librarians who seek to manage library services and resources, but they may not resonate with institutional leaders as well as outcomes-based approaches."[21]

As the availability of online information has increased, the nature of reference services in libraries has changed dramatically, leading to fewer, but often more complex, reference questions.[22] This shift has led many libraries to use new online reference data collection and assessment tools.[23] These new technologies have the potential to capture richer information about reference interactions. Recording information about reference interactions and outcomes is essential for demonstrating the value of the changing nature of reference work. Much of the recent literature illustrates the new complexity in reference interactions, as well as how to track new modes of reference (e.g., online, chat, e-mail).[24] Many libraries have implemented either vendor-provided (e.g., LibStats, LibAnalytics, Gimlet) or locally developed tools for recording reference assessment information. The benefits of using these new methods for library services assessment include continuous data collection, flexibility and mobility in the data-collection process, and increased detail.[25]

In the opening literature review of the section titled "Transforming Reference Services: More Than Meets the Eye," Kawanna Bright, Consuella Askew, and Lori Driver stress that academic librarians need to be engaged in the "transformative" programs happening in higher education institutions that will help demonstrate the value and relevance that reference and research services bring to the student learning experience. While reiterating the urgent need for assessment, they boldly proclaim that "the desk will continue its iconic role in reference service delivery" as long as librarians are willing to adapt based on the needs of patrons. In the second chapter in the section, Corinne Laverty and Elizabeth A. Lee provide one example of innovative adaption and assessment through their use of dialogic mapping in research consultations. In "Dialogic Mapping: Evolving Reference into an Instructional Support for Graduate Research," they present promising findings indicating that the reference interview can enhance student learning through the use of increased dialogue and visuals. They further argue that in today's fast-paced information age, "slow research" through dialogic mapping creates the best conditions for students to construct new knowledge. Finally, in "Does the Reference Desk Still Matter? Assessing the Desk Paradigm at the University of Washington Libraries," Deb Raftus and Kathleen Collins delineate novel assessment measures and outcomes for their research services. Using the Reference Effort Assessment Data (READ) Scale to analyze reference questions at three different campus libraries, they developed a culturally sensitive and context-specific reference model for each library that met the needs of both librarians and patrons.

Oakleaf contends that "just as there are no 'quick fixes' to the problem of demonstrating the value of higher education, there are no simple solutions to the challenge of articulating the value of academic libraries."[26] The models in this section, however, deliver useful strategies and tips for librarians just beginning an assessment program to those ready to engage in more complex correlations of student learning.

PROFESSIONAL COMPETENCIES: SKILLS FOR A NEW GENERATION

The highly changeable nature of higher education makes it necessary for reference librarians not only to adapt through the creation of innovative services but also, just as importantly, to make sure that their professional knowledge and skills are cutting edge. In some cases, this may mean enhancing traditional strengths, such as communication, resource expertise, and technological proficiency, and in others, it may entail branching out into new areas entirely, such as to collaborate in faculty research, data curation, online publishing, and digital scholarship projects, or to learn a second language. As we have seen from the previous sections, librarians will need to develop specific professional competencies to form effective partnerships with campus entities, support an increasingly diverse range of patrons, utilize a broad range of technological tools, and understand assessment planning, measures, and evaluation, and the role that assessment plays in demonstrating the library's contribution to student learning. At the heart of all these efforts will be the librarian's expertise in promoting and advocating for the value of academic libraries.

Laura Saunders approached the issue of new professional competencies head-on by surveying current academic reference librarians and hiring managers about the skills they identified as most crucial. Concentrating on three areas of general, technology, and personal/interpersonal skills, she found that searching proficiency, customer service, familiarity with online resources, software troubleshooting, knowledge of chat/IM and social media technologies, web design, verbal communication skills, listening, approachability, adaptability, and comfort with instruction rated high on the list of desired attributes.[27] Recent studies confirm these findings, with online search skills, verbal communication, and customer service skills maintaining their centrality for current and future requirements; however, additional competencies, such as "understanding the research process and delivering research support, and a growing focus on teaching and instruction,"[28] were also highlighted. With a more targeted focus on developing competencies to meet the needs of a changing student demographic and an increasingly global educational environment, training in cultural competency and cross-cultural communication will be critical.[29] Knowledge of a foreign language will also be important now and over the next decade, according to a cross-national analysis of reference service competencies, but was found to be less so for the English-speaking countries surveyed.[30] In addition, library training programs need to be ongoing to respond effectively to the changing responsibilities and expectations and also should integrate assessment to ensure that they continue to be relevant.[31]

The last section in our volume is concerned with understanding and developing specific competencies for the changing academic reference environment. Melanie Maksin explores the intersection between reference and instruction as illustrated by the emerging model of one-on-one research conversations. In her chapter, "From Ready Reference to Research Conversations: The Role of Instruction in Academic Reference Service," Maksin shows how the emphasis on information literacy and student-focused learning can shape new approaches to the reference interview and be put into practice by looking for teachable moments and cultivating active and more equal partnerships with patrons. Danielle Colbert-Lewis, Jamillah Scott-Branch, and David Rachlin provide a valuable overview of the core, technical, professional, and personal competencies required of reference librarians in "Necessities of Librarianship: Competencies for a New Generation." They discuss the Reference and User Services Association (RUSA) *Professional Competencies for Reference and User Services Librarians* and tie these competencies to the realities of daily practice. Christine Tobias demonstrates how traditional reference skills can be adapted to and enhanced for the online environment in "Professional Competencies for the Virtual Reference Librarian: Digital Literacy, Soft Skills, and Customer Service." With a focus on virtual reference transactions, she addresses the conventions and differences in online communication required by chat and instant messaging, covers topics like how to create a friendly conversational tone and give feedback online, and presents recommendations for overcoming challenges, such as the lack of visual and audio cues and communicative multitasking. Finally, Peggy Keeran's chapter, "Mediating for Digital Primary Source Research: Expanding Reference Services," explores how the increasing availability of online digital primary source documents is altering the research consultations and services offered by humanities librarians. In particular, she notes the blurring of reference and specialist responsibilities, "Because of the prevalence of digital commercially and freely available collections and finding aids, research in and access to primary sources, which was once chiefly the purview of special collection curators and archivists, has pushed the boundaries of what services can be offered by reference librarians." Together, these chapters will lead reference librarians to reevaluate their professional goals and move forward to develop the competencies best suited to current and future needs.

CONCLUSION

For higher education to fulfill its historic role as an engine of social mobility and economic growth, it must continue to change and evolve. This means that academic librarians and reference librarians, in particular, must think creatively about how to continue current reference services, while also ensuring that many more students receive the learning opportunities they deserve. Investments in collaborations with campus partners, innovations in the use of educational technology, improvements in outcomes assessment methods, and enhancements to professional-development programs for librarians are increasingly crucial to humanizing and cultivating research services for all students in the twenty-first-century academic library.

NOTES

1. Allan Gibb, Gay Haskins, and Ian Robertson, "Leading the Entrepreneurial University: Meeting the Entrepreneurial Development Needs of Higher Education Institutions," in *Universities in Change: Managing Higher Education Institutions in the Age of Globalization*, ed. Andreas Altmann and Bernd Ebersberger (New York: Springer, 2013), 9–45.

2. For an in-depth discussion on the needs of today's college students, please see Clayton M. Christensen and Henry J. Eyring, *The Innovative University: Changing the DNA of Higher Education From the Inside Out* (San Francisco: Jossey Bass, 2011), 301–24.

3. Heinz-Dieter Meyer, Edward P. St John, Maia Chankseliani, and Lina Uribe, "The Crisis of Higher Education Access—A Crisis of Justice," in *Fairness in Access to Higher Education in a Global Perspective: Reconciling Excellence, Efficiency, and Justice*, ed. Heinz-Dieter Meyer, Edward P. St. John, Maia Chankseliani, and Lina Uribe (Rotterdam, The Netherlands: Sense Publishers, 2013), 1–11.

4. Association of College and Research Libraries, Research Planning and Review Committee, *Environmental Scan 2013* (Chicago: Association of College and Research Libraries, 2013), accessed March 18, 2014, www.ala.org/acrl/sites/ala.org.acrl/files/content/publications/whitepapers/EnvironmentalScan13.pdf.

5. Rebekah Kilzer, "Reference as Service, Reference as Place: A View of Reference in the Academic Library," *The Reference Librarian* 52, no. 4 (2011): 294.

6. Joan Giesecke, "The Value of Partnerships: Building New Partnerships for Success," *Journal of Library Administration* 52, no. 1 (2012): 36–52; Bethany Latham and Jodi Welch Poe, "The Library as Partner in University Data Curation: A Case Study in Collaboration," *Journal of Web Librarianship* 6, no. 4 (2012): 288–304.

7. Nora F. Belzowski, J. Parker Ladwig, and Thurston Miller, "Crafting Identity, Collaboration, and Relevance for Academic Librarians Using Communities of Practice," *Collaborative Librarianship* 5, no. 1 (2013): 3–15.

8. Giesecke, "The Value of Partnerships," 49.

9. Yvonne Nalani Meulemans and Allison Carr, "Not at your Service: Building Genuine Faculty-Librarian Partnerships," *Reference Services Review* 41, no. 1 (2013): 80–90.

10. ACRL Research Planning and Review Committee, *Environmental Scan 2013*, 2.

11. Emily Love, "A Simple Step: Integrating Library Reference and Instruction into Previously Established Academic Programs for Minority Students," *The Reference Librarian* 50, no. 1 (2009): 4–13; Emily Love, "Building Bridges: Cultivating Partnerships between Libraries and Minority Student Services," *Education Libraries* 30, no. 1 (2007): 13–19; and Scott Walter, "Moving Beyond Collections: Academic Library Outreach to Multicultural Student Centers," *Reference Services Review* 33, no. 4 (2005): 438–58.

12. ACRL Research Planning and Review Committee, *Environmental Scan 2013*, 4.

13. Yunshan Ye, "New Thoughts on Library Outreach to International Students," *Reference Services Review* 37, no. 1 (2009): 8; and Lorrie Knight, Maryann Hight, and Lisa Polfer, "Rethinking the Library for the International Student Community," *Reference Services Review* 38, no. 4 (2010): 581–605.

14. Mark A. Puente, LaVerne Gray, and Shantel Agnew, "The Expanding Library Wall: Outreach to the University of Tennessee's Multicultural/International Student Population," *Reference Services Review* 37, no. 1 (2009): 41.

15. Anne T. Switzer, "Redefining Diversity: Creating an Inclusive Academic Library through Diversity Initiatives," *College and Undergraduate Libraries* 15, no. 3 (2008): 281.

16. Michael Saar and Helena Arthur-Okur, "Reference Services for the Deaf and Hard of Hearing," *Reference Services Review* 41, no. 3 (2013): 434–52; Sue Samson, "Best Practices for Serving Students with Disabilities," *Reference Services Review* 39, no. 2 (2011): 260–77; Pascal Lupien, "GLBT/Sexual Diversity Studies Students and Academic Libraries: A Study of User Perceptions and Satisfaction," *The Canadian Journal of Information and Library Science* 31, no. 2 (2007): 131–47; and Bharat Mehra and Donna Braquet, "Progressive LGBTQ Reference: Coming Out in the 21st Century," *Reference Services Review* 39, no. 3 (2011): 401–22.

17. Larry Johnson et al., *The NMC Horizon Report: 2014 Higher Education Edition* (Austin, TX: The New Media Consortium, 2013), accessed April 19, 2014, www.nmc.org/pdf/2014-nmc-horizon-report-he-EN.pdf.

18. Michael M. Smith and Barbara A. Pietraszewski, "Enabling the Roving Reference Librarian: Wireless Access with Tablet PCs," *Reference Services Review* 32, no. 3 (2004): 249–55.

19. Joan K. Lippincott, "A Mobile Future for Academic Libraries," *Reference Services Review* 38, no. 2 (2010): 205–13.

20. Larry Johnson et al., *The NMC Horizon Report*.

21. Association of College and Research Libraries, *Value of Academic Libraries: A Comprehensive Research Review and Report*, researched by Megan Oakleaf (Chicago: Association of College and Research Libraries, 2010), accessed April 19, 2014, www.ala.org/acrl/sites/ala.org.acrl/files/content/issues/value/val_report.pdf.

22. Sarah M. Philips, "The Search for Accuracy in Reference Desk Statistics," *Community and Junior College Libraries* 12, no. 3 (2005): 49–60.

23. Bella Karla Gerlich and G. Lynn Berard, "Testing the Viability of the READ Scale (Reference Effort Assessment Data): Qualitative Statistics for Academic Reference Services," *College & Research Libraries* 71, no. 2 (2010): 116–37.

24. Joshua Finnell and Walt Fontane, "Reference Question Data Mining: A Systematic Approach to Library Outreach," *Reference & User Services Quarterly* 49, no. 3 (2010):

278–86; and Judith S. Garrison, "Making Reference Service Count: Collecting and Using Reference Service Statistics to Make a Difference," *Reference Librarian* 51, no. 3 (2010): 202–11.

25. Xi Shi and Sarah Levy, "A Theory-Guided Approach to Library Services Assessment," *College & Research Libraries* 66, no. 3 (2005): 266–77.

26. ACRL, *Value of Academic Libraries*.

27. Laura Saunders, "Identifying Core Reference Competencies from an Employers' Perspective: Implications for Instruction," *College & Research Libraries* 73, no. 4 (July 2012): 396–98.

28. Gaby Haddow, "Knowledge, Skills and Attributes for Academic Reference Librarians," *Australian Academic and Research Libraries* 43, no. 3 (September 2012): 243; and Brenda Chawner and Gillian Oliver, "A Survey of New Zealand Academic Reference Librarians: Current and Future Skills and Competencies," *Australian Academic and Research Libraries* 44, no. 1 (2013): 32–37.

29. Lori S. Mestre, "Librarians Working with Diverse Populations: What Impact Does Cultural Competency Training Have on Their Efforts?" *The Journal of Academic Librarianship* 36, no. 6 (2010): 479–88; Dawn Amsberry, "Using Effective Listening Skills with International Patrons," *Reference Services Review* 37, no. 1 (2009): 10–19.

30. Laura Saunders et al., "Culture and Competencies: A Multi-Country Examination of Reference Service Competencies," *Libri: International Journal of Libraries and Information Services* 63, no. 1 (2013): 39.

31. Lily Todorinova and Matt Torrence, "Implementing and Assessing Library Reference Training Programs," *The Reference Librarian* 55, no. 1 (2014): 44.

BIBLIOGRAPHY

Amsberry, Dawn. "Using Effective Listening Skills with International Patrons." *Reference Services Review* 37, no. 1 (2009): 10–19.

Association of College and Research Libraries. *Value of Academic Libraries: A Comprehensive Research Review and Report*. Researched by Megan Oakleaf. Chicago: Association of College and Research Libraries, 2010. Accessed April 19, 2014. www.ala.org/acrl/sites/ala.org.acrl/files/content/issues/value/val_report.pdf.

Association of College and Research Libraries, Research Planning and Review Committee. *Environmental Scan 2013*. Chicago: Association of College and Research Libraries, 2013. Accessed March 18, 2014. www.ala.org/acrl/sites/ala.org.acrl/files/content/publications/whitepapers/EnvironmentalScan13.pdf.

Belzowski, Nora F., J. Parker Ladwig, and Thurston Miller. "Crafting Identity, Collaboration, and Relevance for Academic Librarians Using Communities of Practice." *Collaborative Librarianship* 5, no. 1 (2013): 3–15.

Chawner, Brenda, and Gillian Oliver. "A Survey of New Zealand Academic Reference Librarians: Current and Future Skills and Competencies." *Australian Academic and Research Libraries* 44, no. 1 (2013): 29–39.

Christensen, M. Clayton, and Henry J. Eyring. *The Innovative University: Changing the DNA of Higher Education From the Inside Out*. San Francisco, CA: Jossey Bass, 2011.

Finnell, Joshua, and Walt Fontane. "Reference Question Data Mining: A Systematic Approach to Library Outreach." *Reference & User Services Quarterly* 49, no. 3 (2010): 278–86.

Garrison, Judith S. "Making Reference Service Count: Collecting and Using Reference Service Statistics to Make a Difference." *Reference Librarian* 51, no. 3 (2010): 202–11.

Gerlich, Bella Karla, and G. Lynn Berard. "Testing the Viability of the READ Scale (Reference Effort Assessment Data): Qualitative Statistics for Academic Reference Services." *College & Research Libraries* 71, no. 2 (2010): 116–37.

Gibb, Allan, Gay Haskins, and Ian Robertson. "Leading the Entrepreneurial University: Meeting the Entrepreneurial Development Needs of Higher Education Institutions." In *Universities in Change: Managing Higher Education Institutions in the Age of Globalization*, edited by Andreas Altmann and Bernd Ebersberger, 9–45. New York: Springer, 2013.

Giesecke, Joan. "The Value of Partnerships: Building New Partnerships for Success." *Journal of Library Administration* 52, no. 1 (2012): 36–52.

Haddow, Gaby. "Knowledge, Skills and Attributes for Academic Reference Librarians." *Australian Academic and Research Libraries* 43, no. 3 (September 2012): 231–48.

Johnson, Larry, Samantha Adams Becker, Victoria Estrada, and Alex Freeman. *The NMC Horizon Report: 2014 Higher Education Edition.* Austin, TX: The New Media Consortium, 2013. Accessed April 19, 2014. www.nmc.org/pdf/2014-nmc-horizon-report-he-EN.pdf.

Kilzer, Rebekah. "Reference as Service, Reference as Place: A View of Reference in the Academic Library." *The Reference Librarian* 52, no. 4 (2011): 294.

Knight, Lorrie, Maryann Hight, and Lisa Polfer. "Rethinking the Library for the International Student Community." *Reference Services Review* 38, no. 4 (2010): 581–605.

Latham, Bethany, and Jodi Welch Poe. "The Library as Partner in University Data Curation: A Case Study in Collaboration." *Journal of Web Librarianship* 6, no. 4 (2012): 288–304.

Lippincott, Joan K. "A Mobile Future for Academic Libraries." *Reference Services Review* 38, no. 2 (2010): 205–13.

Love, Emily. "Building Bridges: Cultivating Partnerships between Libraries and Minority Student Services." *Education Libraries* 30, no. 1 (2007): 13–19.

———. "A Simple Step: Integrating Library Reference and Instruction into Previously Established Academic Programs for Minority Students." *The Reference Librarian* 50, no. 1 (2009): 4–13.

Lupien, Pascal. "GLBT/Sexual Diversity Studies Students and Academic Libraries: A Study of User Perceptions and Satisfaction." *The Canadian Journal of Information and Library Science* 31, no. 2 (2007): 131–47.

Mehra, Bharat, and Donna Braquet. "Progressive LGBTQ Reference: Coming Out in the 21st Century." *Reference Services Review* 39, no. 3 (2011): 401–22.

Mestre, Lori S. "Librarians Working with Diverse Populations: What Impact Does Cultural Competency Training Have on Their Efforts?" *The Journal of Academic Librarianship* 36, no. 6 (2010): 479–88.

Meulemans, Yvonne Nalani, and Allison Carr. "Not at your Service: Building Genuine Faculty-Librarian Partnerships." *Reference Services Review* 41, no. 1 (2013): 80–90.

Meyer, Heinz-Dieter, Edward P. St. John, Maia Chankseliani, and Lina Uribe. "The Crisis of Higher Education Access—A Crisis of Justice." In *Fairness in Access to Higher Education in a Global Perspective: Reconciling Excellence, Efficiency, and Justice,* edited by Heinz-Dieter Meyer, Edward P. St. John, Maia Chankseliani, and Lina Uribe, 1–11. Rotterdam, The Netherlands: Sense Publishers, 2013.

Philips, Sarah M. "The Search for Accuracy in Reference Desk Statistics." *Community and Junior College Libraries* 12, no. 3 (2005): 49–60.

Puente, Mark A., LaVerne Gray, and Shantel Agnew. "The Expanding Library Wall: Outreach to the University of Tennessee's Multicultural/International Student Population." *Reference Services Review* 37, no. 1 (2009): 30–43.

Saar, Michael, and Helena Arthur-Okur. "Reference Services for the Deaf and Hard of Hearing." *Reference Services Review* 41, no. 3 (2013): 434–52.

Samson, Sue. "Best Practices for Serving Students with Disabilities." *Reference Services Review* 39, no. 2 (2011): 260–77.

Saunders, Laura. "Identifying Core Reference Competencies from an Employers' Perspective: Implications for Instruction." *College & Research Libraries* 73, no. 4 (July 2012): 390–404.

Saunders, Laura, Serap Kurbanoglu, Mary Wilkins Jordan, Joumana Boustany, Brenda Chawner, Matylda Filas, Ivana Hebrang Grgic, et al. "Culture and Competencies: A Multi-Country Examination of Reference Service Competencies." *Libri: International Journal of Libraries and Information Services* 63, no. 1 (2013): 33–46.

Shi, Xi, and Sarah Levy. "A Theory-Guided Approach to Library Services Assessment." *College & Research Libraries* 66, no. 3 (2005): 266–77.

Smith, Michael M., and Barbara A. Pietraszewski. "Enabling the Roving Reference Librarian: Wireless Access with Tablet PCs." *Reference Services Review* 32, no. 3 (2004): 249–55.

Switzer, Anne T. "Redefining Diversity: Creating an Inclusive Academic Library through Diversity Initiatives." *College and Undergraduate Libraries* 15, no. 3 (2008): 280–300.

Todorinova, Lily, and Matt Torrence. "Implementing and Assessing Library Reference Training Programs." *The Reference Librarian* 55, no. 1 (2014): 37–48.
Walter, Scott. "Moving Beyond Collections: Academic Library Outreach to Multicultural Student Centers." *Reference Services Review* 33, no. 4 (2005): 438–58.
Ye, Yunshan. "New Thoughts on Library Outreach to International Students." *Reference Services Review* 37, no. 1 (2009): 7–9.

Part I

Collaboration: Partnerships for Lifelong Learning

Chapter One

Step Away from the Desk

Re-casting the Reference Librarian as Academic Partner

Michael Courtney and Angela Courtney

A library is a growing organism—S. R. Ranganathan[1]

In April 1968, having already established the Documentation Training and Research Centre at the Indian Statistical Institute in Bangalore as well as receiving the honorific title of National Research Professor in Library Science from the Indian government, Dr. S. R. Ranganathan, long a prognosticator of the evolution of the library's centrality within the college campus, stressed the importance of a close collaboration between librarians and teaching faculty in the overall intellectual and emotional development of the student. Ranganathan called for a reform in consideration of the library's place within higher education and asserted: "[The library] should not any longer be continued as a ritual appendage. It should be woven integratedly into the life of the students and teachers in the university. There should be as much education within the library as within the class room. To effect this, the librarians and the teachers should work in partnership."[2] In this sense, he viewed the librarian's role as one of continuance and supplementation; or, to put it in more direct terms, in as much as higher education trends toward student-centered approaches, so too should it be library-centered and, as such, an intimate and desirable partnership should exist between librarians and teaching faculty. To be certain, such statements may not seem radical within the context of twenty-first-century approaches to academic library reference service. The notions of integrating reference and research services more closely into the campus curriculum, collaborating with external partners in student-centered initiatives, fostering faculty research through enriched and alternative approaches to traditional service models, as well as the

3

now-ubiquitous concept of "embeddedness" that permeates the scholarly literature, are all at the forefront of current scholarly thought within the profession. However, the idea of academic library reference service fundamentally existing as a partnership between the librarian and the end-user, be it student, faculty, community member, or other, is a relatively recent construct, however much it may have been historically implicit.

James I. Wyer, a contemporary of Ranganathan and author of the seminal text *Reference Work*, extended the role of the reference librarian beyond Samuel Swett Green's 1876 plea for personalized service to that of an intermediary between the patron and the resource. In fact, he viewed the reference librarian as an *interpreter*, and pre-supposed the partnership in the actual process of reference librarianship that Robert Taylor was to discuss almost forty years later.[3] Wyer's word choice was deliberate: "to interpret seems a much more exact and satisfying verb than to aid, to help, or to assist, in describing reference work," and "it suggests thoroughness (even in helping) as against superficiality; sympathetic as against perfunctory service; a colleague rather than a clerk; informed leadership rather than a steering committee; in a word, understanding."[4] Robert Taylor viewed this interpretative role directly as a process of *negotiation* between the reference librarian and the patron, emphasizing the necessity of communication in this dialogue, and asserting the process of negotiation leads to problem resolution. He stressed the importance of self-awareness for libraries in such processes and placed this within the context of an ongoing dialogue, further implying the shared roles, on both sides of the reference desk, in the performance of reference service. Ranganathan himself recognized these specific roles, describing the reference librarian as *facilitating* the connection between patron and resource and understanding that, in order to do so, there must be an "intimate communion" between the reference librarian and the patron, at once recognizing the need for personalized service, but emphatically ascribing a relational role, or partnership.[5]

The idea of the reference librarian's role as *facilitator* is perhaps most in line with current ideology and one that necessarily implies the concepts of partnership and collaboration that underpin the evolution of the academic reference librarian in the twenty-first century. R. David Lankes states it succinctly: "In a word, what libraries and librarians do is facilitate."[6] In fact, Lankes provides the following directive that academic reference librarians would do well to acknowledge:

> Revolutions in Egypt, Fab Labs, and being a beacon of community aspirations seem to call for a stronger word, like "empower," "advocacy," or "inspire." And libraries should do all of these. Recall that facilitation is only one part of the larger mission to "improve society through facilitating knowledge creation in their communities." The word improve is key. Improve is active. This

means that facilitation is also active. To facilitate is not to sit back and wait to be asked. . . . No one ever changed the world waiting to be asked. No, you should expect the facilitation of librarians and libraries to be proactive, collaborative, and transformational. Libraries and librarians facilitate knowledge creation, working to make you and your community smarter.[7]

A curious path, indeed, has been followed in library reference service, but one that fully positions the librarian in an evolutionary and now more foundational role: from personal service provider to interpreter, negotiator, facilitator, and, most importantly, partner. Much like Lankes's implicit notion of librarianship as an *active* and transformative experience, the act of *partnering* in the process of academic library reference service connotes a significant change in how to provide reference service, and one that removes the physical limitations of the traditional desk and, in turn, places the librarian within many contextual roles across the academy, while preserving the core foundational aspects from which reference service has evolved.

While there have been many articles published over the past few years about the importance of collaboration and partnership in academic libraries, much of that scholarship has focused specifically on the connections forged in the classroom as teaching faculty and librarians work together toward common goals of information fluency for undergraduate students. The bountiful harvest of success stories with this type of learning-focused collaboration indicates that the role of teacher-librarian, a partner with teaching faculty members, has a natural extension into many other areas of library services. Indeed, the teaching role of the academic reference librarian has a long and fruitful tradition. Raymond C. Davis, librarian at the University of Michigan, saw a real need for instructing students on the use of reference materials and established a course for freshman undergraduates that covered the fundamentals of using the library. Davis's pioneering effort was likely "the first course of its kind to be given to freshman" and was taught from 1879 until his resignation in 1905.[8] Courses of this kind had indeed spread by the latter part of the nineteenth century, and the role of teacher, while not explicit within the fundamental duties of the reference librarian, did begin to receive particular notice, especially within governing texts in the instruction of library reference service.[9] Margaret Hutchins, in describing the reference librarian as teacher, explains that there is a "peculiar interest in undertaking this instruction because [the reference librarian] knows that the more people he can induce and prepare to help themselves the more time he will have to help those who have reference problems too hard to solve by themselves."[10] Ranganathan, for his own part, had spent several years early in his career as a teacher in the Government College, Mangalore, and later the Presidency College, Madras, India. During that time he was instrumental not just in the formations of class libraries, but also in instructing his students in the use of library resources, his earliest foray into providing reference service. In fact, he realized that he "had really integrated in those years the function of a teacher with that of a reference librarian" and found himself to be "spending much of [his] time in the area of overlap between the regions of a teacher and of a reference librarian."[11]

It should come as no surprise, then, as academic library reference service has continued to evolve over the course of almost 140 years, the role of educator has remained constant in all of its many permutations. As the profession shifted into the twenty-first century, James K. Elmborg argued that the reference desk (however one may define it) is, in itself, a "powerful teaching station" and sought out a modern framework for defining the role of reference librarian, or, a new "pedagogy for the reference desk."[12] In fact, Elmborg urges reference librarians to "work on ways to become full partners in the educational enterprise" in order for reference service to remain a viable entity.[13] The current literature is abundant with discussion of the teaching aspect of reference librarians and a new shift in the paradigm: while seemingly a natural extension of academic library reference service, the librarian as educator presents with it a need for training and awareness of educational pedagogy and student learning approaches across the academy. Carol S. Scherrer discovered, in a 2004 study, that reference librarians' roles as teachers had dramatically shifted from traditional bibliographic instruction to curriculum-based classroom instruction, as well as new approaches within online environments. Scherrer reported that "this teaching, moreover, was different from the teaching of the past" and that reference librarians expressed a need for "a conceptual framework of adult learning theory to devise a learning continuum for students and faculty as they progressed in their knowledge, as well as practical tips for improving their teaching in general, such as devising goals for classes, delivering content, and appraising results."[14] With such a perceived shift in the role of the reference librarian on the academic campus, the need for partnering with teaching faculty in assessing the learning outcomes of students across the curriculum, as well as understanding conceptual approaches to teaching in general, is an immediate requirement for fulfilling the necessary (and now required) teaching component of academic library reference. The very notion of librarians and teachers as partners in the process of inquiry-based learning is of high importance across the spectrum, from the K–12 librarian to higher education and beyond. As the idea of *reference services* generally, or the *reference department* specifically, changes from a finite unit to a set of interconnected services shared by staff across disciplines and areas of expertise, the role of the reference librarian becomes less tethered to the physical constraints of the old desk model and requires more of a collaborative partnership both internal and external to the library as we understand it. In fact, Frances Devlin and John Stratton point specifically to the increased demands on academic reference librarians as a call to restructure the very notion of the reference service model. Seeing an expansion of reference librarian roles to include greater emphasis on areas such as "open access publishing, copyright consultancy, data services management, and classroom teaching," traditional staffing models rooted in large part to the decades-old desk and departmental model proved to be great inhibitors to fully realizing the new demands on the academic reference librarian.[15] Stepping away from and beyond the desk, then, proves a necessary evolution of reference service and creates a new collaborative paradigm for the librarians as they venture out into the campus and beyond.

The reference librarian is similarly well positioned to be a partner not only in teaching endeavors, but also in increasingly complex and technical research activities that frequently characterize scholarly publishing in the twenty-first century. As academic libraries regularly confront greater demands on their time, money, and human resources, they also must encourage and support reference librarians and departments to look closely at their own roles within their organization, augmenting traditional strengths to realign with current methodology and anticipate evolving scholarly practices. With the pervasive presence of web technologies, from vendor-developed databases to open-source tools, reference services in academic libraries are undergoing a series of environmental changes with the potential to disrupt or render them redundant both in name and in practice. As Jill Stover concisely and effectively states, "Being strategically different is an absolute necessity for libraries that compete in an increasingly overcrowded marketplace."[16] Foundational reference services need to be examined closely by the librarians themselves in the twenty-first century.

Reference departments should view technology as just another method by which reference librarians can deliver their services, and begin to develop expertise in digital publishing technology that now characterizes the landscape of academic publishing. Traditional strengths will evolve as librarians redefine reference services to play larger and more important roles in the research and teaching activities of students and faculty. Effective and successful reference services programs will continually analyze trends in scholarly publication and teaching to be able to identify where they need to focus their own development, continuing education efforts, and outreach to campus partners. Reference service itself, then, must develop an expanded purview, moving out from and beyond the physical reference desk to become an increasingly active and integral part of the academic research and learning processes, from creatively facilitating research in the ubiquitous composition courses to being important members of digital research project teams. Acknowledging a movement beyond traditional reference librarianship by fostering roles in user education, research partnership and support, and an ever-pressing imperative for both awareness and proficiency of new and emerging technologies, twenty-first-century library reference service is at the cusp of reenvisioning itself to better define roles and services that must adapt and transform in tandem with its surrounding landscape.

In 2009, David Shumaker issued "a call to do something else new as well, to explore new territories outside the library and take new opportunities to build working relationships—true collaboration and partnerships."[17] His cause was embedding librarians, a sometimes successful endeavor over the past few years, but it was accompanied by a wise caveat that reference librarians and departments should not leave behind their traditional strengths and should still respect the library as a place and space. His call and caveat nearly five years later remains pertinent. Now reference librarians have a unique and timely opportunity to cultivate partnerships in research and teaching, not necessarily by embedding themselves outside the library, but rather by becoming integral in the growing digital scholarship endeavors in and out of the classroom. Now is the time, as Yvonne Nalani Meulemans and Allison Carr urge in their article "Not at Your Service: Building Genuine Faculty-Librarian Partnerships," for reference librarians to take active steps to move beyond the reference desk, to cast aside an often-assumed subservience to their teaching and research faculty colleagues.[18]

Reference librarians and departments should take a cue from some of the changes that are currently garnering attention within the library community. For example, Stanford University Libraries' staff focused <digiPrep> workshop series offers staff the opportunity to attend several two-hour training sessions on topics such as project management, digital preservation, and metadata.[19] Acknowledging librarians as researchers in their own right, the intent is to prepare library staff "not only for helping patrons, but also for facilitating staff members' own digital research projects."[20]

A more rigorous program is Columbia University Libraries' Developing Librarian Project, which focuses on subject librarians and digital scholarship.[21] This particular effort is characterized by teamwork, participation, and a belief in the importance of the process, as is communicated in their charter: "A team of scholar librarians will create a digital history of Morningside Heights from 1820–1950. The project is important, but the process of learning emergent technologies and research methods is equally if not more important than the project."[22] Their two-year project will digitize the history of their neighborhood, and in so doing the participants will learn a variety of skills that characterize digital scholarship, including digital publication tools, design principles, metadata, data management, and so on. This project also values traditional research and prioritizes research clearly in the syllabus.[23] While there is emphasis on the Morningside Heights digital history, a more important priority is the learning. Participating librarians not only put their new skills to work immediately, but also reflect on their experiences immediately through their shared blog.[24] This step allows regular assessment of the

Developing Librarian as a learning project, and helps to guide practices as the endeavor moves ahead.

Currently under way at Indiana University is *Research Now*, a partnership between the Reference Services Department and the Digital Collections Services Department to cross-train reference librarians in the processes, tools, and technologies that comprise the works of Digital Collections Services, and to similarly cross-train Digital Collections Services to be able to work with reference and research interactions at a traditional reference desk.[25] The effort was inspired by the concurrent library renovation of the traditional Reference Room into the Scholars' Commons, a space designed to foster academic community building and to nurture digital scholarship. As plans for the renovation and the training were developing, public-service-oriented subject librarians and others asked to be included in the training. The project focuses on documenting library history, and the participating librarians have encouraged the project managers to expand the research purview to include several sessions that cover a range of subject reference tools, an overview of the foundations of reference, the reference interview, archival standards, practice with real reference questions, in addition to digital resources and platforms included in the Stanford and Columbia projects. While the subject and reference librarians have worked together as partners at the reference desk for years at Indiana, another partnership is being forged between public services and digital services. As this partnership develops, an ancillary benefit is the realization by the public services participants that not only are their research and reference skills still vital, but also they are being called on to teach their digital counterparts what to expect while staffing a service point that will address technical and subject research needs. All of these efforts at training and continuing education should ensure that reference departments will become, or maintain, their status as integral players in academic scholarship.

Historically, reference librarians, along with their subject-librarian colleagues, have been the backbone of research in the humanities and social sciences. Yet for several years reference has floundered trying to hold onto traditional strengths—adopting new methods of delivery (notably chat reference) as the simplicity of Internet research and easily accessible library databases have led to fewer users in the library space. Reference librarians and reference departments are research experts, and they should be part of the growing number of collaborative teams of scholars working on projects within the broad arena of digital scholarship. The three projects mentioned above are only a few examples of ways that librarians can and need to empower themselves to become partners in faculty research projects. Echoing Laura Saunders's 2012 survey findings that hiring managers were seeking reference librarians with a "wide range of competencies ranging from facility with technology to interpersonal and communication skills" to effectively answer the needs at a reference desk, it is clear that developing a generalist-level competency with publishing and presentation tools and actively advertising this ability increases the profile and implied value of reference librarians across the campus.[26]

Reference departments are at the center of a series of environmental changes with the potential to disrupt or render them redundant, in name and in practice, if they are unable to exploit the opportunities that are presented as a result of these quick and varied shifts. Having heard the premature call to mourn the death of reference for years, understandably, reference librarians may begin to believe it is inevitable and give in to the prediction. Librarians must heed Jill Stover's call to "recognize what patrons wish to accomplish and where the library fits into the process of achieving those goals."[27] It is imperative for there to be a focus on partnerships that have the potential to propel and sustain reference services, as well as to enable and empower reference departments to increase expertise with new tools and to develop new skills and expertise. Many reference departments already have become campus experts with recent developments, such as bibliographic management tools like Zotero and Mendeley and presentation tools such as Power-Point and Prezi, by conducting workshops and consultations for library users. In other words, reference services have a history of finding a need and then filling it in an expert and professional manner. Reference staff can easily be the de facto experts in publication tools for blogs, wikis, and online book monograph platforms, GIS, text analysis, visualization, and other developing technologies, while still continuing to play to their strengths as expert researchers.

Naturally, time demands on the reference staff can be a concern, one that is only partly mitigated by the recurring invocation of declining demands for reference service. Reference departments, however, must consistently evaluate what they offer in light of what their students and faculty need. To remain viable, reference librarians and departments must be familiar with academic trends and practices on their campuses and look to align their activities with goals, priorities, and strategic directions of the university. This reality may mean reference librarians need to let go of some vestigial activities to make time for more significant pursuits. For example, time spent on developing monthly new books lists may be superseded by time spent developing fluency in and teaching students how to use mobile note-taking tools, online textual analysis programs, or blogging platforms.

To effectively move beyond the desk (and here it is important to note that moving beyond does not mean abandoning the desk, which remains an important part of reference's future), reference services must be redefined. That is to say that reference's traditional strengths in areas such as public service, research methods, expert knowledge of resources, instructional skills, and proficiency with research tools from databases to word processing should be augmented by important larger roles in the research and teaching lives of students and faculty. Now more than ever, strong reference services programs rely on analyzing trends in research, publication, and teaching to identify potential areas for library partnerships and foci for their own continuing development and education. Librarians as individuals and as members of departments should define areas where they think they could be effective partners. By integrating themselves into their academic community, librarians will be able to discern needs on their campus that they can fill. They will often have to avail themselves of continuing-education opportunities in order to meet these demands, but the truth is if libraries do not make the most of these gaps, then such voids will be filled elsewhere. The ability to anticipate, recognize, and act will place as partners librarians in the midst of campus research.

Reference departments must adopt an ongoing transformational process of identifying needs and adapting their strengths to address those gaps. An important part of this continuing progression to foster a vital and vibrant reference department is that individual librarians be encouraged and empowered to play to their own strengths and to seek out partnerships on the campus where they find an unmet demand in an area where they have an interest or ability. Just as Kay Ann Cassell observes that "librarians understand that one model does not fit all users and that they must be flexible in order to meet user needs," all librarians are not going to share the same strengths or abilities.[28] At this point in time, it is crucial, however, that librarians be supported by their institutions in order to enable them to attain the necessary skills to perform as a partner with a faculty member or as a member of a research team. In today's current and quickly changing academic environment, it is imperative that librarians do not fall behind the technology curve.

The swift changes from print to digital scholarship and open-access dissemination will require reference librarians to become proficient in a wide range of digital technologies through which scholarly research is not only conducted, but also composed, designed, and made available. Anticipating and reacting to these developments need not mean a complete change to reference services, but rather enhancing librarians' abilities and with digital technology as well as robust and reciprocal referral services with various campuses services. For example, when confronted with a student who wants to make a map, the reference interview will pull out the details to discover precisely what the student means—the reason, goals, and overarching context for the project. Depending on what the interview reveals in addition to the level of skill of the librarian, next steps could include helping the student with mapping software, an introduction to Google Earth, or a referral to a campus GIS center. A librarian approached by a graduate student looking for an outlet outside of traditional publishing to use as a testing ground for thought and theories could point the student to several blogging platforms.

The librarian should also be able to help the student navigate the development of the blog. A faculty member who feels limited by the confines of traditional publishing may want to develop a multimedia exhibit to supplement the book. A librarian familiar with exhibit platforms such as Omeka has the ability to help the scholar develop an online supplement to the book.

It is also key to remember that the library still exists as a place, one that is significant to academic researchers. The library remains a place where research is done, a place that researchers recognize as a home for their scholarly activities. Academic research in many fields continues to rely on the contents of a library's collections and the expertise of its reference librarians. Reference librarians have to value their own traditional strengths on which their reputations were built, but they also need to act quickly and intelligently in order to recast themselves as partners in the vibrant academic life of their institutions. Stepping away from the reference desk does not necessarily mean leaving the library. Augmenting the traditional reference desk to be prepared to handle questions about digital research tools and processes (GIS, visualization, mark-up, encoding, and so on) would welcome faculty and students to a comfortable and familiar environment where they can locate assistance with technologies that they may find otherwise uncomfortable as they begin to move their own research into what is likely to be a very new arena.

In order to thwart the predictions of their tragic, long-anticipated death, reference departments and librarians need to be proactive. Reference departments cannot wait for something to happen, to be rescued from the brink by administrative intervention. Rather, a reference department and its staff must take control of its current role and reputation and in so doing help to protect its future. Departments must embrace technology beyond simply being expert database searchers, and they also need to illustrate the value of the reference generalist. The combination of a broad familiarity with reference sources and research needs, as well as a solid awareness of and fluency with the proliferation of exciting and always-changing tools that characterize digital scholarly practices is a collaborative service that libraries in general, and reference departments in particular, are uniquely poised to provide support to researchers from undergraduates to faculty.

The basic tenets that have guided reference departments for years should still be the guiding principles going forward. Those principles that were laid out by such luminaries as Green, Mudge, Wyer, Hutchins, Ranganathan, and beyond remain very much central to the mission of library reference service. All would agree, however, that the library is constantly evolving and to remain static would inhibit the very service that we espouse. *Grow, move, change.* Not only is the conceptual reference desk necessary, but it will also become more vital to the daily work and long-term projects that should be intersecting with reference. Moving beyond the desk is indeed a challenge, but if reference departments and librarians choose to take up this challenge, they will find their skills and talents, traditional and digital, to be more important to the academic community than ever.

NOTES

1. S. R. Ranganathan, *The Five Laws of Library Science* (Madras: The Madras Library Association, 1931), 382.

2. S. R. Ranganathan, "Productivity and Partnership in University Education," *Library Herald* 10, no. 1 (1968): 13–14.

3. Robert S. Taylor, "Question-Negotiation and Information Seeking in Libraries," *College & Research Libraries* 29, no. 3 (1968): 178–94.

4. James I. Wyer, *Reference Work* (Chicago: American Library Association, 1930), 5.

5. S. R. Ranganathan, *Reference Service* (London: Asia Publishing House, 1961), 53.

6. R. David Lankes, *Expect More: Demanding Better Libraries for Today's Complex World* (Lexington, KY: CreateSpace, 2012), 42.

7. Ibid.

8. Henry O. Severance, "Raymond C. Davis, 1836–1919," *College & Research Libraries* 2 (1941): 346.

9. "Conference of Librarians," *Library Journal* 22, no. 10 (1897): 165–68.

10. Margaret Hutchins, *Introduction to Reference Work* (Chicago: American Library Association, 1944), 183.

11. Ranganathan, *Reference Service*, 25.

12. James K. Elmborg, "Teaching at the Desk: Toward a Reference Pedagogy," *portal: Libraries and the Academy* 2, no. 3 (2002): 455.

13. Ibid., 464.

14. Carol S. Scherrer, "Reference Librarians' Perceptions of the Issues They Face as Academic Health Professionals," *Journal of the Medical Library Association* 92, no. 2 (2004): 228.

15. Frances Devlin and John Stratton, "Evolving Models of Reference Staffing at the University of Kansas Libraries," *Research Library Issues: A Report from ARL, CNI, and SPARC* 282 (2013): 21.

16. Jill Stover, "Be You; Be Unique: How to Create Competitive Reference Services by Being Strategically Different," in *The Desk and Beyond: Next Generation Reference Services*, ed. Sarah K. Steiner and M. Leslie Madden (Chicago: Association of College and Research Libraries, 2008), 135.

17. David Shumaker, "Who Let the Librarians Out? Embedded Librarianship and the Library Manager," *Reference & User Services Quarterly* 48, no. 3 (2009): 240.

18. Yvonne Nalani Meulemans and Allison Carr, "Not at Your Service: Building Genuine Faculty-Librarian Partnerships," *Reference Services Review* 41, no. 1 (2013): 80–90.

19. Stanford University Libraries, *<digiPrep> Workshops* (2013), accessed December 1, 2013, https://digitalhumanities.stanford.edu/digiPrep.

20. Jacqueline Hettel, "<digiPrep> Workshops: A New SUL Series for Digital Research Best Practices," *Stanford University Libraries News* (August 26, 2013), accessed December 1, 2013, http://library.stanford.edu/news/2013/08/workshops-new-sul-series-digital-research-best-practices.

21. Columbia University Libraries Humanities and History Team, *Breaking the Code: The Developing Librarian Project* (2013), accessed December 1, 2013, http://wwwwww.developinglibrarian.org.

22. Columbia University Libraries Humanities and History Team, "Charter," *Breaking the Code: The Developing Librarian Project* (2013), accessed December 1, 2013, http://wwwwww.developinglibrarian.org/link-to-google-doc-for-developing-our-charter.

23. Columbia University Libraries Humanities and History Team, "Roadmap," *Breaking the Code: The Developing Librarian Project* (2013), accessed December 1, 2013, http://wwwwww.developinglibrarian.org/syllabus.

24. Columbia University Libraries Humanities and History Team, "Four Things," *Breaking the Code: The Developing Librarian Project* (2013), accessed December 1, 2013, http://wwwwww.developinglibrarian.org/category/four_things.

25. Indiana University Libraries, *Research Now: Cross-Training for Digital Scholarship* (2013), accessed December 1, 2013, https://wiki.dlib.indiana.edu/display/SC/Research+Now%3A+Cross-Training+for+Digital+Scholarship+Home.

26. Laura Saunders, "Identifying Core Reference Competencies from an Employers' Perspective: Implications for Instruction," *College & Research Libraries* 73, no. 4 (2012): 401.

27. Stover, "Be You," 142.

28. Kay Ann Cassell, "Meeting Users' Needs through New Reference Service Models," in *Reference Renaissance: Current and Future Trends*, ed. Marie L. Radford and R. David Lankes (New York: Neal-Schuman Publishers, 2010), 159.

BIBLIOGRAPHY

Cassell, Kay Ann. "Meeting Users' Needs through New Reference Service Models." In *Reference Renaissance: Current and Future Trends*, edited by Marie L. Radford and R. David Lankes, 153–60. New York: Neal-Schuman Publishers, 2010.

Columbia University Libraries Humanities and History Team. *Breaking the Code: The Developing Librarian Project*, 2013. Accessed December 1, 2013. www.developinglibrarian.org.

"Conference of Librarians." *Library Journal* 22, no. 10 (1897): 165–68.

Devlin, Frances, and John Stratton. "Evolving Models of Reference Staffing at the University of Kansas Libraries." *Research Library Issues: A Report from ARL, CNI, and SPARC* 282 (2013): 21–24.

Elmborg, James K. "Teaching at the Desk: Toward a Reference Pedagogy." *portal: Libraries and the Academy* 2, no. 3 (2002): 455–64.

Hettel, Jacqueline. "<digiPrep> Workshops: A New SUL Series for Digital Research Best Practices." *Stanford University Libraries News* (August 26, 2013). Accessed December 1, 2013. http://library.stanford.edu/news/2013/08/workshops-new-sul-series-digital-research-best-practices.

Hutchins, Margaret. *Introduction to Reference Work*. Chicago: American Library Association, 1944.

Indiana University Libraries. *Research Now: Cross-Training for Digital Scholarship*, 2013. Accessed December 1, 2013. https://wiki.dlib.indiana.edu/display/SC/Research+Now%3A+Cross-Training+for+Digital+Scholarship+Home.

Lankes, R. David. *Expect More: Demanding Better Libraries for Today's Complex World*. Lexington, KY: CreateSpace, 2012.

Meulemans, Yvonne Nalani, and Allison Carr. "Not at Your Service: Building Genuine Faculty-Librarian Partnerships." *Reference Services Review* 41, no. 1 (2013): 80–90.

Ranganathan, S. R. *The Five Laws of Library Science*. Madras: The Madras Library Association, 1931.

———. "Productivity and Partnership in University Education." *Library Herald* 10, no. 1 (1968): 1–18.

———. *Reference Service*. London: Asia Publishing House, 1961.

Saunders, Laura. "Identifying Core Reference Competencies from an Employers' Perspective: Implications for Instruction." *College & Research Libraries* 73, no. 4 (2012): 390–404.

Scherrer, Carol S. "Reference Librarians' Perceptions of the Issues They Face as Academic Health Professionals." *Journal of the Medical Library Association* 92, no. 2 (2004): 226–32.

Severance, Henry O. "Raymond C. Davis, 1836–1919." *College & Research Libraries* 2, no. 4 (1941): 344–47.

Shumaker, David. "Who Let the Librarians Out? Embedded Librarianship and the Library Manager." *Reference & User Services Quarterly* 48, no. 3 (2009): 239–42, 257.

Stanford University Libraries. *<digiPrep> Workshops*, 2013. Accessed December 1, 2013. https://digitalhumanities.stanford.edu/digiPrep.

Stover, Jill. "Be You; Be Unique: How to Create Competitive Reference Services by Being Strategically Different." In *The Desk and Beyond: Next Generation Reference Services*, edited by Sarah K. Steiner and M. Leslie Madden, 135–47. Chicago: Association of College and Research Libraries, 2008.

Taylor, Robert S. "Question-Negotiation and Information Seeking in Libraries." *College & Research Libraries* 29, no. 3 (1968): 178–94.

Wyer, James I. *Reference Work*. Chicago: American Library Association, 1930.

Chapter Two

The Scholarly Commons

Emerging Research Services for Graduate Students and Faculty

Merinda Kaye Hensley

As reference models change in response to technology and the emerging needs of scholars, academic libraries are exploring innovative ways to more broadly support research activities. The Scholarly Commons (SC) at the University of Illinois at Urbana-Champaign was established to better serve the needs of faculty and graduate students pursuing in-depth research and scholarly inquiry. The suite of services builds on the traditional model of reference by administering on-demand and consultation services, programmatic offerings, a space where researchers can use technology to further their research, and a common entry point that can direct scholars to relevant campus resources and experts. The element that has been most effective in preparing these activities, however, is the development of partnerships with several campus organizations. These collaborations deeply enhance library and campus services provided to a cross-disciplinary learning environment.

Revisioning reference services and creating the Scholarly Commons was part of a larger, systematic review of library services referred to as "New Service Models."[1] After several years of library-wide investigation and discussion, the administration dedicated resources to open a new type of service space during a time of consolidating traditional reference points. Recommendations from October 2008 address growing demand for re-imagined scholarly services:

Scholar Services are understood to encompass traditional Library services for faculty, including research consultation, instructional design, and identification of information resources, as well as emergent service needs, including scholarly communications education, data services, digitization and metadata services, scholarly publishing services, and personal research data management.[2]

In addressing increasing demands from interdisciplinary inquiry, a Scholarly Commons leadership team was assigned to investigate cutting-edge approaches to teaching and research rooted in five core values for the development of new research support including service, innovation, risk-taking, collaboration, and community. It is these values that drive the motivation for evolving traditional reference services in the library. "As important, the design of scholar services programs must be fluid, and its principal players agile, in order to allow for new initiatives to grow as these broader changes continue to unfold."[3] The coordinator was charged with managing resources and building collaborative relationships in an effort to create nimble and forward-thinking services for the campus that support the evolving challenges faced by researchers across disciplines.

The Scholarly Commons opened in August 2010 as a pilot effort in a space on the third floor of the Main Library. While the space was not expansive, it did have interconnected rooms in order to provide consultation services, a modest meeting room, an office with two computer stations that included sound-proofing for web usability purposes, and an office for the coordinator. Services began to expand rapidly, and the Scholarly Commons outgrew its space in less than one year.

During the same time period, reference services continued to change. In late 2011, the library's New Service Model Team acknowledged that in-person reference interactions were declining while virtual questions were increasing exponentially and both venues were seeing an increase in complexity.[4] In response, an implementation team recommended strategies for innovating reference services throughout the library system by consolidating desks into four service points, plus one dedicated space for monitoring virtual reference questions through the online chat system. The Main Library maintained the Information Services Desk in a central location,[5] but staffing changed to reflect the interdisciplinary nature of questions. Librarians across departmental libraries combined to create a "hub" to staff the Information Services Desk along with library staff and graduate assistants from the Graduate School of Library and Information Science. A Reference Services Committee was formed to address staff training and assessment needs. The new unit, Reference, Research, and Scholarly Services, was charged with overseeing the Scholarly Commons, an effort to address the more complex and highly technical questions that were arising in the humanities and social sciences, separated from the constraints of a traditional reference desk.

While the reference desk at Illinois has expanded over the years to multiple venues for offering research assistance (e.g., chat reference and embedded librarians), this model was not robust enough to engage scholars with their increasingly intricate research projects. This type of research most often reflects the intersections between interdisciplinary research and technology. Examples of questions include managing and cleaning data using qualitative and quantitative software programs, creating data-visualization requests for high-quality scanning and OCR technology, using software and collaborative space to perform web usability tests, answering questions related to copyright and author's rights, and much more. The Scholarly Commons began with two existing projects, data services and a series of open workshops that addressed the advanced research and information-management needs of graduate students and faculty.

In March 2012, the Scholarly Commons moved into its current space in the Main Library. Leadership for the Scholarly Commons is currently managed by a pair of coordinators as a portion of their assigned duties. The space includes a dozen public-access computers with a wide variety of research-related software, consultation desks for partners, collaboration space, a reference collection, and four different types of scanners. The Scholarly Commons also manages a large conference room with a touch-screen monitor, an instructional space with computers, and a usability lab outfitted to be nearly soundproof. The Scholarly Commons is open forty hours per week, but opens later in the day and closes in the early evening to better reflect graduate-level research patterns. The space is staffed primarily by students from the Graduate School of Library and Information Science as part of the library's pre-professional assistantship program, who provide a triage of assistance, answering basic questions and connecting more complex questions to the librarians and partners as necessary. When patrons enter the space, they can expect to use technology resources (e.g., software and scanners) with basic assistance from the person staffing the desk, to drop in on data services consultation hours offered five days per week, and to consult the reference collection. The Scholarly Commons does not have an allocated budget at this time; however, a generous gift from the University of Illinois Division of Intercollegiate Athletics (DIA) funds all services, marketing, and outreach activities. The DIA was interested in funding the Scholarly Commons specifically because of its mission to create an innovative space and develop services that address the needs of advanced scholarship.

The following chapter is a case study of the strategic partnerships the Scholarly Commons has developed during its first two years, relationships that have been built on a profusion of services: consultations, learning opportunities in-person and online, a sandbox of hardware and software to explore new research techniques, seminar events, and invited guest speakers. Current areas of specialization include data services, digital humanities, digitization work, scholarly communication and copyright education, web and computer usability, and new efforts in publishing. The following questions will be addressed for each strategic partnership:

- Who is the partner? What is their mission?
- How does the partner's service profile align with the goals of the Scholarly Commons?
- What services are provided?
- Are there identified areas of growth?

The Scholarly Commons continues to make progress toward its initial vision, to "foster the development of a collaborative culture of scholarly inquiry at Illinois by maintaining an environment in which students and scholars can access, and contribute to, the resources made available by academic, research, and support units across campus."[6]

LITERATURE REVIEW

The Scholarly Commons takes inspiration from similar existing services across institutions. One of the most established programs in the country, the University of Virginia's Scholars Lab brings together "digital humanities, geospatial information, and scholarly making and building at the intersection of the digital and physical worlds."[7] The University of North Carolina at Chapel Hill also offers instructional and advanced assistance with data collection, geospatial projects,[8] and scholarly communication.[9] The University of California, Los Angeles, gives scholars access to a data registry, a database for recording the location of data sets for publications and research.[10] Indiana University at Bloomington has recently expanded their Scholars' Commons Series to incorporate seminars on a wide variety of scholarly topics, and a brown bag series on digital libraries, a half-day workshop on getting published in a journal, a digital humanities series on computational techniques, and engagement with Geographic Information Systems (GIS) Day.[11] The University of Kansas's Center for Digital Scholarship[12] and the University of Michigan[13] support digital publishing services, including digital repositories and online publishing systems for journals and monographs.

There are two recent studies in the literature that give an overview of the growth of scholarly services. In a series of interviews with ten libraries, Craig Gibson and Meris Mandernach constructed an overview of innovative reference service models that are emerging to support scholars: libraries are moving toward a staffing model where librarians are available on an on-call basis; librarians are increasingly engaged within departments and being included on research projects; research questions are being answered online and services are being offered at the point of need (e.g., offices, laboratories);

external partnerships involve a trade-off of space; and new spaces are being created to accommodate collaborations and programming.[14] In a similar vein, Lucinda Covert-Vail and Scott Collard systematically review graduate student services, provide specific examples for how libraries are partnering across campus, and point out that "libraries need to exploit all available partnering opportunities in order to identify and market services to graduate students" and "institutions that have created strong partner relationships with academic units cite their effectiveness and value, with non-library partners serving as effective promoters of library resources and services."[15]

PARTNERS ADVISORY BOARD

An advisory board was created in order to keep all external partners up to date on Scholarly Commons activities and to provide a voice for their opinions on past and future services. The partners meet once per year in the spring, a venue to share accomplishments from the past year and an opportunity for input for the coming year, and receive regularly scheduled e-mail updates.

Partner: Applied Technologies for Learning in the Arts and Sciences (ATLAS)[16]
Service area: Data Services
Data services in the Scholarly Commons is led by three entities: the numeric and spatial data librarian, the Data Services Committee, and a partnership with the staff from Applied Technologies for Learning in the Arts and Sciences (ATLAS) in the College of Liberal Arts and Sciences. Prior to its partnership with the library, ATLAS was charged with serving only the College of Liberal Arts and Sciences. However, for the past decade, reference services across disciplines are experiencing growing demand from scholars working on finding, using, managing, and archiving data. The library's partnership with the ATLAS portfolio provides data services to the entire campus: acquiring data sets needed for teaching and research; locating, downloading, and preparing data for secondary analysis; identifying and creating course materials and teaching tools (plus customized data sets drawn from various data repositories); and consulting around software problems with standard statistical packages. Services offered in collaboration with ATLAS and the Scholarly Commons have also expanded to meet research needs for statistical or geospatial analysis.[17]

The Scholarly Commons works closely with the Data Services Committee[18] in order to create a service profile that addresses researchers working with data throughout its life cycle, including the development of data management plans and data curation. The charge of the committee is to investigate best practices pertaining to the provision of numeric and spatial data and assistance offered to data users in the library around multiple topics such as data procurement, access to and reuse of data purchased by the library, training and instruction for data users, and assessment of services; administer the Data Purchase Program; embed and promote data services to the campus; and look for opportunities to collaborate with researchers to strengthen the campus environment for using, documenting, and storing data.[19]

Data services consultation hours are offered four days per week and staffed by trained librarians and ATLAS. Researchers may drop in or make scheduled appointments with a specific expert. The Data Services Committee also administers a data-purchase program each semester, advertising a call for proposals for the purchase of data sets, which are archived and open for use by future researchers. Data literacy is primarily addressed through a series of data-related workshops. The data-centric librarians and ATLAS staff teach workshops on a wide variety of data-related topics. Examples include working with census data, basic GIS training, introduction to data-management plans, and an introduction to the Interuniversity Consortium for Political and Social Research (ICPSR). The Scholarly Commons space supports computers imaged with qualitative and quantitative software packages (e.g., SPSS, SAS, STATA, ArcGIS) and routinely reviews the packages based on feedback and requests.

Data literacy efforts are currently focused on increasing staff training opportunities for subject-specialist librarians, and the creation of expanded in-person and online learning opportunities.

Partner: Survey Research Laboratory[20]
Service area: Data Services
One of the most popular services offered by the Scholarly Commons is the consultation hours staffed by the Survey Research Lab. Established in 1964, the Survey Research Lab administers an array of services dedicated to the process of survey design and analysis. Survey Research Lab services are provided to the University of Illinois system as a for-fee service; however, the Scholarly Commons uses a portion of its funds to buy out staff time for consultations at no cost to graduate students and faculty. The services maintained by the Survey Research Lab staff include sample and questionnaire design, data collection and cleaning of data sets, and analysis of data. Staffing consultation hours one day per week brings visibility to Survey Research Lab expertise and further develops relationships with campus researchers. In turn, the Scholarly Commons purchases access to several qualitative and quantitative data software programs, trains the graduate assistants to answer basic data-related questions, and purchases reference titles at the suggestion of Survey Research Lab staff. In looking toward the future, the partners have considered expanding in-person learning opportunities and workshops on

survey-related topics and offering half-day seminars covering the basics of data collection (e.g., data setup, how to identify and deal with missing data, and basic analysis techniques).

Partner: Campus Information Technologies and Educational Services, Academic Technologies Services[21]
Service area: Teaching and Learning
The Scholarly Commons and campus instructional technology services have a similar educational goal for the academic community, providing scholars with assistance related to managing information through technology. Campus Information Technologies and Educational Services (CITES) is comprised of a division of teaching and learning, Academic Technologies Services. The staff are dedicated to exploring how technology can be leveraged for the university classroom (e.g., course-management systems, implementing the "flipped" classroom, supporting multimedia projects). To date, Academic Technology Services has partnered to offer workshops in the Scholarly Commons classroom on the integration of technology into teaching. Example workshops include how to best use presentation software for teaching and presentations, creating multimedia projects using iPads, and collaborative research strategies through the CITES-managed wiki and cloud computing service. Academic Technology Services, like all partnerships with the Scholarly Commons, benefits by expanding their reach to the campus community by increasing exposure to their services and in taking advantage of the triage system for referrals. In looking to identified areas for growth, the Scholarly Commons aims to work more closely with the Undergraduate Library's Media Commons,[22] a partnership with CITES that supports the creation of digital media.

Partner: Graduate College[23]
Service area: The Savvy Researcher Workshop Series and Campus Outreach
The Graduate College, in working with scholars in over one hundred disciplines, is in a unique position to reach students in all disciplines of a very large campus community, not unlike the mission of the Scholarly Commons.

The Savvy Researcher is an open workshop series that covers the advanced research and information-management needs of graduate students and faculty particularly around using technology in research. The Graduate College cosponsors the Savvy Researcher workshop series by advertising on their website and on a listserv, a weekly message that reaches a large percentage of graduate students. The listserv includes descriptions of offerings for the upcoming week, thereby highlighting the role the Scholarly Commons can play in students' professional development. The Graduate College has also contributed to the educational mission of the Scholarly Commons in developing and co-teaching a workshop related to the job search process. The workshop covers effective job-search strategies and introduces a variety of online tools meant to organize research related to the job hunt. And finally, the Scholarly Commons serves the Graduate College by advising on issues related to copyright concerns for the online submission and archiving process of dissertations. The Scholarly Commons team is currently working with the Graduate College to pioneer a new initiative, the Image of Research.[24] The annual competition, similar to other library awards for research, calls for graduate students to submit imagery related to their research, which will be showcased as an exhibit and online.

Partners: Hathi Trust Research Center[25] and Illinois Program for Research in the Humanities[26] and Institute for Computing in Humanities, Arts, and Social Science[27]
Service area: Digital Humanities
The English and Digital Humanities Librarian and the Scholarly Commons are working to provide a suite of support services related to the digital humanities. The team from the Scholarly Commons and the English and Digital Humanities Librarian meet regularly to discuss current digital humanities projects and to brainstorm ways that they can support increasingly complex digital humanities projects. There are three partners working in this arena: the Illinois Program for Research in the Humanities, the Hathi Trust Research Center, and the Institute for Computing in Humanities, Arts, and Social Science.

First, the goals for the Illinois Program for Research in the Humanities are focused on promoting conversations across the humanities, arts, and social sciences through workshops, fellowships, lectures, and offering some services. There are two projects on the horizon including cosponsoring lectures and exploring options for supporting Scalar,[28] an open-source presentation and publishing service.

Second, the Hathi Trust Research Center works to administer computational access to digital works in the public domain so that scholars can analyze texts and the associated data. The Scholarly Commons has partnered with the Hathi Trust Research Center to arrange front-end documentation, training, and support to scholars worldwide. While this Scholarly Commons project is still in the pilot stage, the plan is to serve as a portal to the Hathi Trust Research Center.

Third, the Institute for Computing in Humanities, Arts, and Social Science administers support for grants to accomplish large-scale humanities projects and provides access to high-performance computing. One of the primary areas of collaboration with the Institute for Computing in Humanities, Arts, and Social Science is to establish support for faculty and graduate students who aren't quite at the level or as comfortable with the tools that the

Institute for Computing in Humanities, Arts, and Social Science uses. The partnership is working to create beginner support in geographic information systems, text mining, network analysis, and so on.

Partner: Office of Undergraduate Research[29]
Service area: Publishing
The Office of Undergraduate Research is a provost initiative to foster collaborative undergraduate research efforts and aid in the development of educational opportunities for faculty and students across disciplines. In partnering with the Scholarly Commons, the Office of Undergraduate Research has allocated resources to archive undergraduate research projects in the institutional repository and in the creation of open-access undergraduate research journals. The Scholarly Commons purchased a hosted installation of Open Journal Systems, an open-source software that curates journals, in order to collect, edit, and publish journal articles. The publishing of original student work affords an opportunity to create information literacy initiatives to address the student as content creator and curator and educate graduate student advisors and faculty members on scholarly communication issues. Current workshop sessions include how to conduct a literature review, citation management, creating posters for the research symposium, and training on scholarly communication issues specific to the needs of undergraduate students (e.g., open access). A third partner in this effort, the University of Illinois Writing Center, provides peer-tutoring training for the undergraduate student editors. The Scholarly Commons reciprocates involvement in undergraduate research twofold: by accepting an invitation to serve on the Office of Undergraduate Research Advisory Board, and by curating a blog that reaches out to undergraduate research and teaching faculty by disseminating research tips and undergraduate research events. Future opportunities for the Scholarly Commons will build on the expansion of publishing efforts beyond journal publications and more educational efforts regarding scholarly communication issues.

Partner: Student Money Management Center[30]
Service area: Teaching and Learning
Academic libraries are increasingly involved with campus partners outside of traditional library-related issues. The Association of College and Research Libraries (ACRL) president, Trevor Dawes, emphasizes, "Being embedded in the academic culture gives us a unique opportunity to provide access to the information, resources, education, and tools that our community members need to make good financial decisions in our increasingly complex global financial ecosystem."[31] The Student Money Management Center, a division of the University Student Financial Services and Cashier Operations, works to provide educational initiatives to improve student understanding of finan-

cial literacy. The Student Money Management Center partners with the Scholarly Commons to offer a variety of workshops in the Scholarly Commons instructional space about information-management issues (e.g., how to protect your online identity and exploring how students' attitudes toward money shape their financial decisions). The Scholarly Commons also developed a bibliography of financial-literacy resources for students.[32] Looking toward the future, the Scholarly Commons is participating in campus-wide efforts to expand financial-literacy education to students at all levels of the university.

Partner: ORCID[33]
Service area: Scholarly Communication
ORCID is an online identification system and central registry that facilitates researchers' ability to navigate their workflow for manuscript submission and grant applications. As online systems continue to expand, researchers are increasingly aware of the responsibility to manage their online presence. This partnership takes the form of a volunteer ambassadorship, with the Scholarly Commons interweaving ORCID throughout workshops and campus-wide outreach efforts. For example, in a session about managing an online scholarly presence, librarians talk about the impact of personal research through online metric systems (e.g., ImpactStory,[34] ORCID). Marketing efforts through posters, website development, handouts, and giveaways are avenues for showcasing the work around the Scholarly Commons' mission to provide education on a wide variety of scholarly communication issues, including bibliometrics.

INTERNAL PARTNERSHIPS

Subject-specialist librarians and Library Information Technology Services are at the heart of the success of the Scholarly Commons. The holistic approach to librarianship requires that all librarians are responsible for data services and scholarly communication within their disciplines, and the Scholarly Commons model administers a solid underpinning of support for gradually learning new skills in emerging research areas. Staff training in the library is two-fold: training is developed for subject librarians from experts in specific areas (e.g., scholarly communication); plus the library purchases access to online training opportunities offered by the ACRL and other similar organizations.

Partner: Library Information Technology Services[35]
Library Information Technology (IT) provides the crux of support essential to running the sandbox environment[36] in the Scholarly Commons. The space

holds a dozen public-access computers, including three Macs, all of which are imaged with software programs not available on other library computers. Examples of software are ABBY FineReader, the Adobe Suite of products, AcrGIS, Atlas.ti, SPSS Statistics, Morae, Oxygen XML editor, Python, R and Rstudio, and much more.[37] In 2012, Library IT and the Scholarly Commons successfully petitioned for a professional staff position to maintain licensing and imaging support for the hardware in the space, as well as to support the large-screen monitor and technology in the conference room and to keep the licenses up to date in the instructional space. Start-up challenges comprised of setting a workflow for establishing a model for the ongoing acquisition, maintenance, support, and renewal of hardware and software. Currently, staff are looking into breaking software down into clusters within the Scholarly Commons space so that not all computers need to have all software programs, many of which take up considerable space on the hard drive. This decision should also offer more flexibility in supporting service programs, including adapting to the needs of teaching faculty as they increasingly incorporate specific software needs into their courses. As an example, a teaching faculty member approached the Scholarly Commons to give students access to QGIS,[38] a free and open-source geographic information systems program. Library IT was able to add the software to the computers on short notice, and the staff responded by learning the basics of QGIS in order to answer basic student questions. The Scholarly Commons is fielding an elevated number of requests to purchase and install software for students to use as part of their courses and this presents a challenge in how many software programs the staff is feasibly able to support. The Scholarly Commons, as a learning and lab space, continues toward a workflow that enables agility in testing new technologies for research as well as for teaching and learning.

Partner: Subject Specialists
The Savvy Researcher workshop series is mainly supported through the work of the subject-specialist librarians and external partners. From 2009 to 2013, the Savvy Researcher has contributed over forty unique workshops to the campus, reaching an average of 1,200 attendees per year. In looking for ways to expand library instruction opportunities, the workshops build on knowledge the librarian brings to the classroom. For example, librarians often assist with classes in demonstrating how to find information related to discipline-related work; however, there is usually little time to teach citation-management skills or to get into the details of data management. Subject librarians take leadership of the Savvy Researcher in specific areas in order to teach a wide variety of workshops related to advanced research and information-management skills. Example workshops include introducing the basics of several citation managers, demonstrating how to negotiate publication agreements, finding government statistics, using digital tools for archival

research, finding grants to support research, practical copyright for teaching and research, current awareness tools, creating research posters, and much more.[39] Almost all of the sessions offer online support through web pages or research guides. New workshops are consistently under development (e.g., bibliometric analysis of research output), with ideas being generated from assisting students in the Scholarly Commons, reference interactions, suggestions from teaching faculty, students, and librarians, and formal assessment techniques. The Savvy Researcher workshop series brings together the expertise of the partners and librarians and is an amplification of the educational mission of the Scholarly Commons.

Another area where subject librarians offer expertise to the campus is web and computer usability. The Digital Resources and Reference Librarian and the Technical Architect for Web Content provide expert support on an as-needed basis. The usability lab offers a space for researchers that is nearly soundproof with a Mac and PC and the corresponding software to perform usability testing. The Scholarly Commons collection development policy also includes web and computer usability.

ASSESSMENT

To assess traditional reference services, the University Library employs the Reference Effort Assessment Data (READ) Scale[40] and inputs data into an online management system, Desk Tracker.[41] The Scholarly Commons has grown steadily since its inception, but gathering assessment data for an innovative and new service has presented significant challenges. Assessment data for the Scholarly Commons looks much different than the data gathered for the Information Services Desk. Traditional reference service questions revolve around locating materials and assisting students with starting a research project. In tracking data for traditional reference services, librarians record the number of questions by assigning a READ Scale number and data related to the type of question (e.g., directional, looking for a specific resource, technical help with computers, research assistance), and a subject area.

In constructing a narrative about how the Scholarly Commons helps researchers, the interactions are more complex, users are usually repeat visitors, and questions are not only heavily technology-based but also vastly unpredictable, making them not easily quantifiable. Researchers often find the Scholarly Commons because they either are facing a technology-centric problem or have a research-related question that has many parts. In response, the Scholarly Commons coordinators modified the assessment input form to more clearly reflect the kinds of interactions faced on a daily basis. To supplement the data gathered by librarians and partners, there are formal assessment paper forms, a brief questionnaire asking patrons about their research and their experience in the Scholarly Commons. The coordinators have also implemented informal assessment strategies and are constantly watching Scholarly Commons' activities in motion, closely monitoring how researchers are interacting with the space and the services they receive from staff and partners.

FUTURE PLANS AND DEVELOPMENT

While the Scholarly Commons provides an entry point for services related to research data stewardship, the eResearch Task Force points out that the library, "cannot advance substantively unless there is both campus-level technical and personnel infrastructure to support data curation and preservation and domain-specific expertise to support research data management, preservation, and sustained access."[42] The eResearch Task Force acknowledges that "services for which campus researchers currently lack support include (a) a robust, secure storage and network infrastructure that is accessible to all campus units, (b) a local research data repository service, (c) data management and publishing services, and (d) data transformation and migration services."[43] The Task Force specifically recommends that the initiative collaborate with a series of campus partners: the Office of the Vice Chancellor for Research, Campus Information Technologies and Educational Services, and the National Center for Supercomputing Applications, as well as the colleges and their respective research centers. The Scholarly Commons will be the hub for research data services and the implementation committee is charged with overseeing the development of library-wide training opportunities, identifying external research data organizations with which the initiative should be engaged, and creating best practices for subject-specialist librarians working with faculty and researchers.[44] Efforts will be spearheaded by a director of research data services, a position that is supported by the University Library and the vice chancellor for research, and two data curation specialists in order to address needs related to data storage, networking, and manipulation and visualization.[45]

CONCLUSION

The overarching goal of the Scholarly Commons is to move from supporting discrete tasks related to technology and research to driving the educational process significantly forward by providing services that support a larger and more holistic picture of digital scholarship. Academic libraries are just beginning to adjust and innovate to the technology challenges our researchers face. The most difficult element of this endeavor is being unable to predict the questions our researchers will ask us; hence the need to prepare broadly. In bringing together partnerships across campus and performing regular environmental scans of our academic communities, the Scholarly Commons is building a community of researchers, one that is attempting to stay on the cutting edge of research endeavors. Our goal is to build on strategic campus partnerships through a combination of consultation services, robust staff training, and information-literacy efforts, in order to construct a foundation in which researchers can continue to collaborate with our knowledge of the research process.

NOTES

1. University Library, "New Service Models," last modified April 24, 2013. www.library.illinois.edu/nsm.
2. University Library, Scholarly Commons Leadership Team, "The Scholarly Commons: Bringing People Together in Support of Scholarship," University of Illinois at Urbana-Champaign, October 3, 2008, accessed September 21, 2013, www.library.illinois.edu/nsm/scholcom/ScholalryCommonsReport.pdf.
3. Ibid., 6.
4. University Library, Reference Services Implementation Team, "Reference Services Implementation Team: Final Report," University of Illinois at Urbana-Champaign, July 2011, accessed September 12, 2013, www.library.illinois.edu/nsm/reference/ReferenceImplementationNSMFinalReport_070611.pdf.
5. The three other in-person desk locations include the Undergraduate Library, Physical Sciences at Grainger Engineering Library, and Life Sciences at the Funk Family ACES Library.
6. University Library, "The Scholarly Commons: Bringing People Together in Support of Scholarship," 1.
7. University of Virginia Library, "Scholars' Lab," accessed December 1, 2013, www.scholarslab.org.
8. The University of North Carolina at Chapel Hill, "GIS & Data Services," accessed December 1, 2013, http://library.unc.edu/services/data.
9. The University of North Carolina at Chapel Hill, "Scholarly Communications Office," accessed December 1, 2013, http://library.unc.edu/scholcom.
10. University of California at Los Angeles, "UCLA Data Registry," accessed December 1, 2013, www.library.ucla.edu/service/data-registry-home.
11. Indiana University at Bloomington, "IU Libraries Scholars' Commons Series," accessed December 1, 2013, http://libprod.lib.indiana.edu/tools/workshops/workshop-listings.
12. The University of Kansas, Center for Digital Scholarship, "Digital Publishing," accessed December 1, 2013, http://cds.lib.ku.edu/services/journal-publishing.
13. University of Michigan Library, "Michigan Publishing," accessed December 1, 2013, www.publishing.umich.edu.
14. Craig Gibson and Meris Mandernach, "Reference Service at an Inflection Point: Transformations in Academic Libraries," in *The Proceedings of the ACRL 2013 Conference*, ed. Dawn M. Mueller (Chicago: ACRL, 2013), 491–99, accessed October 1, 2013, www.ala.org/acrl/sites/ala.org.acrl/files/content/conferences/confsandpreconfs/2013/papers/GibsonMandernach_Reference.pdf.
15. Lucinda Covert-Vail and Scott Collard, "New Roles for New Times: Research Library Services for Graduate Students" (Washington, DC: Association of Research Libraries, 2012), accessed September 21, 2013, www.arl.org/storage/documents/publications/nrnt-grad-roles-20dec12.pdf.

16. University of Illinois, Applied Technologies for Learning in the Arts and Sciences, "ATLAS," accessed December 1, 2013, www.atlas.illinois.edu.

17. University of Illinois Library, "Data Services Task Force," last modified March 9, 2011, accessed August 25, 2014, www.library.illinois.edu/committee/dataservice/dstf.html.

18. Membership includes staff from ATLAS and the Numeric and Spatial Data Librarian, Engineering Research Data Services Librarian, Life Sciences Data Services Librarian, and the Scholarly Commons Coordinators.

19. University of Illinois Library, "Numeric and Spatial Data Services," last modified September 5, 2013, accessed August 25, 2014, www.library.illinois.edu/sc/datagis/index.html.

20. University of Illinois at Chicago, "Survey Research Laboratory," accessed December 1, 2013, www.srl.uic.edu.

21. University of Illinois, Campus Information Technologies and Educational Services, "Online Teaching and Learning," last modified November 21, 2013, accessed August 25, 2014, www.cites.illinois.edu/onlinelearning/index.html.

22. University of Illinois Library, "Media Commons," last modified April 4, 2013, accessed August 25, 2014, www.library.illinois.edu/ugl/mc.

23. University of Illinois at Urbana-Champaign, "The Graduate College," accessed December 1, 2013, www.grad.illinois.edu.

24. Modeled after a similar program at the University of Illinois at Chicago: http://grad.uic.edu/cms/?pid=1000645, accessed December 1, 2013.

25. Hathi Trust Digital Library, "Our Research Center," accessed December 1, 2013, www.hathitrust.org/htrc.

26. University of Illinois, "Illinois Program for Research in the Humanities," accessed December 1, 2013, www.iprh.illinois.edu.

27. University of Illinois, "Institute for Computing in Humanities, Arts, and Social Science," accessed December 1, 2013, http://chass.illinois.edu.

28. The Alliance for Networking Visual Culture, "Scalar," accessed December 1, 2013, http://scalar.usc.edu.

29. University of Illinois at Urbana-Champaign, Office of the Provost, "Office of Undergraduate Research," accessed December 1, 2013, http://provost.illinois.edu/our.

30. University of Illinois at Urbana-Champaign, University Student Financial Services and Cashier Operations, "Student Money Management Center," accessed December 1, 2013, www.studentmoney.uillinois.edu.

31. Trevor A. Dawes, "Libraries, ACRL, and Financial Literacy: Helping Students Make Sound Decisions," *College & Research Libraries News* 74, no. 9 (October 2013): 466–67, accessed November 10, 2013, http://crln.acrl.org/content/74/9/466.full.

32. University of Illinois Library, "Financial Literacy," last modified December 16, 2013, accessed August 25, 2014, http://uiuc.libguides.com/financialliteracy.

33. ORCID, "Connecting Research and Researchers," accessed December 1, 2013, http://orcid.org.

34. ImpactStory, accessed December 1, 2013, http://impactstory.org.

35. University of Illinois Library, "Library IT Help Desk," last modified October 21, 2013, accessed August 25, 2014, www.library.illinois.edu/ithelp.

36. A sandbox environment is a flexible technology-enhanced work environment where the Scholarly Commons partners with Library IT in order to respond as quickly as possible to download new software programs so that researchers can assess its needs in support of their academic work.

37. University of Illinois Library, "Room 306 Main Technology," last modified September 16, 2013, accessed August 25, 2014, www.library.illinois.edu/it/helpdesk/groupspaces/main306sc.html.

38. "QGIS," last modified December 15, 2013, accessed August 25, 2014, www.qgis.org/en/site.

39. University of Illinois Library, "Savvy Researcher Workshops," accessed December 1, 2013, http://illinois.edu/calendar/list/4068.

40. Bella Karr Gerlich, "The READ Scale," accessed December 1, 2013, http://read-scale.org.

41. Compendium Library Services, "Desk Tracker," accessed December 1, 2013, www.desktracker.com.
42. University Library's eResearch Task Force, "eResearch Services at the University Library—Final Report of the Library eResearch Task Force," University of Illinois at Urbana-Champaign, January 16, 2013, accessed August 25, 2014, http://hdl.handle.net/2142/42561.
43. Ibid., 7.
44. Ibid., 3.
45. Ibid., 8.

BIBLIOGRAPHY

Covert-Vail, Lucinda, and Scott Collard. "New Roles for New Times: Research Library Services for Graduate Students." Washington, DC: Association of Research Libraries, 2012. Accessed September 21, 2013. www.arl.org/storage/documents/publications/nrnt-grad-roles-20dec12.pdf.

Dawes, Trevor A. "Libraries, ACRL, and Financial Literacy: Helping Students Make Sound Decisions." *College & Research Libraries News* 74, no. 9 (October 2013): 466–67. Accessed November 10, 2013. http://crln.acrl.org/content/74/9/466.full.

Gibson, Craig, and Meris Mandernach. "Reference Service at an Inflection Point: Transformations in Academic Libraries." In *The Proceedings of the ACRL 2013 Conference*, edited by Dawn M. Mueller, 491–99. Chicago: ACRL, 2013. Accessed October 1, 2013. www.ala.org/acrl/sites/ala.org.acrl/files/content/conferences/confsandpreconfs/2013/papers/GibsonMandemach_Reference.pdf.

University Library, Reference Services Implementation Team. "Reference Services Implementation Team: Final Report." University of Illinois at Urbana-Champaign, July 2011. Accessed September 12, 2013. www.library.illinois.edu/nsm/reference/ReferenceImplementationNSMFinalReport_070611.pdf.

University Library, Scholarly Commons Leadership Team. "The Scholarly Commons: Bringing People Together in Support of Scholarship." University of Illinois at Urbana-Champaign, October 3, 2008. Accessed September 21, 2013. www.library.illinois.edu/nsm/scholcom/ScholalryCommonsReport.pdf.

University Library's eResearch Task Force. "eResearch Services at the University Library—Final Report of the Library eResearch Task Force." University of Illinois at Urbana-Champaign, January 16, 2013. Accessed November 13, 2013. http://hdl.handle.net/2142/42561.

Part II

Diversity: Meeting the Information Needs of a Changing Demographic

Chapter Three

The Rainbow Connection

Reference Services for the LGBT Community in Academic Libraries

Matthew P. Ciszek

Over the past thirty years, the numbers of lesbian, gay, bisexual, and trans-gender (LGBT) students have increased steadily on college and university campuses. Many factors may explain this trend, including growing numbers of LGBT young adults who are more open about their sexual orientation, gender identity, or gender expression at a younger age, a willingness of students to identify openly as a member of the LGBT community in a college or university setting, and a growing acceptance of the LGBT community in wider society. Early attempts to serve this community on campus were most-ly through student-run organizations and resources; however, the late 1980s and 1990s saw higher education begin to devote resources to serving the needs of LGBT students.[1] Colleges and universities also started to create student centers to "provide student services and programs; offer campus-wide support to LGBT students, faculty, staff, their friends, and families; and work to offer opportunities for growth" for the entire institution.[2]

At the same time, there has been a growing interest in the academic study of the LGBT experience. Colleges and universities have created academic programs, curriculum, and courses in LGBT studies, and LGBT-related top-ics are now discussed in many courses and areas throughout a student's academic career. Wider issues in society, such as same-sex marriage, anti-gay bullying, and the fight for nondiscrimination protections for LGBT peo-ple, have increased the profile of the LGBT community. As these issues have taken on a prominence in national conversations, higher education has responded by creating coursework, services, and programs both for the LGBT community and about the LGBT experience.

Academic libraries often have followed the lead of their parent organizations in developing collections, programs, and services to serve the needs of the LGBT community and support research on LGBT-related topics or support LGBT studies curricula. Much of the work in this area has focused on collection development and bibliographic control; there has been scant research or practical examples of the development of reference services and programs geared toward the LGBT community in academic libraries. This chapter offers some best practices for academic libraries seeking to engage and inform the LGBT community on campus by creating reference services and programs that meet their needs.

DEFINITIONS

Although openly lesbian, gay, bisexual, and transgender individuals have become a more visible part of society, confusion still exists about these terms in wider society. Before we can discuss the LGBT community and serving them in an academic library setting, we must define and discuss these terms. The terms *lesbian*, *gay*, and *bisexual* refer to a person's sexual orientation, "an individual's physical and/or emotional attraction to the same and/or opposite gender."[3] The term *transgender* is distinct from sexual orientation and refers to a "broad range of people who experience and/or express their gender differently from what most people expect."[4] *Transgender* refers to either gender identity—"a person's innate, deeply felt psychological identification as male or female, which may or may not correspond to the person's body or designated sex at birth"[5]—or gender expression—"all of the external characteristics and behaviors that are socially defined as either masculine or feminine, such as dress, grooming, mannerisms, speech patterns and social interactions."[6]

The acronym *LGBT* is commonly used, in both the academic literature and the wider society, to identify the community of lesbian, gay, bisexual, and transgender persons. Other terms and acronyms may also be used to refer to this community, including GLBT, LGBTQ, LGBTQIA, sexual minorities, genderqueer, and queer, among others. An effort has been made to be as inclusive as possible in all definitions of the LGBT community, and to use standard acronyms, terms, and definitions. For the purposes of this chapter, the author chooses to use the terms *LGBT* and *LGBT community* as shorthand to refer to all people of varying sexual orientations, sexual minorities, gender identities, and gender expressions.

LITERATURE REVIEW

Library and information science has a long history of publications and research directed at determining the needs of special populations within the community and creating collections, services, and programs to meet these needs. However, even as many LGBT people were becoming more public about their sexual orientation, gender identity, or gender expression over the last thirty years, "little has been written concerning [LGBT] library services compared to other minority groups."[7] This was corrected in the early 1990s as more concerted research dedicated to serving the information needs of the LGBT community in libraries was conducted and published in the professional literature.[8] This research and writing features building collections of LGBT-related materials, with less emphasis on library services and programs for the LGBT community. Additionally, the research in this area has highlighted library types other than academic libraries, with a greater emphasis on research and initiatives in public or school library settings.

One of the first comprehensive works in this area is Cal Gough and Ellen Greenblatt's *Gay and Lesbian Library Service.*[9] The primary emphasis of this book is collection development, material selection, and acquisition of gay- and lesbian-related materials. Less prominence is paid toward library services and programs geared toward the LGBT community. However, in the chapter concerned with gay and lesbian materials in academic libraries, Suzy Taraba goes beyond collection development and stresses that academic libraries must make patrons "aware of the library's collecting efforts so that they will realize that the library can and does support research."[10] Simply providing LGBT-related collections and resources is not enough. Academic libraries also must include "individual contact with faculty and students, reference guides, bibliographies and pathfinders," among other resources.[11]

Notably absent from this seminal work is a treatment of the library and information needs of bisexual and transgender patrons. Meagan Albright states that "many libraries provide service to the lesbian and gay portion of the community, but do not include materials for the transgender" or bisexual segments of the community.[12] While there has been an uptick in research about the information needs of the transgender community in recent years, such as articles by Jami Kathleen Taylor[13] and Angie Beiriger and Rose M. Jackson,[14] even less professional literature covers the information needs of the bisexual community. Articles by Mark Norman[15] and Alfred J. Encarnacion[16] incorporate the bisexual community in larger treatments of the lesbian, gay, and bisexual communities. More recent comprehensive treatments of LGBT issues in libraries consist of Michael A. Lutes and Michael A. Montgomery's chapter on serving the needs of LGBT students in academic libraries[17] and Ellen Greenblatt's updating of her earlier anthology,[18] which contains a chapter on serving the needs of the entire LGBT community in academic libraries.[19]

Building a collection of LGBT-related resources should be followed up with additional resources and services. Finding aids, research guides, and similar materials can be created to provide access and discovery of LGBT collections. Reference and research services may also be developed, including programming and outreach geared toward the LGBT community. Ann Curry's trailblazing study examining public library reference services to gay and lesbian youth[20] was followed by research on the usage of online reference services by LGBT patrons[21] and studies of the circulation of LGBT-related materials at self-checkout stations.[22] Angie Manfredi stresses the need for serving LGBT young adults in public library collections and services,[23] while Tim Gardes looks for ways to serve LGBT students in a library media-center setting.[24] Albright brings much of this research together as she not only outlines programs and services that public libraries should develop for the LGBT community, but also stresses the importance of outreach to the community as well.[25]

While the majority of research into reference and research services has focused mainly on public and school libraries, a handful of research studies LGBT patrons in academic libraries. Library instruction in academic libraries geared toward the LGBT community is discussed in research by Sara McDowell,[26] while Matthew P. Ciszek suggests a relationship between LGBT campus climate and online reference sources in academic libraries.[27] Nanci Milone Hill provides examples of tangible ways that both academic and public libraries are serving the needs of the LGBT community,[28] and Bharat Mehra and Donna Braquet envision reference services for the LGBT community in academic libraries for the twenty-first century.[29] Only through the provision of a balanced program of collections and services geared toward the LGBT community can a library claim to meet the needs of this population.

Before additional collections and services can be developed, librarianship must gauge the needs of the LGBT community. Early research in this area looked inwardly and studied how the profession was serving the community,[30] but evolved into externally focused surveys seeking to identify the information needs of LGBT patrons. One of the first large-scale assessments of the needs of Canadian LGBT students found that more can be done to serve this community, despite general satisfaction with library resources and services.[31] Building on this research, Susann Schaller[32] and Mehra and Braquet[33] have performed surveys of the information needs of the LGBT communities in an academic setting, while Norman has done the same in public libraries.[34] Determining the needs of the LGBT community, through surveys, focus groups, and outreach, makes certain that libraries are building collections and creating services, programs, and resources for this community.

BEST PRACTICES

Create LGBT Research Guides

Academic libraries develop a number of research guides, in print and online formats, on a variety of topics, including specialized subjects and disciplines. While most academic libraries have produced and maintained print research guides for many years, many have now converted these guides to an online format available through the library website for ease of updating and consistency across subjects. Creating a research guide for LGBT-related resources serves as one of the quickest and least difficult means that academic libraries can undertake to provide better services and resources for the LGBT community. A well-written and updated guide to LGBT-related resources not only highlights the materials and resources located in the library's collections, but also guides patrons to external sources of information, many of which may not be widely known or easily accessible.

Moving to an online format for these guides has an added benefit for many LGBT patrons as well. Curry suggests that an online LGBT research guide may be the only resource consulted by these academic library patrons as "the Internet, accessed at home, is now the most vital source of information for college-age LGBT youth."[35] Due to the "anxiety of possible disclosure" of one's sexual orientation or gender identity/expression, LGBT patrons are much more likely to seek information on LGBT-related topics in an online, anonymous manner.[36] A well-written and -researched LGBT research guide takes into consideration the notion that not only are "[LGBT] library users . . . very private about their information needs, but they are not the only ones with these needs."[37] College and university students and faculty outside the LGBT community also may have reference questions and research demands about the LGBT community and LGBT-related topics. Thus, a well-written research guide on LGBT topics can be instrumental in offering resources and information to serve these patrons as well.

The Internet is a rich resource for materials geared toward the LGBT community or dealing with LGBT-related topics. Due to the "abundance of [LGBT]-related resources available on the Internet," academic libraries should make every attempt to collect and highlight "relevant Internet sites to [LGBT] patrons."[38] Academic libraries creating LGBT research guides should carefully review and select Internet sources for inclusion in the guide, and make every attempt to pair complementary sources from the Internet with those the library has in its collections and databases. Special consideration should be given to Internet sites authored by reputable LGBT organizations (i.e., the Human Rights Campaign; the National Lesbian, Gay, Bisexual, and Transgender Task Force; or the GLBT Round Table of the American Library Association) over sites maintained by unaffiliated individuals or less-respected organizations. Research guides at other colleges and universities may also furnish a wealth of additional Internet sources for the creation of a research guide.

Lastly, academic libraries must ensure that LGBT information sources are placed in a separate, top-level research guide to make it straightforward for patrons to find needed information. In a recent study of over 250 academic libraries, 11 percent of the libraries surveyed included LGBT-related topics in another research guide, usually geared toward gender studies or women's studies.[39] While full-text searching of online research guides is becoming more prevalent in academic libraries, most patrons would search for LGBT-related information in a separate guide geared toward these information sources. An immediate association between LGBT topics and the related subject areas of gender studies and women's studies cannot be assumed. This may cause patrons to overlook critical information sources. Academic libraries must create dedicated research guides of LGBT-related sources, and make it as easy as possible to find them.

Appoint a Contact Person for LGBT Resources

Equally important to a well-written and easy-to-locate research guide is identification of a contact person for LGBT resources. Having an LGBT resource "expert" creates a safe and welcoming environment for the LGBT community in the academic library, and offers additional help and support with reference and research needs in this area. Often, patrons have follow-up questions about the sources and additional needs for detailed research help outside the scope of a general research guide. In addition, many LGBT patrons and those researching LGBT topics may look for a "sympathetic ear," a person who has knowledge of the subject matter and a willingness and openness to talk about sensitive subjects without fear of embarrassment or lack of privacy. Selecting a contact person for LGBT resources, making this person available for regular consultation and research questions, and publicizing the availability of this person ensures that the LGBT community and those looking for LGBT-related resources have a dedicated and knowledgeable library professional at their disposal.

In many libraries, this person also authors the LGBT research guide, and/ or has additional knowledge of the LGBT community and LGBT-related resources. However, the library need not recruit a member of the LGBT community to serve in this capacity. Some additional training and experience with LGBT-related topics and information sources, however, is preferable. Most academic libraries building collections in LGBT-related areas will have a selector for these materials, and often this person serves as the library's "expert" in this area as well. Additionally, the contact person does not need to be dedicated to LGBT resources and research questions alone; many libraries will choose to utilize a reference librarian as the point person in a handful of related disciplines. Academic libraries typically assign the responsibilities of serving as an LGBT contact person into diversity librarian positions or group the responsibilities with other allied subject matter, like gender and women's studies. However a library chooses to structure it, "a welcoming, enthusiastic, and compassionate" person to work with the LGBT community on their research needs and others who seek LGBT-related information has a "positive impact" on all patrons.[40]

Offering Alternative Reference and Circulation Services

Reference and public services play a large role in contributing to a welcoming and service-oriented space. However, some members of the LGBT community may feel uncomfortable seeking help from library staff in person for fear of "outing" themselves or embarrassment at asking reference questions about sensitive topics related to sexuality and gender identity/expression. Some academic libraries provide online reference services, and this type of service may prove more useful to the LGBT community. LGBT individuals may also fear asking "sensitive questions," like those relating to LGBT topics, and seek out online sources of assistance due to the anonymity and avoidance of disapproval and social cost that these services accommodate.[41] Online reference may be the only reference help that LGBT students and others seek. Therefore, libraries should ensure that all staff involved in online reference have basic training on terminology and issues related to the LGBT community. More detailed questions and research requests should be handed off to an "expert" in this area to ensure that the reference needs are met in a timely and coordinated manner.

Additionally, research indicates that LGBT-related materials circulate more often when self-checkout machines are available to patrons. Stephanie Mathson and Jeffrey Hancks report that LGBT-related books are more likely to be circulated using an unmediated self-checkout machine than at the circulation desk in an academic library for many of the same reasons that online reference services are preferred by the LGBT community.[42] LGBT patrons appreciate this additional means of circulating LGBT-related materials. Self-checkout machines negate fears of disclosure to peer students that may be working at an academic library circulation desk or others on the library staff. This research underscores the need for libraries to be aware of and sensitive to LGBT patrons while providing alternative avenues for service in the form of online or self-service amenities.

Highlight LGBT Collections and Resources

Building a collection of LGBT-related resources is important, but academic libraries should build awareness of these among the LGBT community and all users of the library. Creating LGBT research guides and selecting and introducing "experts" in the library who can assist with LGBT-related research are good starts, but an academic library seeking to serve the needs of the community will also want to showcase these collections and resources. While "books and resources for LGBT patrons are an integral part of the library's collection," programming and outreach to LGBT patrons is equally vital.[43] Angie Manfredi suggests that "once titles with [LGBT] content have become part of your collection, the next step in advocating and integrating is to add them to the standard repertoire of your cumulative work as a . . . librarian."[44] Often this work of marketing collections, programming, and outreach will take many forms in an academic library.

One of the easiest and most straightforward means of informing patrons of LGBT collections and increasing awareness of the LGBT community is through library displays. The purpose of this is not only to "highlight titles with [LGBT] content," but also to "emphasize that your library is committed to integrated library service to all your patrons."[45] Many academic libraries create displays around Black History Month, Hispanic Heritage Month, and other celebrations of diversity throughout the year. Academic libraries seeking to serve the LGBT community may consider displays to celebrate LGBT History Month in October or LGBT Pride Month in June. An additional idea may be to display a number of "banned" LGBT materials during Banned Books Week. Libraries will want to ensure that the LGBT community and LGBT materials are given equal time and space in library displays. Catherine Ritchie and Dale McNeill give the clearest justification for why we should be actively promoting LGBT-related materials in academic libraries:

> Along with all the other population groups a public library serves, a library's [LGBT] patrons deserve to see themselves reflected in a facility's displays, as so African Americans, Asian Americans, Latinos, and aficionados of gardening, mystery novels, or true crime accounts. To exclude any single population from representation is prejudicial and a violation of the Library Bill of Rights.[46]

If we "actively promote parts of our collection and programs to other members of the community, but ignore the LGBT population, we are in effect practicing a form of censorship."[47]

Programming and outreach has typically been the purview of public libraries, but developing these efforts in academic libraries does much to serve the LGBT community on campus as well as the larger LGBT community surrounding the college or university. Academic libraries should consider sponsoring speakers from the LGBT community to talk about diversity and the LGBT experience. Authors of LGBT literature and research, often from the institution's own faculty, can be invited to give lectures, book signings, or poetry readings at the library. Coordinated events between the library and the campus LGBT center during a library open house or LGBT History Month are an excellent way to highlight services and resources of both the center and the library. Although many academic libraries do some of these activities, more can always be done to provide outreach and programming for the LGBT community.[48]

Partner with LGBT Organizations

Outreach and programming are two important dimensions of greater partnership between an academic library and LGBT library users. Libraries should seek not only to make relevant collections, resources, and services available to LGBT students, faculty, and staff, but also to partner with campus organizations and organizations in the wider community in order to determine the information needs of LGBT patrons and build support of the library among the LGBT community. Albright suggests that libraries "should not only provide basic services to the LGBT community[;] they should also perform outreach . . . to determine further needs and services"[49] the academic library can make available to these patrons. Some academic libraries offer "roving reference services" in LGBT student centers to reach out to this student population, while others make reference materials authored by national LGBT organizations available on the library's website or in the reference area. Partnering with campus LGBT centers to catalog and highlight collections of LGBT-related materials located outside the library can be a means to increase awareness of resources on campus. Consulting with national and local LGBT organizations, as well as discussions with LGBT students, faculty, and staff, offers a wealth of information to library staff and administration on how to offer comprehensive services to the LGBT community, and incorporate them into the library on a broad scale.[50]

Building support for the academic library among LGBT patrons is critical to meeting their needs. Alvin M. Schrader calls on libraries to "proceed systematically and build on community support" when working with the LGBT students, faculty, and staff.[51] Reaching out to the LGBT community "spreads the word that the . . . library is listening," and introduces the library as a "positive source of information."[52] Making personal connections with members of the LGBT community and LGBT organizations provides great promotion of the library's LGBT collections and services, but also serves as a rich source of speakers and programming ideas geared toward LGBT people and those interested in the subject matter.[53] Greater collaboration between the library and the LGBT community is beneficial to both, and warrants that the needs of all patrons are being met.

Develop LGBT-Related Library Instruction

Meeting the information needs of the LGBT community extends to library instruction as well. Library instruction must be "inclusive, not heterosexist, and meet the information needs of all students for LGBT materials."[54] Efforts should be made to include LGBT topics and sources in general library instruction to familiarize all library patrons with the LGBT community and their issues. Academic libraries may want to consider creating library workshops targeting LGBT information sources, which may be offered in conjunction with an LGBT-related class, or as a stand alone workshop for interested students, faculty, and staff. Emphasis should be given not only to LGBT-related materials, but also to the terminology used by LGBT people and difficulties that nonstandard terminology creates for finding information, especially online. Library instruction can serve as an important tool for raising awareness of not only LGBT-related sources of information but also the LGBT community among the academic community-at-large.

Formal, in-class instruction is not the only means an academic library can utilize to educate its patrons about LGBT issues. Often the most profound library instruction takes place in the "teachable moments" at the reference desk or during a one-on-one research-assistance session. Students and faculty who may not have time to attend a dedicated class on LGBT topics will most certainly benefit from librarians knowledgeable on these topics who can expand and deepen research in this area. LGBT patrons who may be reticent about attending a public workshop, but who may need detailed research help and instruction in LGBT-related materials, may find this more private means of instruction preferable. Finally, including instruction on LGBT topics in the day-to-day activities of the reference desk enriches the overall diversity of the academic library and ensures that the information needs of the LGBT faculty, staff, and students are being met, while also expanding the horizons of the college or university community as a whole.

CONCLUSION

Academic libraries must opt for a "holistic strategy in providing library services and collections" to the LGBT community.[55] Building collections of LGBT-related materials is an excellent start, but to fully meet the needs of LGBT patrons and others seeking LGBT-related information, libraries must also develop reference resources, services, and programs. Some best practices have been identified in this chapter to assist academic libraries in doing so. Building and maintaining top-level research guides on LGBT-related topics is critical to direct patrons to resources and collections. Developing knowledgeable reference staff and appointing a "point person" for LGBT resources reinforces the commitment to serving the needs of LGBT persons.

Offering alternative circulation and reference services that allow LGBT patrons to preserve anonymity overcomes trepidations about "outing oneself," while highlighting LGBT collections and providing LGBT programming and services allows those patrons who are more open about their sexuality, gender identity, and gender expression to see themselves in the larger institution. Partnering with LGBT organizations leads to better reference service and richer collections, services, and programs in the academic library. Finally, library instruction can be used, both in classroom settings and through "teachable moments" at the reference desk, to increase understanding of LGBT issues among the wider academic community.

Following these best practices ensures that the academic library is meeting its "obligation to challenge the myths and misconceptions that prevail about LGBT patrons and their information needs."[56] LGBT students, faculty, and staff are present on every college and university campus. Academic libraries in the twenty-first century must engage and inform this growing community by creating relevant and forward-looking reference services and programs, and educate all students about LGBT issues through allowing the stories and experiences of the LGBT community to be disseminated widely.

NOTES

1. Michael J. Cuyjet, Mary F. Howard-Hamilton, and Diane L. Cooper, eds., *Multiculturalism on Campus: Theory, Models, and Practices for Understanding Diversity and Creating Inclusion* (Sterling, VA: Stylus, 2011), 297.

2. Ibid.

3. "Sexual Orientation and Gender Identity: Terminology and Definitions," Human Rights Campaign, accessed January 5, 2014, www.hrc.org/resources/entry/sexual-orientation-and-gender-identity-terminology-and-definitions.

4. Ibid.

5. Ibid.

6. Ibid.

7. Steven Joyce, "Lesbian, Gay, and Bisexual Library Service: A Review of the Literature," *Public Libraries* 39, no. 5 (2000): 270.

8. Ibid., 271.

9. Cal Gough and Ellen Greenblatt, eds., *Gay and Lesbian Library Service* (Jefferson, NC: McFarland, 1990).

10. Suzy Taraba, "Collecting Gay and Lesbian Materials in an Academic Library," in *Gay and Lesbian Library Service*, ed. Cal Gough and Ellen Greenblatt (Jefferson, NC: McFarland, 1990), 34.

11. Ibid.

12. Meagan Albright, "The Public Library's Responsibilities to LGBT Communities: Recognizing, Representing, and Serving," *Public Libraries* 45, no. 5 (2006): 54.

13. Jami Kathleen Taylor, "Targeting the Information Needs of Transgender Individuals," *Current Studies in Librarianship* 26, no. 1/2 (2002): 85–109.

14. Angie Beiriger and Rose M. Jackson, "An Assessment of the Information Needs of Transgender Communities in Portland, Oregon," *Public Library Quarterly* 26, no. 1–2 (2007): 45–60.

15. Mark Norman, "OUT on Loan: A Survey of the Use and Information Needs of Users of the Lesbian, Gay, and Bisexual Collection of Brighton and Hove Libraries," *Journal of Librarianship and Information Science* 31, no. 4 (1999): 188–96.

16. Alfred J. Encarnacion, "The Essentiality of G/L/B/T Collections in Public Libraries," *Bookmobile and Outreach Services* 8, no. 1 (2005): 7–22.

17. Michael A. Lutes and Michael A. Montgomery, "Out in the Stacks: Opening Academic Library Collections to Lesbian, Gay, Bisexual, and Transgender Students," in *Working with Lesbian, Gay, Bisexual, and Transgender Students: A Handbook for Faculty and Administrators*, ed. Ronni L. Sanlo, 105–13 (Westport, CT: Greenwood Press, 1998).

18. Ellen Greenblatt, ed., *Serving LGBTIQ Library and Archives Users: Essays on Outreach, Service, Collections and Access* (Jefferson, NC: McFarland, 2011).

19. K. L. Clarke, "LGBTIQ Users and Collections in Academic Libraries," in *Serving LGBTIQ Library and Archives Users: Essays on Outreach, Service, Collections and Access*, ed. Ellen Greenblatt, 81–112 (Jefferson, NC: McFarland, 2011).

20. Ann Curry, "If I Ask, Will They Answer?: Evaluating Public Library Reference Service to Gay and Lesbian Youth," *Reference & User Services Quarterly* 45, no. 1 (2005): 65–74.

21. Samantha Thompson, "'I Wouldn't Normally Ask This . . . ': Or, Sensitive Questions and Why People Seem More Willing to Ask Them at a Virtual Reference Desk," *The Reference Librarian* 51, no. 2 (2010): 171–74.

22. Stephanie Mathson and Jeffrey Hancks, "Privacy Please? A Comparison Between Self-Checkout and Book Checkout Desk Circulation Rates for LGBT and Other Books," *Journal of Access Services* 4, no. 3–4 (2006): 27–37.

23. Angie Manfredi, "Accept the Universal Freak Show," *Young Adult Library Services* 7, no. 4 (2009): 26–31.

24. Tim Gardes, "Serving Lesbian, Gay, Bisexual, Transgendered, and Questioning Teens in Your Library Media Center," *CSLA Journal* 32, no. 1 (2008): 23–24.

25. Albright, "The Public Library's Responsibilities to LGBT Communities," 52–56.

26. Sara McDowell, "Library Instruction for Lesbian, Gay, Bisexual, and Transgendered Students," in *Teaching the New Library to Today's Users*, ed. Trudi E. Jacobson and Helene C. Williams (New York: Neal-Schuman, 2000), 71–86.

27. Matthew P. Ciszek, "Out on the Web: The Relationship between Campus Climate and GLBT-Related Web-Based Resources in Academic Libraries," *Journal of Academic Librarianship* 37, no. 5 (2011): 434.

28. Nanci Milone Hill, "Out and About: Serving the GLBT Population @ Your Library," *Public Libraries* 46, no. 4 (2007): 18–24.

29. Bharat Mehra and Donna Braquet, "Progressive LGBTQ Reference: Coming Out in the 21st Century," *Reference Services Review* 39, no. 3 (2011): 401–22.

30. Eric Bryant, "Pride and Prejudice," *Library Journal* 120, no. 11 (1999): 37–39.

31. Pascal Lupien, "LGBT/Sexual Diversity Studies Students and Academic Libraries: A Study of User Perceptions and Satisfaction," *The Canadian Journal of Information and Library Science* 31, no. 2 (2007): 131–47.

32. Susann Schaller, "The Information Needs of LGBTQ College Students," *Libri* 61, no. 2 (2011): 100–111.

33. Mehra and Braquet, "Progressive LGBTQ Reference," 401–22.

34. Norman, "OUT on Loan," 188–96.

35. Curry, "If I Ask, Will They Answer?," 66.

36. Schaller, "The Information Needs of LGBTQ College Students," 109.

37. Linda B. Alexander and Sarah D. Miselis, "Barriers to GLBTQ Collection Development and Strategies for Overcoming Them," *Young Adult Library Services* 5, no. 3 (2007): 44.

38. Cal Gough and Ellen Greenblatt, "Barriers to Selecting Materials about Sexual and Gender Diversity," in *Serving LGBTIQ Library and Archives Users: Essays on Outreach, Service, Collections and Access*, ed. Ellen Greenblatt (Jefferson, NC: McFarland, 2011): 168.

39. Ciszek, "Out on the Web," 434.

40. Curry, "If I Ask, Will They Answer?," 73.

41. Thompson, "I Wouldn't Normally Ask This . . . ," 171–74.

42. Mathson and Hancks, "Privacy Please?," 27–37.

43. Hill, "Out and About: Serving the GLBT Population @ Your Library," 21.

44. Manfredi, "Accept the Universal Freak Show," 27.

45. Ibid., 28.

46. Catherine Ritchie and Dale McNeill, "LGBTQ Issues in Public Libraries," in *Serving LGBTIQ Library and Archives Users*, ed. Ellen Greenblatt (Jefferson, NC: McFarland: 2011), 66.

47. Hill, "Out and About: Serving the GLBT Population @ Your Library," 24.

48. Ibid., 21.

49. Albright, "The Public Library's Responsibilities to LGBT Communities," 53.

50. Ibid.

51. Alvin M. Schrader, "Challenging Silence, Challenging Censorship, Building Resilience: LGBTQ Services and Collections in Public, School and Post-Secondary Libraries," *Feliciter* 55, no. 3 (2009): 109.

52. Ritchie and McNeill, "LGBTQ Issues in Public Libraries," 61.

53. Ibid., 68.

54. McDowell, "Library Instruction for Lesbian, Gay, Bisexual, and Transgendered Students," 75.

55. Schrader, "Challenging Silence, Challenging Censorship, Building Resilience," 109.

56. Jennifer Downey, "Public Library Collection Development Issues Regarding the Information Needs of GLBT Patrons," *Progressive Librarian* 25 (2005): 91.

ADDITIONAL RESOURCES

American Library Association. "Gay, Lesbian, Bisexual, and Transgender Round Table (GLBTRT)." Accessed February 28, 2014. www.ala.org/glbtrt/glbtrt.

———. "Office of Literacy and Outreach Services' List of LGBT Resources." Accessed February 28, 2014. http://delicious.com/alaolos/GLBT.

———. "Out in the Library: Materials, Displays and Services for the Gay, Lesbian, Bisexual, and Transgender Community." Accessed March 1, 2014. www.ala.org/advocacy/intfreedom/iftoolkits/glbttoolkit/glbttoolkit.

———. "Over the Rainbow Books: A Book List from the Gay, Lesbian, Bisexual, and Transgender Round Table of the American Library Association." Accessed March 1, 2014. www.glbtrt.ala.org/overtherainbow.

———. "Stonewall Book Awards." Accessed March 1, 2014. www.ala.org/glbtrt/award.

EBSCO Industries Inc. "LGBT Life: LGBT Journals, Magazines and Newspapers." Accessed February 28, 2014. www.ebscohost.com/academic/lgbt-life.

Lambda Literary Foundation. "Lambda Literary: The Leader in LGBT Book Reviews, Author Interviews, Opinion, and News Since 1989." Accessed February 28, 2014. www.lambdaliterary.org.

Pennsylvania State University, LGBTA Student Resource Center and the Consortium of Higher Education LGBT Resource Professionals. "LGBTQ Architect." Accessed on February 28, 2014. http://architect.lgbtcampus.org.

Policy Institute of the National Gay and Lesbian Task Force. "Transgender Equality: A Handbook for Activists and Policymakers." Accessed March 1, 2014. www.thetaskforce.org/downloads/reports/reports/TransgenderEquality.pdf.

Transgender Law and Policy Institute. "Ways that U.S. Colleges and Universities Meet the Day-to-Day Needs of Transgender Students." Accessed March 1, 2014. www.transgenderlaw.org/college/guidelines.htm.

BIBLIOGRAPHY

Albright, Meagan. "The Public Library's Responsibilities to LGBT Communities: Recognizing, Representing, and Serving." *Public Libraries* 45, no. 5 (2006): 52–56.

Alexander, Linda B., and Sarah D. Miselis. "Barriers to GLBTQ Collection Development and Strategies for Overcoming Them." *Young Adult Library Services* 5, no. 3 (2007): 43–49.

Beiriger, Angie, and Rose M. Jackson. "An Assessment of the Information Needs of Transgender Communities in Portland, Oregon." *Public Library Quarterly* 26, no. 1–2 (2007): 45–60.

Bryant, Eric. "Pride and Prejudice." *Library Journal* 120, no. 11 (1999): 37–39.

Ciszek, Matthew P. "Out on the Web: The Relationship between Campus Climate and GLBT-Related Web-Based Resources in Academic Libraries." *Journal of Academic Librarianship* 37, no. 5 (2011): 430–36.

Clarke, K. L. "LGBTIQ Users and Collections in Academic Libraries." In *Serving LGBTIQ Library and Archives Users: Essays on Outreach, Service, Collections and Access*, edited by Ellen Greenblatt, 81–112. Jefferson, NC: McFarland, 2011.

Curry, Ann. "If I Ask, Will They Answer?: Evaluating Public Library Reference Service to Gay and Lesbian Youth." *Reference & User Services Quarterly* 45, no. 1 (2005): 65–74.

Cuyjet, Michael J., Mary F. Howard-Hamilton, and Diane L. Cooper, eds. *Multiculturalism on Campus: Theory, Models, and Practices for Understanding Diversity and Creating Inclusion*. Sterling, VA: Stylus, 2011.

Downey, Jennifer. "Public Library Collection Development Issues Regarding the Information Needs of GLBT Patrons." *Progressive Librarian* 25 (2005): 86–95.

Encarnacion, Alfred J. "The Essentiality of G/L/B/T Collections in Public Libraries." *Bookmobile and Outreach Services* 8, no. 1 (2005): 7–22.

Gardes, Tim. "Serving Lesbian, Gay, Bisexual, Transgendered, and Questioning Teens in Your Library Media Center." *CSLA Journal* 32, no. 1 (2008): 23–24.

Gough, Cal, and Ellen Greenblatt. "Barriers to Selecting Materials about Sexual and Gender Diversity." In *Serving LGBTIQ Library and Archives Users: Essays on Outreach, Service, Collections and Access*, edited by Ellen Greenblatt, 165–73. Jefferson, NC: McFarland, 2011.

———, editors. *Gay and Lesbian Library Service.* Jefferson, NC: McFarland, 1990.

Greenblatt, Ellen, ed. *Serving LGBTIQ Library and Archives Users: Essays on Outreach, Service, Collections and Access.* Jefferson, NC: McFarland, 2011.

Hill, Nanci Milone. "Out and About: Serving the GLBT Population @ Your Library." *Public Libraries* 46, no. 4 (2007): 18–24.

Human Rights Campaign. "Sexual Orientation and Gender Identity: Terminology and Definitions." Accessed January 5, 2014. www.hrc.org/resources/entry/sexual-orientation-and-gender-identity-terminology-and-definitions.

Joyce, Steven. "Lesbian, Gay, and Bisexual Library Service: A Review of the Literature." *Public Libraries* 39, no. 5 (2000): 270–79.

Lupien, Pascal. "LGBT/Sexual Diversity Studies Students and Academic Libraries: A Study of User Perceptions and Satisfaction." *The Canadian Journal of Information and Library Science* 31, no. 2 (2007): 131–47.

Lutes, Michael A., and Michael A. Montgomery. "Out in the Stacks: Opening Academic Library Collections to Lesbian, Gay, Bisexual, and Transgender Students." In *Working with Lesbian, Gay, Bisexual, and Transgender Students: A Handbook for Faculty and Administrators*, edited by Ronni L. Sanlo, 105–13. Westport, CT: Greenwood Press, 1998.

Manfredi, Angie. "Accept the Universal Freak Show." *Young Adult Library Services* 7, no. 4 (2009): 26–31.

Mathson, Stephanie, and Jeffrey Hancks. "Privacy Please? A Comparison between Self-Checkout and Book Checkout Desk Circulation Rates for LGBT and Other Books." *Journal of Access Services* 4, no. 3–4 (2006): 27–37.

McDowell, Sara. "Library Instruction for Lesbian, Gay, Bisexual, and Transgendered Students." In *Teaching the New Library to Today's Users*, edited by Trudi E. Jacobson and Helene C. Williams, 71–86. New York: Neal-Schuman, 2000.

Mehra, Bharat, and Donna Braquet, "Progressive LGBTQ Reference: Coming Out in the 21st Century." *Reference Services Review* 39, no. 3 (2011): 401–22.

Norman, Mark. "OUT on Loan: A Survey of the Use and Information Needs of Users of the Lesbian, Gay, and Bisexual Collection of Brighton and Hove Libraries." *Journal of Librarianship and Information Science* 31, no. 4 (1999): 188–96.

Ritchie, Catherine, and Dale McNeill. "LGBTQ Issues in Public Libraries." In *Serving LGBTIQ Library and Archives Users*, edited by Ellen Greenblatt, 59–69. Jefferson, NC: McFarland, 2011.

Schaller, Susann. "The Information Needs of LGBTQ College Students." *Libri* 61, no. 2 (2011): 100–111.

Schrader, Alvin M. "Challenging Silence, Challenging Censorship, Building Resilience: LGBTQ Services and Collections in Public, School and Post-Secondary Libraries." *Feliciter* 55, no. 3 (2009): 107–9.

Taraba, Suzy. "Collecting Gay and Lesbian Materials in an Academic Library." In *Gay and Lesbian Library Service*, edited by Cal Gough and Ellen Greenblatt, 25–37. Jefferson, NC: McFarland, 1990.

Taylor, Jami Kathleen. "Targeting the Information Needs of Transgender Individuals." *Current Studies in Librarianship* 26, no. 1/2 (2002): 85–109.

Thompson, Samantha. "'I Wouldn't Normally Ask This . . . ': Or, Sensitive Questions and Why People Seem More Willing to Ask Them at a Virtual Reference Desk." *The Reference Librarian* 51, no. 2 (2010): 171–74.

Chapter Four

Reference Services in a Shifting World

Other Languages, Other Services

Valeria E. Molteni and Eileen K. Bosch

Driven primarily by Latino immigration and population growth, the use of Spanish has become an integral part of many aspects of life in the United States, including higher education. As more Latinos graduate from K–12 schools, the number of Latinos attending college is expected to increase. The authors of this chapter, two librarians from California State University, Long Beach (CSULB), and from San José State University (SJSU) will seek to address this shifting demographic and the information needs of a rising number of Spanish-speaking college students. In addition, they will discuss how different translation practices and the use of patrons' native languages can augment traditional reference services, in-person research consultations, and virtual reference services—whether asynchronous (e-mail) or synchronous (chat and video chat)—to this growing population of library patrons who may be language students, foreign students, or bilingual citizens. Furthermore, the chapter will show different strategies and approaches for providing enhanced reference services to a user population with diverse cultural and language backgrounds.

LITERATURE REVIEW

Latinos are one of the largest and fastest-growing minority groups in the United States according to the 2010 Census. Latinos represent 16 percent of the U.S. population and by 2050, it is estimated that this number will increase to 30 percent. Since Latinos are a fairly young population, with one in four youth under the age of eighteen and one in five K–12 school-aged children, the U.S. Census Bureau predicts that, by 2020, almost one in four college-aged adults will be Latino. Despite the steady and growing numbers of Latino students, Latinos have the lowest educational attainment rate compared to other minority groups; only 19 percent of Latinos have a college degree, compared to 42 percent of white Americans and 26 percent of African Americans. From all the states in the country, California has the largest gap between Latino (15.5 percent) and white (50 percent) adults with degrees.

As this diverse population is reaching the academy, higher educational systems and academic libraries have been trying to address these demographic changes. Much research has been produced to understand this new reality. Julie Renee Posselt and Kim R. Black[1] have studied the success of a specific program oriented to reach minorities in doctoral programs: the McNair Scholar Program. In the study, the authors confirm previous findings that academic activities and other university support services increase the probability of retention and academic achievement for minorities and first-generation students.[2] This is especially significant for the Latino/a population as this group is paradigmatic regarding their needs for success in the academic system. For example, researchers look at cultural congruity and psychological well-being as a measure of academic persistence,[3] and they note that Latino students experience alienation from an educational system that is foreign to them,[4] and also that they do not feel that their identity as bilingual students is respected.[5]

In spite of being the fastest-growing minority group in higher education, Latinos are also the highest risk to drop out, especially during their first year of college.[6] Overall, only thirteen out of one hundred Latinos have a four-year college degree. Because many are first-generation students, they rarely have the support of their families to engage in the college experience. Furthermore, they face obstacles such as the high cost of college education, family, and work obligations, as well as lack of information about available financial aid and academic support to pursue their academic goals.[7]

According to the American Library Association (ALA), about 21 million people in the United States speak limited or no English, 50 percent more than a decade ago. As a result, libraries need to develop services for non-English-speaking patrons, such as: immigrants, international students, heritage language learners (a language learned in the home environment), and international visitors.

Due to these factors, academic libraries can be a very intimidating place for Latino students. They experience challenges of dealing with cultural and linguistic barriers, and feelings of social isolation that complicate the process of acculturation to higher education.[8] According to the study conducted by Dallas Long, Latino college students use academic libraries less often, do not frequently ask for librarian assistance, use academic libraries later in their studies, and do not fully understand the range of resources that academic libraries can provide to them in support of their academic studies (reference services, consultations with subject librarians, interlibrary loan services, or research databases).[9] In addition, the study found that Latino students perceive libraries as a space for cultural support based on their public library experiences. In other words, Latino students try to mirror in academic libraries the sense of community and social connections they find in public libraries, such as speaking Spanish with library staff or having access to library materials in Spanish. These cultural identity issues were found in the study conducted by Susan Luévano-Molina, who surveyed Mexican resident users of public libraries in southern California.[10] The findings pointed out that for Latinos, "the public library fulfills a need for the positive reinforcement of the communities' cultural and educational activities."[11]

With this in mind, there has been a national push in the library profession to engage in broader discussions about the inadequacy of library services for multicultural patrons, especially for the growing demographic of Latinos. As a result, in 2012, the Association of College and Research Libraries (ACRL) published the *Diversity Standards: Cultural Competency for Academic Libraries*. Spearheaded by the Racial and Ethnic Diversity Committee, the ACRL developed these standards based on the 2001 National Association of Social Workers' *NASW Standards for Cultural Competence in Social Work Practice*. These standards provide a cultural competence framework to support libraries and librarians in becoming more knowledgeable of the cultural and language differences of multicultural library users.[12] Furthermore, noticing the inadequacy of library services for Latinos and diverse populations of library users, Patricia Montiel-Overall has proposed a framework for developing cultural competence for library and information science professionals and identified three domains in which cultural competence can be developed: cognitive, interpersonal, and environmental.[13]

CASE STUDIES

CSULB and SJSU are two of the largest campuses of the California State University (CSU) system, which—with its 23 campuses, 437,000 students, and 47,000 faculty members—is one of the largest institutions of public higher education in the nation.[14]

CSULB is the second-largest campus of the twenty-three campuses in the CSU system, and one of the largest universities in the state of California by enrollment—undergraduate and graduate—with a total number of 36,279 students for the fall 2012 semester. The university is located three miles from the Pacific Ocean in the southeastern coastal tip of Los Angeles County. Additionally, it has one of the West Coast's most racially diverse student bodies, and *Diverse Issues in Higher Education* has ranked it ninth in the nation in conferring baccalaureate degrees to minority students.[15] It is also a Hispanic-Serving Institution (HSI), which is defined as a nonprofit institution that has at least 25 percent Hispanic full-time equivalent enrollment, and, of that Hispanic enrollment, at least 50 percent are low income. CSULB obtained its HSI eligibility status in fall 2005 when 8,663 Latino/a students enrolled at the campus, representing 25.1 percent of undergraduate and graduate students. In fall of 2012, Latino/a student enrollment increased to 33.3 percent.[16]

SJSU is located in downtown San José, California, in the heart of Santa Clara County. As of fall 2012, the university had 30,448 students and 1,978 faculty on campus. From July 1, 2011, to June 30, 2012, SJSU awarded 4,900 bachelor's degrees and 2,716 master's degrees.[17] Founded in 1857 as Minns' Evening Normal School, the university is the oldest public university in the state of California.[18] In addition, it is in the top five biggest campuses of the CSU system. The academic data from 2012–2013 show that the university is highly diverse[19]; ethnic minorities represent 58 percent of the total population. The diverse ethnicity of SJSU is distributed as follows: Asian students (33 percent) make up the largest minority, followed by Latino students (21 percent), then African American students (3 percent), and American Indian students (0.33 percent).

University Library, California State University, Long Beach

The CSULB University Library opened in 1972 and experienced a major remodeling from 2006 to 2007. The library has grown from a one-room building to a six-story building with a seating capacity near four thousand. In addition to the library's collection of 1.4 million volumes, the remodeling included an automated book storage and retrieval structure called Online Remote Collection Access (ORCA). It consists of about five thousand metal bins stacked in six rows holding more than eight hundred thousand books/bound journals. The library also has self-serve checkout kiosks available on several floors to help users avoid long lines at the main circulation desk. Patrons can simply scan their ID cards, check out a book, and print the due date receipt.

Serving more than thirty-six thousand campus users, the reference desk is a very busy and fast-paced place, physically and virtually. During April 5, 2011, to August 23, 2012, the library registered more than eight thousand reference transactions including in-person, on-call, e-mail, phone, and chat reference through the consortium QuestionPoint 24/7/IM. In order to expand reference services in digital form, the CSULB Library initiated a virtual reference service, the "Got Questions?" system, through LibAnswers to allow for e-mail, SMS, Twitter, chat, and FAQ virtual reference transactions.

CSULB librarians work closely with faculty by promoting information-literacy instruction, orientations, and reference services to students. Librarians embed information literacy into the curriculum by creating research guides, producing instructional videos in Jing (a video capture software), and developing library tutorials in Prezi (a cloud-based presentation software). In 2012, the library recorded 728 library presentations, including course-related instruction, one-shot library instruction, and orientations to the campus community.[20]

With a large Spanish-speaking community on campus, one of the authors used Spanish to facilitate and promote positive learning and nurturing opportunities during reference interactions at the desk, library instruction, or office hours with patrons in order to lower users' library anxiety levels.[21] To create a welcoming environment, the author used strategies from Carol Collier Kuhlthau's study, which stresses the importance of using affective learning in libraries:

> In the process of doing library research, most people commonly experience certain feelings. Uncertainty, confidence, interest, concern, apprehension, impatience, curiosity, satisfaction and numerous other feelings all play a part in the research process. Feelings, however, are rarely considered when students are learning to use libraries.[22]

After learning from the chair of the Romance, German, Russian Languages and Literature (RGRLL) Department that about 85 percent of the students were first-generation students and Spanish heritage language learners,[23] the RGRLL librarian started to promote library services in Spanish in an effort to improve the educational experience of students of this department. By imparting information-literacy skills in the students' native languages during library instruction, the librarian enabled Spanish-speaking students to become more receptive to acquiring new library research skills and applying that knowledge to their other courses in English as a result.

In collaboration with a RGRLL faculty member, the RGRLL librarian developed a bilingual (Spanish/English) information-literacy module for one Spanish intermediate-level literature course. In general, the module addressed the three common domains for academic success and persistence of Latino/a students: psychological, social, and cultural.[24] Additionally, the module followed the tenets of information literacy set by the *ACRL Information Literacy Competency Standards for Higher Education*:

> Gaining skills in information literacy multiplies the opportunities for students' self-directed learning, as they become engaged in using a wide variety of information sources to expand their knowledge, ask informed questions, and sharpen their critical thinking for still further self-directed learning.[25]

This module was a series of workshops in Spanish integrating course content with library research and writing skills using affective learning. All of the sessions consisted of identifying and targeting pre-identified problem areas, emphasizing the importance of effective library research (finding, assessing, evaluating, creating, and using information ethically) and developing good writing practices (drafting, revising, and editing). Since many RGRLL students had never used the CSULB library or any other academic library before, the librarian organized targeted tours focusing on reference, circulation, and collections areas with which students needed to become familiar. These library orientations introduced students to CSULB library services and resources, demonstrated how to use critical library collections to identify the works and literary criticism of important authors, and showed students how to use search strategies to find journal articles. The sessions were designed to engage students in searching the library's catalog and databases to locate their library materials, but they also required students to explore the physical library and bring library materials to the class. Even though this exercise seemed to be too simple, it provided students the chance to explore the library on their own and also gave them a sense that academic libraries are not that intimidating. All workshops were conducted in Spanish to allow students to develop information literacy and research skills without any language barriers. By using library search worksheets and hands-on activities, the faculty member and the librarian were able to promote critical-thinking activities that empowered students to become more independent in their ability to access, analyze, evaluate, and use information effectively for research and writing, thereby increasing their responsibility for their own learning.

Students evaluated the library workshops through print and electronic surveys after the sessions. These surveys implied that once students felt comfortable and familiar with the Spanish-speaking librarian, they were more likely to ask for help at the reference desk. The surveys also suggested that students who benefited from multiple reference and research consultation assistance reported having greater confidence in their research and writing skills and in their use of bibliographic sources.

Follow-up reference interactions were conducted at the reference desk and via synchronous/asynchronous research consultations. In-depth research consultations enabled students to refine their thesis statements and enhance their search strategies by working face-to-face with the librarian. All reference encounters lasted between thirty minutes to one hour. For the most part, the individual research consultations allowed Spanish-speaking students to clarify any confusion around library concepts while also reducing library anxiety.

The students' learning experience was facilitated through the following factors: (1) instruction and reference services in their native language; (2) a nurturing learning environment; and (3) a visible and strong faculty and librarian collaboration. These factors, when combined with a pedagogical approach that is mindful of the importance of affective learning, not only address the students' academic needs but also are aimed toward a wider understanding of what information is, what it does, and how it can be applied. In other words, to accomplish the central mission of higher education in developing lifelong learners, librarian-faculty collaborations that embrace openness to and awareness of cultural differences can foster deep personal and professional growth for students beyond the classroom.

Martin Luther King Jr. Library, San José State University

The Martin Luther King Jr. Library at San José State University is a shared building that combines the San José State University Academic Library with the main branch of the San José Public Library. The MLK Library houses 1.9 million items, and has eight floors, six classrooms, thirty-six meeting rooms (two twelve-person capacity), four special collections rooms, a Cultural Heritage Center, and a Children's Room. A highly diverse population of students, faculty, staff, and community users share the library spaces. These groups have in common not only shared spaces, but also collections and information resources. This cooperative endeavor, which began in 1997 and was one of the largest in the country, has made groundbreaking news in major library journals.[26]

Reference services in this setting are unique. Considerable planning was required before the library opening.[27] Preparation started in 1999 and finished when the library opened its doors on August 1, 2003. The MLK library has several reference desks; the main one is located on the second floor and is staffed with public and academic librarians from Sunday through Saturday. The second desk is located on the third floor and is operated only by public librarians. In addition, another reference desk is situated on the fifth floor, which is run by academic librarians on a reduced schedule. Therefore, academic librarians at SJSU's MLK Library provide reference services not only to a culturally, socioeconomically, and ethnically diverse campus population, but also to the highly diverse public community of the city of San José. The duel reference environment can be quite challenging; as Christina Peterson was quoted, "Academic reference librarians value their expertise in a subject area. Public reference librarians value their generalist abilities."[28]

Additionally, academic reference librarians offer reference services in other venues and settings beyond the reference desk. These services focus only on the SJSU community and they include virtual reference (synchronous and asynchronous) and personal consultations. Research appointments are conducted in the office of the Academic Liaison librarian, and are for in-depth research consultations: papers, final projects, thesis development, and faculty research projects.

In the fall of 2010, Valeria E. Molteni, Crystal Goldman, and Enora Oulc'hen surveyed 744 SJSU students regarding use of the physical space of the SJSU MLK Library among other variables.[29] The study showed that 78 percent of the surveyed SJSU students use the library space. Additionally, this sample data, which included demographic information and students' languages, showed that even though the most represented populations were Asian, white Americans, and Latino (in that order), the second most common language among the students who use the Martin Luther King Jr. Library was Spanish (38 percent among the sample).[30]

These data support the decision of Valeria Molteni, who since the beginning of her position at San José State University in 2009 elected to offer services in Spanish as a strategy to reach the Latino/a population. This choice was reinforced by previous experiences, where the author gave information-literacy sessions and references services in Spanish in another university of the CSU system: California State University, Dominguez Hills.[31] These practices have shown that the use of Spanish could aid in the creation of a relaxed environment during the reference interview. In addition, as the liaison librarian for the Linguistics and Language Development Department, she also speaks Spanish with students who are interested in practicing their language skills.

The establishment of bilingual reference services is an informal endeavor, where the librarian provides the service regardless of the type of patron (public or academic) or reference need. As it was explained above, the reference desk at the Martin Luther King Jr. Library serves a very diverse population. At the desk, the author employs bilingual services spontaneously and reaches the Spanish-speaking population using different strategies, such as: (1) identifying lack of skills using the English language (mainly this applies to public patrons), (2) noticing how the user pronounces specific words that come from Spanish (this is very easy since the state of California has a lot of geographical names in Spanish—e.g., *Arrastradero* Road), and (3) observing when patrons ask about specific topics related to the Latino/a population or to the Spanish language. The librarian also offers research consultations to faculty and students in her office. Usually these appointments are to follow up information literacy sessions; in fact, many students decide to speak Spanish in these appointments and meet with the librarian because of her bilingual proficiency. Students prefer meetings conducted in Spanish when they want to talk in their mother tongue or when they want to expand their vocabulary if they speak Spanish as a heritage language or as a second language. For example, graduate students of Speech Pathology might choose consultations in Spanish in order to increase their language proficiency to prepare for future work with bilingual patients. Asynchronous reference services (e-mails) are also written in Spanish, usually this happens after a previous contact between the librarian and the patron. Regarding synchronous references services (chat, Google+, and Skype), the employment of bilingual services is rare; the methodology applied in this type of reference interaction is very similar to the one at the reference desk. The author obtains hints through written communication that indicate that the user prefers to correspond in Spanish.

In all the cases mentioned above, the librarian continuously responds to the level of language fluency depending on the proficiency of the user. This is accomplished during the reference interview by adjusting to the patron's vocabulary and grammar level, using analogies relevant to Spanish dialects, and understanding the patrons' desire to speak Spanish as needed. For the author, these interactions present an interesting opportunity to use her bilingual abilities to (1) establish a rapport with her patrons, (2) create a comfortable environment that reduces library anxiety, and (3) improve patrons' language abilities when they speak Spanish as a heritage language or as a second language. These experiences are reflected in Valeria E. Molteni's statistics from January to November 2013. The data show that 5 percent of the total reference services (transactions at the reference desk, e-mails, and individual consultations) were delivered in Spanish.[32]

COMMON APPROACHES

The above case studies describe the continuous work of two academic librarians building on a framework of cultural competence, defined as the ability to understand the needs of a multiethnic population,[33] when offering bilingual consultations to diverse (e.g., Spanish-speaking) students during reference services. Both librarians display a common approach in offering bilingual reference services in support of their disciplines, and their techniques are based on building *cultural appreciation*, a genuine empathy and care for the informational needs of patrons, and a keen desire to provide positive library interactions to bilingual students. As demonstrated in figure 4.1, the authors developed a bilingual information literacy model for this framework in 2010.[34] In examining this model, the authors postulate that in order to improve the sense of belonging and academic persistence of bilingual students in academic libraries, specifically Spanish-speaking students, academic librarians need to focus on five factors: (1) accept bilingualism as a cultural value, (2) have the capacity to find analogies among the different Spanish dialects, (3) be flexible, (4) be fluent and have the ability to code-switch, and (5) be open to and aware of cultural differences.

A recent American Library Association survey points out that 88.9 percent of the academic librarians employed are white or Caucasian and that

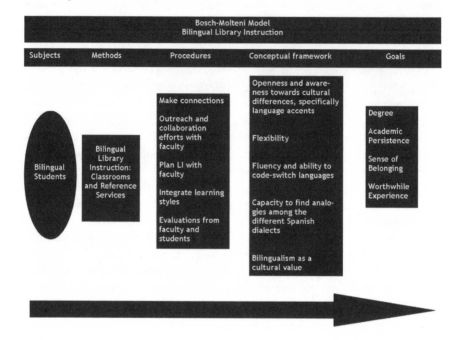

Figure 4.1.

only 1.9 percent self-identified as Latino/a academic librarians.[35] As such, these numbers suggest that it might be difficult for Latino/a college students to connect and navigate in academic libraries where librarians don't seem to be aware of the cultural differences. As Denice Atkins and Lisa Hussey state, "For students from a nondominant culture, knowing how to use the library resources is not only merely about finding information but also about navigating culture."[36] One of the main reasons why the authors provided reference services in other languages was to develop a framework that would prepare heritage-learner students to learn information literacy skills by creating a welcoming environment that enables students to be more receptive to learning new knowledge. Given the drastic demographic changes and increase in the number of international students using academic libraries, the authors would like to advocate for more librarians with second-language abilities (including professional training) to address the cultural and multilingual needs of library patrons who are language students, international students, or bilingual citizens who have been underserved by traditional reference services.

The choice of using Spanish (or any other language) in reference services is usually made in the moment that the service is being provided, primarily for the following reasons: (1) limited English-language skills of the user, (2) as an affective learning strategy that helps diverse students build rapport with the reference service provider, and (3) as a space for transferring skills in the case of patrons that speak Spanish as a heritage language or as a second language. In some instances, the librarian employs the patron's mother tongue to ensure the reference interview and the information delivered is well understood. Since both of these academic libraries are part of large public institutions, many of the patrons who come to the reference desk requesting a specific fact or information are Latino community members nonaffiliated with the institutions. On other occasions, the authors use Spanish to foster emotional connections that alleviate library anxiety and facilitate the transfer of information and knowledge. College students are the predominant population in this cluster. In addition, reference consultations are offered as a follow-up to library instruction sessions. The practice of using patrons' native language during reference interactions, such as Spanish, has a positive emotional impact on library users, especially when users feel the librarian shares their same culture and values. This service promotes and cultivates the creation of a safe space for learning to occur, as well as promotes positive library experiences.[37]

In addition, librarians need to be cognizant of users' Spanish-language ability levels. As a technique, the librarians have adjusted their level of Spanish vocabulary to match the user's level of fluency and command of the spoken language. In order to determine the level of fluency, the librarians employed similar techniques, such as the use of a calm voice and gradually speeding up the conversation. Spanish is the second world language regarding native speakers and international communication,[38] but it is not a monolithic language and it has many dialects and regional differences. For that reason, the authors employ a meta-Spanish: a type of language that can be used across different populations, searching always for analogies among Spanish-language dialects and translating library jargon to Spanish terms. For example, the word in Spanish for library is *biblioteca* not "libreria" (bookshop); this is a very common mistake for a person who has Spanish as a heritage language.

IMPLICATIONS AND CONCLUSION

To better serve the influx of library patrons with different cultural and language backgrounds, academic librarians need to rethink the English-only paradigm. While the recommendations below are specific to bilingual services, they can also be used to address the needs of other diverse populations, including disabled patrons and those with speech, hearing, and visual difficulties (e.g., sign language, Braille).

The following recommendations are intended to help academic librarians develop effective strategies to serve culturally and linguistically diverse users new to the higher education system in the United States:

- Provide a means to reduce first-generation students' cultural shock toward the complexities of the higher education system.
- Make an effort to learn cultural, language, and communication differences.
- Create specific multilingual learning objects for reference services (e.g., tutorials, research guides, or websites as necessary).
- Provide bilingual research help in the language of users: face-to-face, virtual chat, IM, or e-mail reference services.
- Understand nonverbal communication styles (e.g., facial expressions, physical gestures, eye contact, voice tone) that reflect an understanding of the user's language.
- Don't be afraid to consider alternative ways to communicate (e.g., tablet, writing) when facing accent/pronunciation impediments.
- Create a list of librarians and library staff proficient in other languages, including sign language.

With the globalization of higher education, changing demographics, and the increasing diversity of college students, it is becoming more important for academic libraries to develop greater awareness of the heritage of other cultures,[39] and establish policies that integrate multilingual services as an integral part of every library's services.[40] Being aware of cross-cultural communication is an essential part of our duties as academic librarians, and it should be one of our top priorities as the numbers of international and diverse students increase in the United States. Even though the Association of Colleges and Research Libraries (ACRL) has recently published the *Diversity Standards for Cultural Competency for Academic Libraries*,[41] little has been written about instruction or reference services in other languages for academic libraries.[42] However, there seems to be a push for the provision of more multilingual librarians and library staff as shown in the *Guidelines for the Development and Promotion of Multilingual Collections and Services* and the *Diversity Standards: Cultural Competency for Academic Libraries*.[43]

As a result, more research needs to be conducted on reference services to culturally and linguistically diverse patrons, particularly on the effectiveness of these standards for academic libraries.

NOTES

1. 1 Julie Renee Posselt and Kim R. Black, "Developing the Research Identities and Aspirations of First-Generation College Students: Evidence from the McNair Scholars Program," *International Journal for Researcher Development* 3, no. 1 (2012): 26–48.

2. Ebelia Hernández, Michael Mobley, Gayle Coryell, En-Hui Yu, and Gladys Martinez, "Examining the Cultural Validity of a College Student Engagement Survey for Latinos," *Journal of Hispanic Higher Education* 12, no. 2 (2013): 153–73.

3. Alberta Gloria, Jeanette Castellanos, and Veronica Orozco, "Perceived Educational Barriers, Cultural Congruity, Coping Responses and Psychological Well Being of Latina Undergraduates," *Hispanic Journal of Behavioral Sciences* 27, no. 2 (2005): 161–83.

4. Veronica Orozco, "Ethnic Identity, Perceived Social Support, Coping Strategies, University Environment, Cultural Congruity, and Resilience of Latina/o College Students," Order No. 3275216, Ohio State University, 2007. http://search.proquest.com.libaccess.sjlibrary.org/docview/304833020?accountid=10361; and William Jason Stegemoller, "Latino Students and Biliteracy at a University: Literacy Histories, Agency, and Writing," Order No. 3392484, University of Illinois at Urbana-Champaign, 2009. http://search.proquest.com.libaccess.sjlibrary.org/docview/304895607?accountid=10361.

5. Elaine Fredericksen, "Language as Power for Hispanic Students in Higher Education," *Journal of Hispanic Higher Education* 1, no. 3 (2002): 211–24.

6. Deborah Santiago, "What Works for Latino Students in Higher Education," Washington: Excelencia in Education, accessed November 14, 2013, www.edexcelencia.org/research/2013-what-works-latino-students-higher-education.

7. Michelle Camacho Liu, "Investing in Higher Education for Latinos: Trends in Latino College Access and Success," accessed November 14, 2013, www.ncsl.org/documents/educ/trendsinlatinosuccess.pdf.

8. Denice Adkins and Lisa Hussey, "The Library in the Lives of Latino College Students," *Library Quarterly* 76, no. 4 (10, 2006): 456–80; Katherine S. Dabbour and James David Ballard, "Information Literacy and US Latino College Students: A Cross-Cultural Analysis," *New Library World* 112, no. 7/8 (2011): 347–64; Sharon Elteto, Rose M. Jackson, and Adriane Lim, "Is the Library a 'Welcoming Space'?: An Urban Academic Library and Diverse Students Experiences," *portal: Libraries and the Academy* 8, no. 3 (2008): 325–37; and Jacqueline Solis and Katherine S. Dabbour, "Latino Students and Libraries: A US Federal Grant Project Report," *New Library World* 107, no. 1/2 (2006): 48–56.

9. Dallas Long, "Latino Students' Perceptions of the Academic Library," *The Journal of Academic Librarianship* 37, no. 6 (2011): 504–11.

10. Susan Luévano-Molina, "Mexican/Latino Immigrants and the Santa Ana Libraries: An Urban Ethnography," in *Immigrant Politics and the Public Library,* ed. Susan Luévano-Molina (Westport, CT: Greenwood, 2001), 43–63.

11. Luévano-Molina, "Mexican/Latino Immigrants and the Santa Ana Libraries: An Urban Ethnography," 57.

12. American Library Association, "Diversity Standards: Cultural Competency for Academic Libraries," accessed November 18, 2013, www.ala.org/acrl/standards/diversity.

13. Patricia Montiel-Overall, "Cultural Competence: A Conceptual Framework for Library and Information Science Professionals," *The Library Quarterly* 79, no. 2 (2009): 175–204.

14. California State University, "Analytic Studies," accessed April 18, 2014, www.calstate.edu/as.

15. California State University, Long Beach, "*U.S. News & World Report* Ranks CSULB 4th Public University Best in West," *Leadership Update,* accessed October 19, 2013, www.csulb.edu/sites/leadership/fall-2012/u-s-news-world-report-ranks-cal-state-long-beach-4th-best-public-regional-university-in-west-in-2013-best-colleges-guide.

16. California State University, Long Beach, "Ethnic and Gender Distribution of Students, University Total: Fall 2012," *Institutional Research and Assessment On Demand Reporting,* accessed November 16, 2013, http://daf.csulb.edu/offices/univ_svcs/institutionalresearch/ondemand/index.php?sas=1&term=20124&report=enr&college=ut&dept=999.

17. San José State University, "About SJSU: Facts & Figures," accessed April 18, 2014, www.sjsu.edu/about_sjsu/facts_and_figures.

18. San José State University, "Timeline," accessed November 10, 2013, www.sjsu.edu/about_sjsu/history/timeline/1857.

19. San José State University, "About SJSU: Facts & Figures."

20. California State University, "CSU Annual Library Statistic Report 2011–2012," accessed February, 27, 2014, www.calstate.edu/library/content/statistics/documents/2011-2012LibraryStatisticsReport.pdf.

21. Janet Sawyer, Tahereh Zianian, Nina Evans, and David Gillham, "Improving Teaching and Learning in a Regional University Campus through a Focus on the Affective Domain," *Australian and International Journal of Rural Education* 22, no. 3 (2012): 37–51.

22. Carol Collier Kuhlthau, "Feelings in the Library Research Process," *Arkansas Libraries* 42, no. 2 (1985): 23.

23. In general, the term *heritage language learner* refers to a person acquiring a language in the home environment and who has a cultural connection to that language. Andrew Lynch, "Toward a Theory of Heritage Language Acquisition: Spanish in the United States," in *Mi Lengua: Spanish as a Heritage Language in the United States,* ed. Ana Roca and M. Cecilia Colombi, 25–50 (Washington: Georgetown University Press, 2003).

24. Susan Luévano, Tiffini Travis, and Eileen Wakiji, "Academic Libraries: Pathways to Transforming Teaching, Learning, and Relationships in Chicano and Latino Studies," in *Pathways to Progress: Issues and Advances in Latino Librarianship*, ed. John Ayala and Salvador Güereña, 45–57 (Santa Barbara, CA: Libraries Unlimited, 2012).

25. Association of College and Research Libraries, "Information Literacy Competency Standards for Higher Education," accessed December 30, 2013, www.ala.org/acrl/standards/informationliteracycompetency, 5.

26. George M. Eberhart, "Three Plans for Shared-Use Libraries in the Works," *American Libraries* 30, no. 1 (1999): 21–23; Andrew Albanese, "Joint San José Library Opens," *Library Journal* 128, no. 14 (2003): 17; and Walt Crawford, "The Philosophy of Joint-Use Libraries," *American Libraries* 34, no. 11 (2003): 83.

27. Daniane Mizzy, "Yours, Mine, and Ours: Reinventing Reference at San José," *College & Research Libraries News* 66, no. 8 (September, 2005): 598–99; Paul Kauppila, Sandra E. Belanger, and Lisa Rosenblum, "Merge Everything It Makes Sense to Merge: The History and Philosophy of the Merged Reference Collection at the Dr. Martin Luther King, Jr. Library in San José, California," *Collection Management* 31, no. 3 (2006): 33–57; and Harry Meserve, "Evolving Reference, Changing Culture: The Dr. Martin Luther King, Jr. Library and Reference Challenges Ahead," *The Reference Librarian,* no. 93 (2006): 23–42.

28. Daniane Mizzy, "Yours, Mine, and Ours," 599.

29. Valeria E. Molteni, Crystal Goldman, and Enora Oulc'hen, "Experiences of the Student Population at an Urban University: How Do They Use a Joint Library?," *portal: Libraries and the Academy* 13, no. 3 (2013): 233–56.

30. Valeria E. Molteni, "The Library as Space of Learning: Who Is Using It?," poster, Joint Conference of Librarians of Color (JCLC), Kansas City, MO, September 19–23, 2012.

31. Valeria E. Molteni and Eileen Bosch, "Building and Designing Bridges: Enabling Bilingual Academic Learning Experiences," *Librarian as Architect: Planning, Building and Renewing: Thirty-Sixth National LOEX Library Instruction Conference Proceedings* (Ypsilanti, MI: University Library, Eastern Michigan University by LOEX Press, 2010), 41–44; and Isabel Espinal, Susan Luévano, Laura Maldonado, and Valeria E. Molteni, "Latino Information Literacy: Models for Success," round table, First Joint Conference of Librarians of Color: Gathering at the Waters, Embracing Our Spirits, Telling Our Stories, Dallas, TX, October 12–15, 2006.

32. There are two other librarians at the SJSU library who are fluent in Spanish, but they do not keep statistics of their reference consultations delivered in Spanish.

33. Montiel-Overall, "Cultural Competence," 176.

34. Molteni and Bosch, "Building and Designing Bridges: Enabling Bilingual Academic Learning Experiences," 43.

35. American Library Association, Office of Diversity & Office of Research and Statistics, "Diversity Counts," accessed October 25, 2013, www.ala.org/offices/diversity/diversitycounts/divcounts.

36. Adkins and Hussey, "The Library in the Lives of Latino College Students," 473.

37. Eileen K. Bosch and Valeria E. Molteni, "Connecting to International Students in Their Languages: Innovative Bilingual Library Instruction in Academic Libraries," in *International Students and Academic Libraries: Initiatives for Success*, ed. Pamela Jackson and Patrick Sullivan, 135–50 (Chicago: ACRL, 2011).

38. Instituto Cervantes, "El Español: Una Lengua Viva: Informe 2012," in *Centro Virtual Cervantes, El Español en el Mundo: Anuario 2012*, accessed November 7, 2013, http://cvc.cervantes.es/lengua/anuario/anuario_12/i_cervantes/p01.htm.

39. Association of College and Research Libraries, "Diversity Standards: Cultural Competency for Academic Libraries."

40. American Library Association, Reference Services Section of the Reference and User Services Association, "Guidelines for the Development and Promotion of Multilingual Collections and Services," accessed December 30, 2013, www.ala.org/rusa/resources/guidelines/guidemultilingual.

41. Association of College and Research Libraries, "Diversity Standards: Cultural Competency for Academic Libraries."

42. Bosch and Molteni, "Connecting to International Students," 136.

43. American Library Association, Reference Services Section of the Reference and User Services Association, "Guidelines for the Development and Promotion of Multilingual Collections and Services"; and Association of College and Research Libraries, "Diversity Standards: Cultural Competency for Academic Libraries."

BIBLIOGRAPHY

Adkins, Denice, and Lisa Hussey. "The Library in the Lives of Latino College Students." *Library Quarterly* 76, no. 4 (2006): 456–80.

Albanese, Andrew. "Joint San José Library Opens." *Library Journal* 128, no. 14 (2003): 17.

American Library Association, Office of Diversity and Office of Research and Statistics, "Diversity Counts." Accessed October 25, 2013. www.ala.org/offices/diversity/diversitycounts/divcounts.

American Library Association, Reference Services Section of the Reference and User Services Association. "Guidelines for the Development and Promotion of Multilingual Collections and Services." Accessed December 30, 2013. www.ala.org/rusa/resources/guidelines/guidemultilingual.

Association of College and Research Libraries. "Diversity Standards: Cultural Competency for Academic Libraries (2012)." Accessed November 18, 2013. www.ala.org/acrl/standards/diversity.

———. "Information Literacy Competency Standards for Higher Education." Accessed December 30, 2013. www.ala.org/acrl/standards/informationliteracycompetency.

Bosch, Eileen K., and Valeria E. Molteni. "Connecting to International Students in Their Languages: Innovative Bilingual Library Instruction in Academic Libraries." In *International Students and Academic Libraries: Initiatives for Success*, edited by Pamela Jackson and Patrick Sullivan, 135–50. Chicago: ACRL, 2011.

California State University. "Analytic Studies." Accessed April 18, 2014. www.calstate.edu/as.

———. "CSU Annual Library Statistic Report 2011–2012." Accessed February, 27, 2014. www.calstate.edu/library/content/statistics/documents/2011-2012LibraryStatisticsReport.pdf.

California State University, Long Beach. "*U.S. News & World Report* Ranks CSULB 4th Public University Best in West." *Leadership Update.* Accessed October 19, 2013. www.csulb.edu/sites/leadership/fall-2012/u-s-news-world-report-ranks-cal-state-long-beach-4th-best-public-regional-university-in-west-in-2013-best-colleges-guide.

————. "Ethnic and Gender Distribution of Students, University Total: Fall 2012." *Institutional Research and Assessment On Demand Reporting*. Accessed November 16, 2013. http://daf.csulb.edu/offices/univ_svcs/institutionalresearch/ondemand/index.php?sas=1& term=20124&report=enr&college=ut&dept=999.

Camacho Liu, Michelle. "Investing in Higher Education for Latinos: Trends in Latino College Access and Success." Accessed November 14, 2013, www.ncsl.org/documents/educ/trendsinlatinosuccess.pdf.

Crawford, Walt. "The Philosophy of Joint-Use Libraries." *American Libraries* 34, no. 11 (2003): 83.

Dabbour, Katherine S., and James David Ballard. "Information Literacy and US Latino College Students: A Cross-Cultural Analysis." *New Library World* 112, no. 7/8 (2011): 347–64.

Eberhart, George M. "Three Plans for Shared-Use Libraries in the Works." *American Libraries* 30, no. 1 (1999): 21–23.

Elteto, Sharon, Rose M. Jackson, and Adriane Lim. "Is the Library a 'Welcoming Space'?: An Urban Academic Library and Diverse Students Experiences." *portal: Libraries and the Academy* 8, no. 3 (2008): 325–37.

Espinal, Isabel, Susan Luévano, Laura Maldonado, and Valeria E. Molteni. "Latino Information Literacy: Models for Success." First Joint Conference of Librarians of Color: Gathering at the Waters, Embracing Our Spirits, Telling Our Stories, Dallas, TX, October 12–15, 2006.

Fredericksen, Elaine. "Language as Power for Hispanic Students in Higher Education." *Journal of Hispanic Higher Education* 1, no. 3 (2002): 211–24.

Gloria, Alberta, Jeanette Castellanos, and Veronica Orozco. "Perceived Educational Barriers, Cultural Congruity, Coping Responses and Psychological Well Being of Latina Undergraduates." *Hispanic Journal of Behavioral Sciences* 27, no. 2 (2005): 161–83.

Hernández, Ebelia, Michael Mobley, Gayle Coryell, En-Hui Yu, and Gladys Martinez. "Examining the Cultural Validity of a College Student Engagement Survey for Latinos." *Journal of Hispanic Higher Education* 12, no. 2 (2013): 153–73.

Instituto Cervantes. "El Español: Una Lengua Viva: Informe 2012." In *Centro Virtual Cervantes, El Español en el Mundo: Anuario 2012*. Accessed November 7, 2013. http://cvc.cervantes.es/lengua/anuario/anuario_12/i_cervantes/p01.htm.

Kauppila, Paul, Sandra E. Belanger, and Lisa Rosenblum. "Merge Everything It Makes Sense to Merge: The History and Philosophy of the Merged Reference Collection at the Dr. Martin Luther King, Jr. Library in San José, California." *Collection Management* 31, no. 3 (2006): 33–57.

Kuhlthau, Carol Collier. "Feelings in the Library Research Process." *Arkansas Libraries* 42, no. 2 (1985): 23–26.

Long, Dallas. "Latino Students' Perceptions of the Academic Library." *The Journal of Academic Librarianship* 37, no. 6 (2011): 504–11.

Luévano, Susan, Tiffini Travis, and Eileen Wakiji. "Academic Libraries: Pathways to Transforming Teaching, Learning, and Relationships in Chicano and Latino Studies." In *Pathways to Progress: Issues and Advances in Latino Librarianship*, edited by John Ayala and Salvador Güereña, 45–57. Santa Barbara, CA: Libraries Unlimited, 2012.

Luévano-Molina, Susan. "Mexican/Latino Immigrants and the Santa Ana Libraries: An Urban Ethnography." In *Immigrant Politics and the Public Library*, edited by Susan Luévano-Molina, 43–63. Westport, CT: Greenwood, 2001.

Lynch, Andrew. "Toward a Theory of Heritage Language Acquisition: Spanish in the United States." In *Mi Lengua: Spanish as a Heritage Language in the United States*, edited by Ana Roca and M. Cecilia Colombi, 25–50 (Washington: Georgetown University Press, 2003).

Meserve, Harry. "Evolving Reference, Changing Culture: The Dr. Martin Luther King, Jr. Library and Reference Challenges Ahead." *The Reference Librarian* no. 93 (2006): 23–42.

Mizzy, Daniane. "Yours, Mine, and Ours: Reinventing Reference at San José." *College & Research Libraries News* 66, no. 8 (September, 2005): 598–99.

Molteni, Valeria E. "The Library as Space of Learning: Who Is Using It?" Joint Conference of Librarians of Color (JCLC), Kansas City, MO, September 19–23, 2012.

Molteni, Valeria E., Crystal Goldman, and Enora Oulc'hen. "Experiences of the Student Population at an Urban University: How Do They Use a Joint Library?" *portal: Libraries and the Academy* 13, no. 3 (2013): 233–56.

Molteni, Valeria E., and Eileen Bosch. "Building and Designing Bridges: Enabling Bilingual Academic Learning Experiences." In *Librarian as Architect: Planning, Building and Renewing: Thirty-Sixth National LOEX Library Instruction Conference Proceedings*, 41–44. Ypsilanti, MI: University Library, Eastern Michigan University by LOEX Press, 2010.

Montiel Overall, Patricia. "Cultural Competence: A Conceptual Framework for Library and Information Science Professionals." *The Library Quarterly* 79, no. 2 (2009): 175–204.

Orozco, Veronica. "Ethnic Identity, Perceived Social Support, Coping Strategies, University Environment, Cultural Congruity, and Resilience of Latina/o College Students." Order No. 3275216, Ohio State University, 2007. http://search.proquest.com.libaccess.sjlibrary.org/docview/304833020?accountid=10361.

Posselt, Julie Renee, and Kim R. Black. "Developing the Research Identities and Aspirations of First-Generation College Students: Evidence from the McNair Scholars Program." *International Journal for Researcher Development* 3, no. 1 (2012): 26–48.

San José State University. "About SJSU: Facts & Figures." Accessed March 20, 2013. www.sjsu.edu/about_sjsu/facts_and_figures.

———. "Timeline." Accessed November 10, 2013. www.sjsu.edu/about_sjsu/history/timeline/1857.

Santiago, Deborah. "What Works for Latino Students in Higher Education." Washington: Excelencia in Education. Accessed November 14, 2013. www.edexcelencia.org/research/2013-what-works-latino-students-higher-education.

Sawyer, Janet, Tahereh Zianian, Nina Evans, and David Gillham. "Improving Teaching and Learning in a Regional University Campus through a Focus on the Affective Domain." *Australian and International Journal of Rural Education* 22, no. 3 (2012): 37–51.

Solis, Jacqueline, and Katherine S. Dabbour. "Latino Students and Libraries: A US Federal Grant Project Report." *New Library World* 107, no. 1/2 (2006): 48–56.

Stegemoller, William Jason. "Latino Students and Biliteracy at a University: Literacy Histories, Agency, and Writing." Order No. 3392484, University of Illinois at Urbana-Champaign, 2009. http://search.proquest.com.libaccess.sjlibrary.org/docview/304895607?accountid=10361.

U.S. Census Bureau. "*2010 Demographic Profile: CA-Long Beach City.*" Accessed February 27, 2014. www.census.gov/popfinder.

Chapter Five

As Needs Change, So Must We

A Case Study of Innovative Outreach to Changing Demographics

Li Fu

USD AS A CHANGEMAKING CAMPUS

The University of San Diego (USD) is a Roman Catholic, private residential school. It was founded in 1949 and has an enrollment of 8,321, including 33 percent minority students and 7 percent international students. USD is committed to advancing academic excellence, expanding knowledge, fostering a diverse and inclusive community, and preparing students for compassionate service.[1]

The university library, Copley Library, serves the USD community through four departments: Access and Outreach Services (AOS), Archives and Special Collections, Reference, and Technical Services. Open over one hundred hours each week, Copley houses more than five hundred thousand volumes and is a member of regional and national consortia. Library faculty are liaisons who offer specialized and extensive reference, research, and instructional services.[2]

Recognized as a Community Engagement Institution by the Carnegie Foundation, USD has been a member of Ashoka's Changemaker Campus Consortium since 2011. Ashoka was launched in 2008, and it offers the Changemaker Campus designation to leading institutions in socially innovative education. These institutions share a vision for higher education to become the next global driver of social change by transforming the educational experience into a world-changing experience.

Created in the fall of 2011, the USD Changemakers Hub (HUB) links the library and members from all over campus to promote entrepreneurship, collaboration, and innovation for positive social change at USD. A main focus of the HUB is to empower and enable the USD community to learn about themselves, to be inspired, and to experience changemaking in action. By engaging the entire community, the HUB develops opportunities to generate ideas and projects across campus to address social issues at the local, national, and global level. As a promoter of the changemaking philosophy, the university believes everyone can make a difference and everyone can be a changemaker. Through its multidisciplinary approach, the HUB creates, connects, collaborates, and catalyzes change.

The purpose of this case study is to report on the innovative changes and improvements Copley Library has made to outreach services in response to various demographic changes. The article discusses how the librarians of Copley Library respond to changing needs by engaging diversity, reaching out to the underserved, and initiating demographic-specific services. Librarians by profession, educators by approach, and changemakers in practice, they proactively reach above and beyond with innovative outreach services by establishing relationships with both academic and nonacademic units on campus to promote and publicize library resources and services.

CHANGING DEMOGRAPHICS

According to the USD *Quick Facts*, from 2003 to 2013 (see table 5.1 for 2013 numbers), the international student population has more than doubled from 3 percent to 7 percent and the percentage of minority students at USD has increased by 8 percent. Before the international student population grew significantly, the library did not offer services that were tailored to the needs of international students and only a few of these students would come in on their own to explore what the library had to offer. Many were surprised to learn they could take books out of the library, and most were unaware that Interlibrary Loan (ILL) services were available to them as well. Others, especially those from the Business School and the English Language Academy, had difficulty understanding citations and syllabi. Through workshops and face-to-face interactions, librarians understood most international students struggled with how Americans think and write in academic settings, which are different from the norm in their countries. It was also observed that many international students were shy and were often intimidated to initiate a dialog when using the library. Due to language barriers and cultural differences, many international students showed no confidence in their English speaking; so although they had questions and needed help, they never knew how to ask or whom to ask for help.

In addition to serving academic units, the librarians realized that there was no library liaison assigned to serve the more than one hundred nonacademic offices and centers on campus. Through informal librarian interactions and a short survey conducted in 2013 on the needs of library users, they noted that, of the 205 people who participated, almost 31 percent were staff and administrators from nonacademic units. The feedback from this group confirmed that they were noticeably underserved. In casual conversations, the librarians heard again and again that "I have been at USD for many years, but this is the first time I knew of the library's wonderful resources" and "I had no idea I could do that with your resources." Many nonacademic employees at the university were not aware of the library services to which they were entitled.

Traditionally, library services were offered in-house and at the service desk. In the past, access and circulation services librarians did not need to reach out to provide services beyond the circulation desk. At USD, Copley was not known for culturally sensitive services and did not extensively engage students through student organizations or extra curricula programs. As the campus culture is continuously becoming more diverse, learning styles

Table 5.1. Race/Ethnicity of Students: USD Counts and Ranges

2013	Undergrad	Paralegal	Graduate	Law*	Total
Total students enrolled	5,665	162	1,612	882	8,321
Minority students	34%	49%	32%	31%	33%
White only	55%	49%	55%	56%	54%
Unknown	5%	2%	10%	9%	6%
International on visa	7%	0%	8%	5%	7%
Percent:	100%	100%	100%	100%	100%
Multiple categories	**Undergrad**	**Paralegal**	**Graduate**	**Law***	**Total**
	17%	12%	9%	5%	14%
Ethnicity	**Undergrad**	**Paralegal**	**Graduate**	**Law***	**Total**
Hispanic or Latino	8–19%	12–31%	8–13%	8–11%	8–17%
Race	**Undergrad**	**Paralegal**	**Graduate**	**Law***	**Total**
American Indian or Alaska Native	<1–3%	<1–3%	1–2%	<1–2%	<1–2%
Asian	6–11%	7–12%	9–11%	14–16%	7–11%
Black or African American	3–5%	6–7%	4–7%	2–3%	3–5%
Hawaiian or Other Pacific Islander	<1–1%	<1–1%	<1–1%	<1–1%	<1–1%
White	55–69%	49–61%	50–58%	56–60%	54–66%

are changing and information-seeking behavior is evolving. Patrons are no longer satisfied with the in-house services. They expect access outside of traditional settings, and seek services that are tailored to their changing needs. They require access to information 24/7 and cannot rely on just a physical place with limited hours and personnel that cannot speak their language or help them with access or research questions.

LITERATURE REVIEW

In the field of library and information science, many studies examine how to assess user needs, how to structure effective liaison programs, how to develop partnerships, and how to evaluate outreach services. Literature on adopting and applying a changemaking philosophy has yet to emerge; however, the USD librarians identified a few relevant articles documenting similar outreach activities to assist with transforming their services.[3] For example, Connie Ury and Carolyn Johnson describe how they develop social relationships with students and faculty and use those contacts to get connected. They also collaborate with other student-support service units on campus as part of new outreach strategies. Further, Lara Ursin Cummings advocates reaching out beyond the traditional library liaison relationship to produce unexpected partnerships across campus with diverse groups. At her institution, they connect to students in dorms, in the Athletics Department, in the TRiO program, and at campus events. Kate Saylor, Anna Ercoli Schnitzer, Nancy Allee, and Jane Blumenthal also describe how they create transformational outreach programs in the Health Sciences Library for community members, including people with disabilities, professionals in the public health practice community, and students and teachers at public schools.[4]

From the reviewed literature, librarians can learn that innovative outreach service efforts are undertaken by individuals who are always anticipating users' needs—be they the needs of students in general, faculty, student athletes, disabled students, or even parents who are very involved with their children's lives.[5] For example, Mae L. Rodney writes about the "One Book, One Community" program on her campus, which fosters discussion among first-year college students in the freshman seminars and other learning communities. This program helps build a sense of belonging, encourages the formation of new communities, and even opens up communication on sensitive issues.[6] In addition, Molly Strothmann and Karen Antell discuss their success of having a live-in librarian in residence halls to facilitate programming and outreach activities, such as banned-books discussion, research rescue, and library tours. They note that while many librarians have established a presence in academic departments, other places on campus, like student unions, computer labs, and residence halls, have received limited attention as outreach venues.[7]

By expanding the environments in which outreach services are offered, librarians gain new perspectives on ways to respond to users' needs. Beyond changing the location and settings of outreach services, we must also begin to recognize the impact that changing demographics on university campuses have on changing users' needs. Alex Byrne traces the development of integrated approaches to supporting international students. Initiatives include forming a team of specialist librarians, creating guides in the languages other than English most frequently spoken by students, establishing an innovative International Cultural and News Centre, offering information-literacy programs in students' native languages, and training all library staff on cultural awareness.[8] Today's multicultural campuses lead Nancy Fawley to call for librarians to understand the cultural aspects in developing outreach in such settings. She emphasizes that differences in educational philosophies, students' previous scholastic training, and cultural differences as well as individual motivation are all factors that may affect a students' ability to succeed in an American academic environment. For students that may be also participating in a school's English as a Foreign Language program, there are additional challenges around improving their literacy skills.[9] Providing services based on cultural services and languages may serve to establish a connection, as examined by Eileen K. Bosch and Valeria E. Molteni.[10] Libraries on campus can provide the missing link for many of these students who are struggling with finding adequate resources while studying in a foreign culture. The University of Florida Libraries contributes extensively to the campus-wide International Education Week (IEW), and Alena Aissing addresses the positive impact that library involvement has had on the events.[11] For libraries to truly anticipate and address changing users' needs, we as librarians must begin to create multifaceted library outreach programs as described by Merinda Kaye Hensley and Emily Love. They state that a multifaceted library outreach program has six elements: staff development, partnerships, outreach, instruction, student needs, and assessment. As international students transition to their new campus, they have varying levels of need. Hensley and Love encourage library faculty and staff to build on diverse campus communities to help them provide the support needed. Librarians must now build on both internal library and external campus resources to design outreach programs that address changing users' needs.[12]

Ury and Johnson advance that while the demand for face-to-face interaction has declined, information-seeking behavior continues to change. They assert that "the historical model of the library as a place where information is housed and the librarians are available for consultations is no longer reflective of the references services environment."[13] Outreach service has been adopted by default in order to serve users who choose not to go to the library.

Librarians have learned to meet their users where they are, including but not limited to online research institutes, dormitories, teaching departments and programs, career services, athletics, student clubs, and Greek associations.[14] According to Jamie Hazlitt and Courtney Hoffner, university staff can be an invisible patron group, often forgotten as campus outreach typically focuses on faculty and students. They found that staff members may not realize that the library can be a rich employee benefit for them and their families, and the library also missed out on a valuable opportunity to connect with users in student affairs, academic departments, athletics, and everywhere in between.[15]

The evolution of library services continues to be studied. Innovative methods for evaluating, adapting, and expanding services should become a new norm, along with improved librarian training and enhanced use of liaisons to the wider campus and community.[16] Research projects ought to continue in order to document academic libraries' efforts to serve their users' needs. Academic librarians are at a crossroads—there has never been a time when technology, combined with advocacy, can so greatly enhance library services to users and nonusers alike.

REACHING IN, OUT, AND BEYOND

Under new leadership, the Copley Library has expanded services over the past three years. There have been improvements in outreach, collaboration, and overall operations of library services. A head of AOS was hired to oversee both access and outreach. Three of the seven AOS staff members, including a faculty librarian, a visiting librarian, and a library assistant, were assigned liaison or reference librarian responsibilities. Librarians at Copley Library are liaisons to at least one department or office on campus; as such, librarians develop relationships with both academic and nonacademic units to promote and publicize resources and services. In addition, librarians working in the Technical Services and Archives and Special Collections all liaise and reach out to specific departments. With this reorganization, access, liaison, reference, and outreach services are seamlessly joined together to support library outreach.

The 2013 theme of the American Library Association (ALA) encouraged libraries to provide services that empower their users to change their lives through education. Inspired and motivated by this message, librarians at Copley Library believe libraries change lives and librarians are changemakers. Copley librarians now make an extra effort to attract more international students into the library. To tailor library services to this population, the outreach librarian has become an advisor to student organizations and has proactively implemented a series of initiatives to help international students.

An event series titled "How We Can Help You Succeed" has been launched, which includes an orientation for incoming international students, research skills workshops for current international students, and an invited speaker series about Optional Practical Training (OPT), which allows international students to work in the United States up to a total of twelve months full-time in their field of study.[17] By working closely with the International Office (IO), the outreach librarian regularly attends events and activities, such as the IO weekly coffee hour and new-student orientations.

A newly designed "Research Skills Workshop for International Students" has been a hit. Structured just for international students, it helps students understand how critical it is for them to learn research skills to support academic or work-related projects. The workshop focuses on how to search and do research, how to cite sources and write papers, how to better adapt to the American campus environment, and even how to make friends with American students. As one of the best-attended workshops, more sessions have been added in order to accommodate the increased demand. With flexible time and more dates to choose from, including evenings and weekends, a growing number of students are now able to attend. Registration fills up quickly, and some students have to be put on the waitlist.

Upon request, customized consultations and open hours for drop-ins and face-to-face assistance are also made available for non-English speakers. Tours and on-demand sessions are routinely provided for newcomers, international students, and nontraditional users. Librarians present tips and guidance to the attendees on college-level research in American universities. Informal gatherings, group discussions, casual meetings, and one-on-one conversations in all formats are also offered to engage participation. Games and prizes have proven effective for generating increased interest; food and drink are always popular as well.

Librarians have also partnered with teaching faculty to help international students fit into the mainstream of campus culture. With faculty from the School of Business Administration, a Student Social Gathering was held. During the International Education Week, the outreach librarian worked with music faculty and co-organized a Music Night that was hosted by musicians from Mexico, Indonesia, China, and the United States. Further, the Cross Culture Tea Time (CCTT) is a product of collaboration between the outreach librarian and language faculty. Intended to be a language-buddy program that helps Chinese learners and English-language learners pair up and learn from each other, the event has turned out to be so popular that it has since developed into a signature event attended by students, faculty, and staff. In addition, a wide range of diverse student organizations participated, including: the Student Outreach and Recruitment (SOAR), the United Front Multicultural Center (UFMC), the International Student Organization (ISO), Associated Students (AS), the Black Student Union (BSU), the Asian Students Association (ASA), and the Center for Awareness, Service and Action (CASA), to name a few.

By working with faculty advisors of various student organizations, the outreach librarian has successfully organized a Culture Exchange Festival. This event engaged a large audience of students, faculty, and staff, as well as off-campus communities. More than 130 people came from ASA, CSSA, ISO, SOAR, Taiwan Student Association (TSA), and UFMC. Other participants also include USD Chinese as well as American faculty and staff from various disciplines, neighbors from around USD, and those from University of California at San Diego. Interesting programs were offered such as speed dating, charades, calligraphy, paper cutting, chess, and poker, to name a few. There were giveaways and prizes to raise excitement and engagement, such as brushes for calligraphy, bookmarks, chopsticks, keychains, fans with Chinese characters, pens, mugs, cups, and notebooks.

In addition, the outreach librarian participated in the Internationalization of the Curriculum faculty workshop during International Education Week. As a result, internationalized components have been incorporated into the syllabus of the three-unit Library Research Methods 101 course, and the learning outcomes reflect globalization in education. Library Research Methods 101 is one of two courses in Library Science (LIBR), the other class is Information Literacy and Research Strategies 103. As an elective course for undergraduate students, LIBR 101 instructs students in the use of library resources to find and evaluate information across disciplines both within the library and on the Internet. It teaches students how to effectively gather information in diverse formats in order to support their educational and research needs. Topics include, but are not limited to, formulating research questions, evaluating information, understanding the ethical uses of information, and using effective search methods and citation practices.[18]

No longer focusing solely on staffing the service desk and providing traditional services, librarians now reach out to the Center of Inclusion and Diversity and the United Front Multicultural Center[19] for engaging diverse students. Librarians also play significant roles in working with the Disabilities Office to accommodate students with special needs, such as those with learning, as well as physical, disabilities. Window-Eyes has been installed on the library's computers to enable full access to Windows PCs via speech and/ or Braille for people who are visually impaired. For Apple users, librarians help them explore the built-in features specially designed for those who are physically challenged. By working with the Associated Student Organization, librarians strive to meet the needs of all students, including international, multicultural, and nontraditional (e.g., working professionals and parent students) patrons.

Every semester, the library initiates a wide variety of services and programs that enrich the student experience. Alcalá Bazaar is a campus-wide orientation event when staff have an opportunity to welcome new students and connect them with the library. The event has been around for years; however, librarians have only recently become involved. By setting up a booth, librarians are able to talk face-to-face with patrons, introducing the library and highlighting services. Promotional materials distributed at Alcalá Bazaar, such as flyers, brochures, customized business cards, copyright bookmarks, workshop posters, and postcards for Copley Facebook and Twitter, have proven effective for publicizing library services. Patrons appreciate the information and handouts received at the Bazaar, and the library sees more new patrons in return. Other effective events include: President's Welcome Weekend, Homecoming Open House, International Scholars sessions, undergraduate and graduate student orientations, and the Chinese New Year Celebration.

Copley Library serves as the heart of the university, but also reaches across campus to engage all of the university community. Besides the academic programs, the outreach librarian liaises to all nonacademic units, a diverse body that has different needs and expectations of the library. With Human Resources, for example, librarians work to support a different patron population of staff, administrators, part-time and full-time employees, and those working overseas. Workshops have been especially designed for staff and administrators who are traditionally underserved, and topics range from copyright to mobile apps to RapidILL. With the Center for Education Excellence, they extend faculty technology support to staff, and with the Continuing Education Department, they provide online and distance education services. Librarians reach out to the Athletics Department to facilitate co-curricular activities. During the finals period, the library collaborates with the Wellness, Health and Recreation Center on stress-relief programs and resources. Copyright outreach is yet another example of a successful partnership; Copley Library works with Information Technology Services, the Law Library, and even the University General Counsel to educate the campus in creating and successfully implementing copyright policies.

While supporting students and faculty, the library also vigorously reaches out to the community and beyond. Off-campus activities that are a part of Copley's community outreach include the Annual Linda Vista Multi-Cultural Fair and Parade,[20] a yearly event that takes place right in the backyard of USD. By organizing a group of volunteers to assist with the fair, the outreach librarian begins to make connections with the neighborhood community. Some activities include visiting the Bayside Community Center (BCC) and attending the Linda Vista Community meetings, when the outreach librarian pays regular visits to BCC and promotes the library services at the community meetings. In addition, Copley has provided library tours to high school students, prospective parents, and the neighborhood community. A recent example is tours and information sessions to GenerateHope, an organization that supports trafficked young women to discover freedom.[21] By connecting with the users in this group, the outreach librarian promotes the library services and helps them with their information needs.

DISCUSSION

Adapting to new needs is essential, and outreach services are in a key position to model and accomplish this for their libraries. This case study illustrates that librarians can serve as educators by embracing the changemakers' philosophy and practice. They can make a difference by incorporating diversity into traditional services. When users change, librarians need to as well. Everyone can be a change leader, be on a change team, and become a change agent as long as they strive for growth, improvement, and relevancy. By joining the university-wide changemaking learning community, librarians have collaborated with campus partners and improved services to all of the university's library users, making a noticeable and meaningful impact. To succeed with their patrons, USD librarians will continue to employ the changemaking philosophy in reference outreach efforts.

As the student body reflects the profile of an increasingly diverse American population, new library services are in demand. While the university patrons are the primary reason for the library's existence, the partnership of Reference with Outreach Services has generated targeted support to the underserved. Revising how librarians conduct business may seem like a monumental undertaking, particularly at the beginning of the effort. Yet, after barely three years of hard work, more outreach continues to be needed to make patrons feel welcome in the library and educate them about the services and benefits offered. The efforts in changemaking continue to be a work in progress, but building connections with people and partnerships with campus offices and programs, along with internal library collaborations, makes all of the difference.

Finally, new competencies and skill sets have come to the librarians' attention. Because librarians are playing more diverse roles, they need to grow and change themselves first. They must change their mindset in order to facilitate the institutional change needed to respond to the increasing diversity of learners. With more responsibilities, they are expected to play multiple roles as research facilitators, instructors, advisors, and liaisons to campus and community organizations. As new learners face the daunting expectations of a technology-rich environment, the role of the librarian must evolve and become that of the educator—to guide and to lead. They need to constantly renew and reposition themselves in the changing landscape. It is only by integrating new skills into traditional expertise that librarians can fast-track their success. To provide the best services to the changing campus population, they need to look for more effective ways to bring about small changes to daily operations. Continued innovation, adaptation, and learning can create long-lasting improvements and enable twenty-first-century librarians to meet the ever-changing needs of their patrons.

NOTES

I would like to thank my late husband, Henry, for his devoted support throughout my career and the writing of this article. I would also like to recognize Alma Ortega, who contributed to the conception and editing of this work.

1. University of San Diego, "QuickFacts: Enrollment by College/School," University of San Diego, accessed December 2, 2013, www.sandiego.edu/facts/quick/current/school.php.

2. University of San Diego, "Copley Library," University of San Diego, accessed February 7, 2014, www.sandiego.edu/library.

3. Connie Ury and Carolyn Johnson, "Reference Beyond the Walls of the Library: Interacting with Faculty and Students in the 21st Century," *The Reference Librarian* 40, no. 83/84 (2003): 203–18; Lara Ursin Cummings, "Bursting Out of the Box: Outreach to the Millennial Generation through Student Services Programs," *Reference Services Review* 35, no. 2 (2007): 285–95.

4. Kate Saylor, Anna Ercoli Schnitzer, Nancy Allee, and Jane Blumenthal, "A Transformational Outreach Program for an Academic Health Sciences Library," *College & Research Libraries News* 72, no. 2 (2011): 86–89.

5. Cummings, "Bursting Out of the Box," 293.

6. Mae L. Rodney, "Building Community Partnerships," *College & Research Libraries News* 65, no. 3 (2004):130–55.

7. Molly Strothmann and Karen Antell, "The Live-In Librarian: Developing Library Outreach to University Residence Halls," *Reference & User Services Quarterly* 50, no. 1 (2010): 48–58.

8. Alex Byrne, "An Integrated Approach to Supporting International Students at the University of Technology, Sydney in Australia," in *International Students and Academic Libraries: Initiatives for Success*, ed. Pamela A. Jackson and Patrick Sullivan (Chicago: Association of College and Research Libraries, 2011), 201–11.

9. Nancy Fawley, "Addressing Academic Integrity: Perspectives from Virginia Commonwealth University in Qatar," in *International Students and Academic Libraries: Initiatives for Success*, ed. Pamela A. Jackson and Patrick Sullivan (Chicago: Association of College and Research Libraries, 2011), 151–64.

10. Eileen K. Bosch and Valeria E. Molteni, "Connecting to International Students in Their Languages: Innovative Bilingual Library Instruction in Academic Libraries," in *International Students and Academic Libraries: Initiatives for Success*, ed. Pamela A. Jackson and Patrick Sullivan (Chicago: Association of College and Research Libraries, 2011), 135–50.

11. Alena Aissing, "International Education Week: Celebrating the Benefits of International Education and Exchange," in *International Students and Academic Libraries: Initiatives for Success*, ed. Pamela A. Jackson and Patrick Sullivan (Chicago: Association of College and Research Libraries, 2011), 83–91.

12. Merinda Kaye Hensley and Emily Love, "A Multifaceted Model of Outreach and Instruction for International Students," in *International Students and Academic Libraries: Initiatives for Success*, ed. Pamela A. Jackson and Patrick Sullivan (Chicago: Association of College and Research Libraries, 2011), 115–34.

13. Ury and Johnson, "Reference Beyond the Walls of the Library," 216.

14. Paulita Aguilar et al., "Reference as Outreach: Meeting Users Where They Are," *Journal of Library Administration* 51, no. 4 (2011): 343–58; Amy Gratz and Julie Gilbert, "Meeting Student Needs at the Reference Desk," *Reference Services Review* 39, no. 2 (2011): 423–38; Pali U. Kuruppu, "Evaluation of Reference Services: A Review," *The Journal of Academic Librarianship* 33, no. 3 (2007): 368–81.

15. Jamie Hazlitt and Courtney Hoffner, "Supporting our Invisible Patrons: Engaging Staff on a University Campus," poster, California Academic and Research Libraries Conference, San Diego, CA, April 5–7, 2012.

16. Kuruppu, "Evaluation of Reference Services: A Review," 368–81; Frada Motzenger, Bridgette T. Sanders, and Jeannie M. Welch, "Restructuring a Liaison Program in an Academic Library," *College & Research Libraries* 61, no. 5 (2000): 432–40; Cynthia C. Ryans, Raghini S. Suresh, and Wei-Ping Zhang, "Assessing an Academic Library Liaison Programme," *Library Review* 44, no. 1 (1995):14 –23.

17. U.S. Citizenship and Immigration Services (USCIS), "F-1 Optional Practical Training (OPT)," accessed March 17, 2014, www.uscis.gov/eir/visa-guide/f-1-opt-optional-practical-training/f-1-optional-practical-training-opt.

18. University of San Diego, "Academic Course Catalogs," University of San Diego, accessed March 17, 2014, www.sandiego.edu/catalogs/undergraduate/LibraryScience.php.

19. University of San Diego, "United Front Multicultural Center," University of San Diego, accessed February 7, 2014, www.sandiego.edu/unitedfront.

20. Linda Vista Multi-Cultural Fair Inc., "29th Annual Linda Vista Multi-Cultural Fair and Parade," Linda Vista Multi-Cultural Fair Inc., accessed February 17, 2014, www.lindavistafair.org.

21. GenerateHope, "GenerateHope," accessed March 27, 2014, http://generatehope.org.

BIBLIOGRAPHY

Aguilar, Paulita, Kathleen Keating, Suzanne Schadl, and Johann Van Reenen. "Reference as Outreach: Meeting Users Where They Are." *Journal of Library Administration* 51, no. 4 (2011): 343–58.

Aissing, Alena. "International Education Week: Celebrating the Benefits of International Education and Exchange." In *International Students and Academic Libraries: Initiatives for Success*, edited by Pamela A. Jackson and Patrick Sullivan, 83–91. Chicago: Association of College and Research Libraries, 2011.

Ashoka, U. "Changemaker Campus." Accessed December 2, 2013. http://ashokau.org/programs/changemaker-campus.

Bosch, Eileen K., and Valeria E. Molteni. "Connecting to International Students in Their Languages: Innovative Bilingual Library Instruction in Academic Libraries." In *International Students and Academic Libraries: Initiatives for Success*, edited by Pamela A. Jackson and Patrick Sullivan, 135–50. Chicago: Association of College and Research Libraries, 2011.

Byrne, Alex. "An Integrated Approach to Supporting International Students at the University of Technology, Sydney in Australia." In *International Students and Academic Libraries: Initiatives for Success*, edited by Pamela A. Jackson and Patrick Sullivan, 201–11. Chicago: Association of College and Research Libraries, 2011.

Cummings, Lara Ursin. "Bursting Out of the Box: Outreach to the Millennial Generation through Student Services Programs." *Reference Services Review* 35, no. 2 (2007): 285–95.

Fawley, Nancy. "Addressing Academic Integrity: Perspectives from Virginia Commonwealth University in Qatar." In *International Students and Academic Libraries: Initiatives for Success*, edited by Pamela A. Jackson and Patrick Sullivan, 151–64. Chicago: Association of College and Research Libraries, 2011.

Gratz, Amy, and Julie Gilbert. "Meeting Student Needs at the Reference Desk." *Reference Services Review* 39, no. 2 (2011): 423–38.

Hazlitt, Jamie, and Courtney Hoffner. "Supporting our Invisible Patrons: Engaging Staff on a University Campus." Poster at the California Academic and Research Libraries Conference, San Diego, CA, April 5–7, 2012.

Hensley, Merinda Kaye, and Emily Love. "A Multifaceted Model of Outreach and Instruction for International Students." In *International Students and Academic Libraries: Initiatives for Success*, edited by Pamela A. Jackson and Patrick Sullivan, 115–34. Chicago: Association of College and Research Libraries, 2011.

Kuruppu, Pali U. "Evaluation of Reference Services: A Review." *The Journal of Academic Librarianship* 33, no. 3 (2007): 368–81.

Linda Vista Multi-Cultural Fair Inc. "29th Annual Linda Vista Multi-Cultural Fair and Parade." Linda Vista Multi-Cultural Fair Inc. Accessed February 17, 2014. www.lindavistafair.org.

Motzenger, Frada, Bridgette T. Sanders, and Jeannie M. Welch. "Restructuring a Liaison Program in an Academic Library." *College & Research Libraries* 61, no. 5 (2000): 432–40.

Rodney, Mae L. "Building Community Partnerships." *College & Research Libraries News* 65, no. 3 (2004):130–55.

Ryans, Cynthia C., Raghini S. Suresh, and Wei-Ping Zhang. "Assessing an Academic Library Liaison Programme." *Library Review* 44, no. 1 (1995): 14–23.

Saylor, Kate, Anna Ercoli Schnitzer, Nancy Allee, and Jane Blumenthal. "A Transformational Outreach Program for an Academic Health Sciences Library." *College & Research Libraries News* 72, no. 2 (2011): 86–89.

Strothmann, Molly, and Karen Antell. "The Live-In Librarian: Developing Library Outreach to University Residence Halls." *Reference & User Services Quarterly* 50, no. 1 (2010): 48–58.

University of San Diego. "Academic Course Catalogs." University of San Diego. Accessed March 17, 2014. www.sandiego.edu/catalogs/undergraduate/LibraryScience.php.

———. "Changemaker Hub." University of San Diego. Accessed February 7, 2014. http://sites.sandiego.edu/changemaker.

———. "Copley Library." University of San Diego. Accessed February 7, 2014. www.sandiego.edu/library.

———. "QuickFacts: Enrollment by College/School." University of San Diego. Accessed December 2, 2013. www.sandiego.edu/facts/quick/current/school.php.

———. "United Front Multicultural Center." University of San Diego. Accessed February 7, 2014. www.sandiego.edu/unitedfront.

Ury, Connie and Carolyn Johnson. "Reference Beyond the Walls of the Library: Interacting with Faculty and Students in the 21st Century." *The Reference Librarian* 40, no. 83/84 (2003): 203–18.

U.S. Citizenship and Immigration Services (USCIS). "F-1 Optional Practical Training (OPT)." U.S. Citizenship and Immigration Services. Accessed March 17, 2014. www.uscis.gov/eir/visa-guide/f-1-opt-optional-practical-training/f-1-optional-practical-training-opt.

Part III

Technology: Reference Service Beyond the Library Walls

Chapter Six

Roving Reference

Taking the Library to Its Users

Zara Wilkinson

The twenty-first-century academic library must, first and foremost, serve twenty-first-century academic library users. Susan Gardner and Susanna Eng describe millennials as technology veterans who have experience with new communication modes and new technologies.[1] They have high expectations and expect library services, like everything else, to be customizable and adaptable. Traditional library services may lack this necessary adaptability. Instead, they tend to reinforce the "hierarchical role of librarians as gatekeepers and guides to information."[2] Alternative reference models, such as virtual reference and roving reference, present an opportunity to upset the hierarchical model of reference, which is predicated on the presumption that students know what sort of information they want, where to get it, and who to ask. Virtual reference, provided through e-mail, chat, text message, and even social media, has received a lot of attention from academic librarians who are looking to keep up with the next wave of library services. Although virtual reference is incredibly important for serving off-campus and distance students, Michel Atlas stresses that while an increase in online services conveniences our users, "the actual effect is to remove ourselves from potential personal interaction with our patrons and increase the amount of time we spend in our offices."[3] As Anne Moore and Kimberly Wells assert, "Students still need and expect face-to-face assistance."[4]

To provide this face-to-face assistance, as well as to combat decreasing reference desk statistics, many libraries are exploring roving reference, which refers to a number of activities that center around librarians leaving behind the traditional reference desk model, at least for a small time. Darcy

Del Bosque and Kimberly Chapman distill this away-from-desk reference into three simple categories:

1. prescheduled time periods where a library offers reference services at student support facilities or in dormitories;
2. prescheduled time slots where a librarian offers subject-specific reference service or office hours in an academic department; and
3. a roving service away from the reference desk, but within the library building, including computer laboratories that may be administered separately from the library.[5]

Although Del Bosque and Chapman designate only the last, a service within the library, as roving, all three of the reference models described can be defined as part of a big-picture understanding of roving reference. In its simplest form, then, roving reference can be described as a reference model in which librarians move—or rove—and approach their patrons, rather than remaining stationary and waiting to be approached. Michael Smith and Barbara Pietrazewski sum up the roving reference philosophy quite nicely: "If these students won't come to us, perhaps we should go to them."[6] Roving reference programs have been documented at Utica College,[7] George Washington University,[8] Texas A&M,[9] Towson University,[10] University of Northern British Columbia,[11] Southern Illinois–Carbondale,[12] and the University of Maryland Baltimore County,[13] among others.

Roving reference is a way to combat what might be called the library *catch 22*: the only patrons who come to the reference desk for help are those patrons who already know to come to the reference desk for help. As Sarah Archer and Melissa Cast note, the traditional reference desk model requires the student (or faculty member, or other patron) to come forward.[14] No matter how welcoming, warm, and friendly a librarian at the reference desk may be, walking up to a stranger and admitting a lack of knowledge is not easy for even the most gregarious person. Furthermore, it is an unfortunate truth that not all librarians are warm and welcoming all of the time. Even if they are not rude or otherwise unfriendly, a librarian at the reference desk often checks e-mail or completes other work, and as a result he or she may be seen by a patron as unapproachable. Roving reference is essentially a form of outreach, in which librarians attempt to reach (and help) the patrons who don't know where or how to ask for help.

Katherine Penner notes that the current movement toward flexible, personal library space gives students the ability to "transform or personalize" their library surroundings, but as they do so, they are less likely to uproot themselves and move to a designated reference desk to ask for help.[15] As Judith Trump and Ian Tuttle point out, students may also see going to the reference desk as a hardship, even when they are inside the library already:

"In some libraries students may risk losing their seat at a computer terminal . . . or they may be at a terminal on a floor without a service desk where the old adage 'out of sight, out of mind' often applies."[16] For example, in Moore and Wells's study, students expressed a desire not to have to move from or possibly surrender their seats:

> One respondent declared [roving reference] was "helpful because if I need help, I might not want to get up and lose my place, or I might not know who to see." Another student said, "I appreciate the offer. I think it is great, especially for people who do not want to lose their spot, leave their stuff unattended, or are too timid to ask for help."[17]

TECHNOLOGY

Roving reference is in some ways old-fashioned, with its focus on physical space and face-to-face interaction. That said, the success or failure of a roving reference endeavor depends on the available technology. While roving reference programs have certainly been around longer than mobile technologies, mobile technology is a major reason why roving reference has been increasingly popular in recent years. Mobile devices have improved in leaps and bounds, and as a result, they are becoming more well-suited for use in roving reference programs, particularly in academic libraries. Phyllis Rudin argues that academic roving reference could not really catch on until technology made a dynamic, instructional reference interaction possible away from the confines of the desk:

> In a university setting, though, where teaching patrons how to navigate the library's systems and structures is part and parcel of the roving reference service, a BlackBerry-sized device, designed for individual use, would make demonstrating databases and library catalogues a difficult proposition.[18]

Academic librarians have a much different expectation of reference and instructional services than do public librarians. For example, academic reference is in very large part about the *process* as much as it is about the *product*—that is, reference is as much about teaching a student how to use a specific academic database as it is about helping the student find a specific article. Reference interviews are intended to be instructional, leaving students with a greater knowledge of how the research process works and strong preparation for the next research assignment and the next search for relevant information. Due to this teaching component, the mobile experience must be as close to the nonmobile or "normal" experience as possible.

Penner provides an excellent example of how technological change has made roving reference services more efficient. She describes the Roving Librarian Project at the Elizabeth Dafoe Library at the University of Manitoba, in which librarians with mobile devices roved during time periods that were known to include heavy library use. When the program began in 2005, the laptops were larger, required a cart, and had low power efficiency. In 2009, netbooks were introduced, and these devices offered more portability and a longer battery life. However, in 2010, the library experimented with two newer mobile devices, a Google Android mobile phone and an Apple iPod Touch. Although Penner reports that both of these devices offered maximum mobility, each had difficulties accessing the campus wireless network on all floors of the library building. Eventually, the Roving Librarian Project decided to use an Apple iPhone as their mobile device, with the added benefit that the iPhone could access a 3G network when the campus wireless network was otherwise not an option.[19]

The release of the iPad and the iPad Mini has made roving reference easier than ever. Megan Lotts and Stephanie Graves as well as Joanna Gadsby and Shu Qian report the use of iPads for roving reference.[20] While an iPhone is a good option for roving reference, iPhones are expensive, small, and are most effective with a data plan. The Apple iPad is a tablet that can be used on a wireless Internet connection or with a purchased data plan. The iPad offers many of the benefits of the iPhone as well as some improvements: it is lightweight and easily carried, but has a larger screen than the iPhone, allowing the user experience to more closely resemble that of a full-size computer. By using an iPad (or a competitor's tablet, such as the Microsoft Surface), librarians can travel within the library or across campus and still have reliable access to e-mail, the library's website, and electronic resources.

Many librarians argue that using an iPad or other comparable product for roving reference has other benefits as well. The University of Maryland, Baltimore County, for example, performs roving reference with a 3G-enabled iPad, but the iPad also has at least one in-house use: by connecting to the 3G service instead of the on-campus network, librarians are able to better understand the problems that off-campus users have when accessing electronic resources.[21] Lotts and Graves note that librarians at Southern Illinois–Carbondale are allowed to take their iPads to conferences, enabling them to write notes, access the Internet, and stay in touch with the office while they are away. They also mention that using iPads allows librarians who do not have mobile devices for personal use to become familiar with popular technology.[22] As these devices become increasingly ubiquitous, patrons will use them to access library resources, and it will only help librarians to become familiar with the mobile user experience.

ROVING AS REFERENCE

Roving reference can be located as an extension of consultation-based reference services. John Cruickshank and David Nowak describe a shift toward this sort of service model, based on the efforts of librarians at the Mississippi State University Libraries.[23] Librarians gathered information from patrons in order to determine what services were needed both through formal meetings and, because of the proximity of the library to the targeted department, through more casual interactions in hallways and other locations. They also investigated faculty's database-searching habits and determined that faculty members were not all competent in online searching. As a result of this information gathering, Mississippi State University librarians directed their service and philosophy toward a "consultative reference service model based upon a firm knowledge of patrons' need and expectations."[24] This consultative model included personal meetings with faculty and an electronic reference room that facilitated one-on-one interactions between students and librarians. Roving reference operates under the same principles as these services, but makes them mobile, either within the library building or at another location on campus.

Roving reference outside of the library often takes the form of what Rudin calls "library outposts" or "roving writ large,"[25] spaces in academic or social areas in which librarians set up shop in order to provide research assistance. Described by Del Bosque and Chapman, the University of Texas at San Antonio Library devised a comprehensive system to offer research assistance and outreach at multiple locations around campus. The University of Texas at San Antonio developed library outposts at locations such as the tutoring and advising center, the Writing Center, student apartments and residence halls, and a computer lab. The librarians involved in the study observed that their roving reference experiences were different depending on the type of location in which they occurred. Librarians also had to adapt to the more casual environment, as many students in the residence hall spaces were engaging in recreational activities rather than academic ones: "Librarians were guests in the students' home [residence halls], so to speak, and many students were curious as to the librarians' presence."[26] In this model, roving reference was combined with in-library services as Drop-In Tours and Library Crash Courses, library-focused services that gave students the opportunities to join scheduled tours or to receive library instruction on specific, predetermined topics.

While Del Bosque and Chapman document roving reference services within both academic and social spaces, other librarians focus primarily on academic spaces. Claire Holmes and Lisa Woznicki, for example, describe two different approaches to roving reference at Towson University. Blending the social and the academic, one librarian scheduled weekly ninety-minute visits to a café within her liaison department's building; the "walk in" model allowed for unscheduled and organic interactions with students. Another librarian decided to combine a weekly two-hour visit to a departmental computer lab with the option of arranging a special appointment elsewhere in the building.[27] The option of a private appointment or follow-up consultation proved important for both models. Similarly, Moore and Wells describe how two librarians share office hours in a building that houses courses in both of their liaison disciplines. Together, the librarians are able to provide assistance to students in the same location five days a week. In an interview, one of the two librarians expressed to Moore and Wells that the questions she received were quite varied: "The questions she gets range from citation issues to 'how do I start this research with this bit of information' to in-depth support where she makes an appointment to meet with the student [later]."[28]

Another form of roving reference involves exchanging library spaces for departmental spaces: embedding librarians into academic departments. Rudin depicts this phenomenon as a rather logical extension of the existing liaison model, in which academic librarians who are subject specialists are assigned the corresponding academic department.[29] Liaison librarians are generally responsible for all instruction and collection development related to that department. Liaison librarians may also have a myriad of other duties: organizing events or exhibits, distributing relevant information to faculty, and assisting faculty with their own research or tenure documentation. Embedding librarians into academic departments is intended to strengthen this relationship by adding geographical proximity, as well as to make it easier and more convenient for faculty and graduate students to take advantage of the librarians' expertise. Archer and Cast emphasize the need for a librarian to be mobile in order to assist faculty members at the point of need—in their offices:

> "Going Where the Questions Are" can be accomplished by going directly to faculty offices to answer questions. If a faculty member is having difficulty using electronic reference tools from her office, go to the professor's office and provide a little one-on-one tutoring. One librarian at Northeastern State University took an ERIC thesaurus to the faculty member's office and talked the professor through the research process.[30]

While some libraries have experimented with assigning liaison librarians permanent office space in their associated departments, rather than or in addition to within the library walls, the less-dramatic approach involves setting limited office hours similar to the office hours kept by teaching faculty.

In this model, a liaison librarian would arrange to be present within an academic department for a certain amount of hours per week, during a scheduled time period. Faculty and graduate students, as well as some undergraduate students who frequent the department—perhaps for their own professors' office hours—would then come to expect to see the librarian at a specific time, and will then know exactly when and where to go for help. However, unlike teaching faculty office hours, liaison librarians may not want to confine themselves to an actual office. While an office does promise higher degrees of both comfort and privacy, residing in an office requires librarians to rely exclusively on others to come see them. There may be little point in trading a traditional reference desk or liaison model, in which the librarian waits for a student or faculty member to come into the library for help, for a similar situation in another building. Instead, A. Ben Wagner and Cynthia Tysick emphasize that one of the biggest benefits of holding office hours within academic departments is serendipity:

> It was clear from both verbal and nonverbal cues that many of the questions and interactions would never have taken place had so much as an e-mail or phone call been required. The most common opening line ran something like this, "I was just passing by and was wondering if . . ."[31]

Many of these students asked their question only because they were speaking with a librarian at exactly the right moment, demonstrating the value in having librarians stationed away from the library.

Roving reference within the library is often used to supplement reference services at the reference desk. Sometimes, however, roving is part of an attempt to revolutionize reference services. Megan Dempsey describes how librarians at Raritan Valley Community College have rejected the traditional reference desk format as the sole point of contact for student assistance and developed a replacement that blended many different alternative reference formats. Their redesigned reference service includes core daytime reference desk hours staffed by adjunct librarians and a referral system. The referral system features a check-out desk as the first point of contact with students; the staff members at the check-out desk are expected to answer all questions except those related to library databases, the library catalog, or specific class assignments. Questions not answered at the check-out desk are referred to "on call" full-time librarians or, if staffed, to the reference desk. When not answering referred questions, "on call" librarians are expected to be in their offices, logged into the virtual reference system. At the same time, they also incorporate elements of the roving reference model:

> We also realized it was essential for on-call librarians to roam the library frequently during their shift. The concept of the roving librarian integrated nicely into our new format, giving us the opportunity to stay in touch with what is happening in all areas of the library, continue to monitor noise levels and prevent complaints, and assist students in an unintimidating way at their workstations.[32]

This blended model, with roving reference bundled into the core duties of a reference librarian, requires librarians to be flexible and adaptable, but also to juggle multiple responsibilities at once.

ROVING AS INSTRUCTION

Although roving reference, as evidenced by its name, is often described as the reference desk gone mobile, it can also be seen as an increased opportunity for instruction. Jeanne Galvin, for example, sees roving reference as point-of-need instruction,[33] suggesting that it might be a more natural corollary to information-literacy instruction than to traditional reference. Similarly, Sandy Campbell and Debbie Fyfe argue that one of the results of a shift from traditional desk to roving reference "was that many of the reference questions turned into one-on-one instructional sessions."[34] They locate roving reference as a form of instruction in which librarians are impromptu teachers of everything from basic computer use to in-depth research tools: "We have no lesson plans and no preparation time, we don't know what we're going to be teaching next, and there is no set amount of time allocated to delivering this uncertain curriculum."[35]

One of the interesting results of the Del Bosque and Chapman study is that librarians did not feel that the success of the program needed to be measured by the amount of questions answered. Rather, "they felt that *fewer, lengthier* [emphasis added] transactions with patrons were successful, and that they were able to reach students who might not feel comfortable approaching a librarian for help in a traditional setting."[36] The emphasis on a smaller number of longer, more in-depth transactions supports the assertion that roving reference is actually a form of highly personalized instruction. Eileen Kramer, for example, reports of the roving reference initiative at Utica College: "Roving reference offers a greater chance for librarians to teach users the techniques that make improved searching possible."[37] The Utica librarians also found that the roving librarian answered more sophisticated questions that required more "professional activity,"[38] while at the reference desk librarians tended to answer questions about finding known items or specific resources.

The highly instructional nature of roving reference suggests some policy initiatives. If nothing else, the experiences of researchers quoted above and others suggest that librarians and library administrators should not be too quick to dismiss roving reference efforts with low numbers of questions answered. However, this is not the only implication for library policies and procedures, especially those related to reference desk staffing. Take, for example, virtual or chat-based "real-time" reference: one might imagine short interactions and short answers, sprinkled with links to appropriate web resources and little else. However, Patricia Johnston indicates that 60 percent of questions answered by the University of New Brunswick's virtual reference service required some form of instruction.[39] Kate Shaw and Amanda Spink outline some of the varied models for virtual reference provision, including hiring additional staff in order to manage virtual reference services in a way that does not unfairly burden reference librarians.[40] Instead of introducing virtual reference as a duty to be performed while sitting at an already-busy reference desk, increased staffing allows virtual reference to become a fully realized task separate from traditional reference. Few librarians have suggested the same of roving reference, although it embodies the same instructional potential as virtual reference and an equal, if not greater, time commitment. If already-overworked librarians, especially academic librarians who may hold faculty status and must therefore fulfill tenure requirements, balk at the thought of taking on the time- and energy-intensive task of a concerted roving reference program, a potential solution could be to hire additional professional staff for whom roving reference would represent a large portion of their job duties.

ROVING AS MARKETING

Roving reference is also very useful as a form of outreach and marketing. In addition to presenting an opportunity to provide research assistance and point-of-need instruction, roving reference is an opportunity to reach students who do not ordinarily come into the library. Roving reference can also be used to serve students who use the physical library building, but do not take advantage of the existing services offered by librarians. Brent Nunn and Elizabeth Ruance, in their discussion of how to market reference librarians to their users, point out that roving reference is particularly valuable because of the difficulty inherent in marketing services rather than goods. As they describe, roving reference has as its chief goal "making nonlibrary users aware of what the library can offer."[41] The benefit of this sort of marketing is that it is cumulative; the results are not directly tied to the amount of people who take advantage of the services during any particular time frame. As Del Bosque and Chapman note, "Rather than being a heavily used service for solving information needs, these additional services [...] becomes [sic] a marketing tool promoting the library in general. . . . These services showed students that the library consists of people who want to help them."[42]

Roving also represents a way to market libraries and librarians to other, nonstudent populations on campus. Reports from librarians like Holmes and Woznicki demonstrate that increased campus visibility is one of the most important benefits of roving reference. Getting librarians out of the library and into other campus spaces generates goodwill and gets librarians noticed by faculty and campus administrators:

> The . . . librarian was praised by her dean and a department chair. . . . Many faculty members stopped to say they endorsed the service in their work with students. . . . One department chair mentioned the service during a national accreditation site visit. In another case, an associate dean e-mailed the librarian stating that seeing the students engaged with her was "uplifting."[43]

Wagner and Tysick echo these findings: "The librarians were completely unprepared for the significant good will generated among the faculty. . . . One librarian received a warm, thank-you e-mail just for announcing the office hours before they had even begun."[44] Similarly, Gadsby and Qian mention that UMBC's roving reference program garnered positive feedback from the provost of the university, who witnessed a reference interaction while passing by with prospective students.[45] In these particular examples, roving reference functioned as a highly visible example of the service provided by librarians at these universities. These faculty members and university administrators might not have otherwise had the opportunity to witness firsthand a librarian interacting with a student, or to interact with a librarian themselves. By implementing roving reference, librarians can make a positive impression on the campus community and cement partnerships with teaching faculty and administrators.

CONCLUSION

Advances in technology, and particularly the introduction of the tablet computer, have made roving reference an enticing proposition for academic libraries. When academic librarians rove to other locations on campus, students who never would have stood up and walked to the reference desk can still receive professional, personalized research help. Roving reference targets the student who does not come into the library and who therefore may not know what the library can offer. In this respect, roving reference, by reaching out specifically to users who may not have received previous library instruction, can combat library anxiety. As defined by Atlas, library anxiety is "characterized by feeling that one's library skills are inadequate compared to those of one's peers, that this inadequacy is shameful and should be hidden, and that one's inadequacy is revealed by asking questions."[46] Indeed, particularly in academic libraries, many patrons can be afraid to reveal their ignorance, either of basic library knowledge or skills, or of the requirements of their research paper or project. Roving librarians, removed from the reference desk, have the time and the flexibility to offer these students one-on-one instruction on whatever topic or tool they require.

One of the important take-away messages of the literature on roving reference is that it is not a replacement for other types of reference. Roving reference is a supplement to the traditional reference desk, an academic library's established instruction program, and other existing and emerging outreach activities. As Penner states, "It is not a matter of changing the level of instruction that we give them or abandoning methods that have worked for us in the past. It may simply be a matter of adding to what we have already established, or perhaps modifying those services to adapt to the changing landscape of our users."[47] By getting librarians out of the library and into other campus spaces, roving reference often causes librarians to become more visible to faculty, campus administrators, and other university offices. Roving programs market the library and its librarians to both students and faculty and can be used to cultivate the image of a helpful, supportive entity on campus. When implemented in addition to desk-based and virtual reference services, roving reference increases the amount of people who receive research assistance from a librarian, garners goodwill toward the library on campus, and makes the library a friendlier, more approachable place.

NOTES

1. Susan Gardner and Susanna Eng, "What Students Want: Generation Y and the Changing Function of the Academic Library," *portal: Libraries & the Academy* 5, no. 3 (2005): 405–20.

2. Judith F. Trump and Ian P. Tuttle, "Here, There, and Everywhere: Reference at the Point-of-Need," *Journal of Academic Librarianship* 27, no. 6 (2001): 464.

3. Michel Atlas, "Library Anxiety in the Electronic Era, Or Why Won't Anybody Talk to Me Anymore?" *Reference & User Services Quarterly* 44, no. 4 (2005): 315.

4. Anne Cooper Moore and Kimberly A. Wells, "Connecting 24/5 to Millennials: Providing Academic Support Services from a Learning Commons," *The Journal of Academic Librarianship* 35, no. 1 (2009): 84.

5. Darcy Del Bosque and Kimberly Chapman, "Your Place Or Mine? Face-to-Face Reference Services Across Campus," *New Library World* 108, no. 5/6 (2007): 248.

6. Michael M. Smith and Barbara A. Pietraszewski, "Enabling the Roving Reference Librarian: Wireless Access with Tablet PCs," *Reference Services Review* 32, no. 3 (2004): 250.

7. Eileen Kramer, "Why Roving Reference: A Case Study in a Small Academic Library," *Reference Services Review* 24, no. 3 (1996): 67–80.

8. Martin Courtois and Maira Liriano, "Tips for Roving Reference," *College & Research Libraries News* 61, no. 4 (2000): 289.

9. Smith and Pietraszewski, "Enabling the Roving Reference Librarian."

10. Claire Holmes and Lisa Woznicki, "Librarians at Your Doorstep: Roving Reference at Towson University," *College & Research Libraries News* 71, no. 11 (2010): 582–85.

11. Kealin McCabe and James MacDonald, "Roaming Reference: Reinvigorating Reference through Point of Need Service," *Partnership: The Canadian Journal of Library & Information Practice & Research* 6, no. 2 (2011): 1–15.

12. Megan Lotts and Stephanie Graves, "Using the iPad for Reference Services: Librarians Go Mobile," *College & Research Libraries News* 72, no. 4 (2011): 217–20.

13. Joanna Gadsby and Shu Qian, "Using an iPad to Redefine Roving Reference Service in an Academic Library," *Library Hi Tech News* 29, no. 4 (2012): 1–5.

14. Sarah Archer and Melissa Cast, "Going Where the Questions Are: Using Media to Maintain Personalized Contact in Reference Service in Medium-Sized Academic Libraries," *The Reference Librarian* 31, no. 65 (1999): 39–50.

15. Katherine Penner, "Mobile Technologies and Roving Reference," *Public Services Quarterly* 7, no. 1 (2011): 27.

16. Trump and Tuttle, "Here, There, and Everywhere," 464.

17. Moore and Wells, "Connecting 24/5," 82.

18. Phyllis Rudin, "No Fixed Address: The Evolution of Outreach Library Services on University Campuses," *The Reference Librarian* 49, no. 1 (2008): 62.

19. Penner, "Mobile Technologies," 28–29.

20. Lotts and Graves, "Librarians Go Mobile," 217–20; Gadsby and Qian, "Using an iPad," 1–5.

21. Gadsby and Qian, "Using an iPad," 3.

22. Lotts and Graves, "Librarians Go Mobile," 220.

23. John Cruickshank and David Nowak, "Marketing Reference Resources and Services through a University Outreach Program," *Reference Librarian*, no. 73 (2001): 265–80.

24. Ibid., 276.

25. Rudin, "No Fixed Address," 62.

26. Del Bosque and Chapman, "Your Place or Mine?," 256.

27. Holmes and Woznicki, "Librarians at Your Doorstep," 582–85.

28. Moore and Wells, "Connecting 24/5," 78.

29. Rudin, "No Fixed Address," 68.

30. Archer and Cast, "Going Where the Questions Are," 41.

31. A. B. Wagner and Cynthia Tysick, "Onsite Reference and Instruction Services," *Reference & User Services Quarterly* 46, no. 4 (2007): 63.

32. Megan Dempsey, "Blending the Trends: A Holistic Approach to Reference Services," *Public Services Quarterly* 7, no. 1 (2011): 12.

33. Jeanne Galvin, "Alternative Strategies for Promoting Information Literacy," *The Journal of Academic Librarianship* 31, no. 4 (2005): 354.

34. Sandy Campbell and Debbie Fyfe, "Teaching at the Computer: Best Practices for One-on-One Instruction in Reference," *Feliciter* 48, no. 1 (2002): 26.

35. Ibid.

36. Del Bosque and Chapman, "Your Place or Mine?," 256.

37. Kramer, "Why Roving Reference," 74.

38. Ibid., 79.

39. Patricia Johnston, "Digital Reference as an Instructional Tool: Just in Time and Just Enough," *Searcher* 11, no. 3 (2003): paragraph 7.

40. Kate Shaw and Amanda Spink, "University Library Virtual Reference Services: Best Practices and Continuous Improvement," *Australian Academic & Research Libraries* 40, no. 3 (2009): 196–97.

41. Brent Nunn and Elizabeth Ruance, "Marketing Gets Personal: Promoting Reference Staff to Reach Users," *Journal of Library Administration* 52, no. 6–7 (2012): 577.

42. Del Bosque and Chapman, "Your Place or Mine?," 260.

43. Holmes and Woznicki, "Librarians at Your Doorstep," 584.

44. Wagner and Tysick, "Onsite Reference," 63.

45. Gadsby and Qian, "Using an Ipad," 4.

46. Atlas, "Library Anxiety, 315.

47. Penner, "Mobile Technologies," 32.

BIBLIOGRAPHY

Archer, Sarah Brick, and Melissa Cast. "Going Where the Questions Are: Using Media to Maintain Personalized Contact in Reference Service in Medium-Sized Academic Libraries." *The Reference Librarian* 31, no. 65 (1999): 39–50.

Atlas, Michel. "Library Anxiety in the Electronic Era, Or Why Won't Anybody Talk to Me Anymore?" *Reference & User Services Quarterly* 44, no. 4 (2005): 314–19.

Campbell, Sandy, and Debbie Fyfe. "Teaching at the Computer: Best Practices for One-on-One Instruction in Reference." *Feliciter* 48, no. 1 (2002): 26–28.

Courtois, Martin, and Maira Liriano. "Tips for Roving Reference." *College & Research Libraries News* 61, no. 4 (2000): 289.

Cruickshank, John L., and David G. Nowak. "Marketing Reference Resources and Services through a University Outreach Program." *Reference Librarian*, no. 73 (2001): 265–80.

Del Bosque, Darcy, and Kimberly Chapman. "Your Place or Mine? Face-to-Face Reference Services Across Campus." *New Library World* 108, no. 5/6 (2007): 247.

Dempsey, Megan. "Blending the Trends: A Holistic Approach to Reference Services." *Public Services Quarterly* 7, no. 1 (2011): 3–17.

Gadsby, Joanna, and Shu Qian. "Using an iPad to Redefine Roving Reference Service in an Academic Library." *Library Hi Tech News* 29, no. 4 (2012): 1–5.

Galvin, Jeanne. "Alternative Strategies for Promoting Information Literacy." *The Journal of Academic Librarianship* 31, no. 4 (2005): 352–57.

Gardner, Susan, and Susanna Eng. "What Students Want: Generation Y and the Changing Function of the Academic Library." *portal: Libraries & the Academy* 5, no. 3 (2005): 405–20.

Holmes, Claire, and Lisa Woznicki. "Librarians at Your Doorstep: Roving Reference at Towson University." *College & Research Libraries News* 71, no. 11 (2010): 582–85.

Johnston, P. E. "Digital Reference as an Instructional Tool: Just in Time and Just Enough." *Searcher* 11, no. 3 (2003): n.p.

Kramer, Eileen H. "Why Roving Reference: A Case Study in a Small Academic Library." *Reference Services Review* 24, no. 3 (1996): 67–80.

Lotts, Megan, and Stephanie Graves. "Using the iPad for Reference Services: Librarians Go Mobile." *College & Research Libraries News* 72, no. 4 (2011): 217–20.

McCabe, Kealin, and James R. W. MacDonald. "Roaming Reference: Reinvigorating Reference through Point of Need Service." *Partnership: The Canadian Journal of Library & Information Practice & Research* 6, no. 2 (2011): 1–15.

Moore, Anne Cooper, and Kimberly A. Wells. "Connecting 24/5 to Millennials: Providing Academic Support Services from a Learning Commons." *The Journal of Academic Librarianship* 35, no. 1 (2009): 75–85.

Nunn, Brent, and Elizabeth Ruane. "Marketing Gets Personal: Promoting Reference Staff to Reach Users." *Journal of Library Administration* 52, no. 6–7 (2012): 571–80.

Penner, Katherine. "Mobile Technologies and Roving Reference." *Public Services Quarterly* 7, no. 1 (2011): 27–33.

Reynolds, Marianne. "Operation Rover." *Library Journal* 130, no. 7 (2005): 62.

Rudin, Phyllis. "No Fixed Address: The Evolution of Outreach Library Services on University Campuses." *The Reference Librarian* 49, no. 1 (2008): 55–75.

Shaw, Kate, and Amanda Spink. "University Library Virtual Reference Services: Best Practices and Continuous Improvement." *Australian Academic & Research Libraries* 40, no. 3 (2009): 192–205.

Smith, Michael M., and Barbara A. Pietraszewski. "Enabling the Roving Reference Librarian: Wireless Access with Tablet PCs." *Reference Services Review* 32, no. 3 (2004): 249–55.

Trump, Judith F., and Ian P. Tuttle. "Here, There, and Everywhere: Reference at the Point-of-Need." *Journal of Academic Librarianship* 27, no. 6 (2001): 464–66.

Wagner, A. B., and Cynthia Tysick. "Onsite Reference and Instruction Services." *Reference & User Services Quarterly* 46, no. 4 (2007): 60–65.

Chapter Seven

Connecting Questions with Answers

Ellie Dworak and Carrie Moore

The term *frequently asked questions* (FAQ) brings to mind library websites circa 1995. These first attempts at providing reference help via the broad reach of the Internet were generally comprised of a list of questions hyperlinked to answers farther down the page. These early FAQs were of uncertain value, though they held the promise of a core principal of librarianship: access to information.[1] Fast-forward to 2013, and FAQs have become a much more sophisticated instrument. The expectation of an FAQ now is that it be database-driven and searchable, combining the simplicity of a search engine while losing none of the specificity innate to library research. Is this an achievable goal? Yes and no, as this chapter will demonstrate. Regardless, it is a necessary objective, one that meets the needs of library users and leverages the knowledge of reference staff.

On an anecdotal level, the need for unmediated access to information in an academic library context has grown with the technology. As "most every action in the modern academic library can be performed without the need for mediation,"[2] there is less tolerance for those situations, which do require facilitation. The authors see local evidence of this in the results of our library's biannual LibQual+ surveys,[3] which demonstrate a steady rise in the desire for independent access to information, and to information resources that are not bound by place or time. While libraries are increasingly able to meet the need for remote access, the complexity of searching for and finding information resources has been amplified by multiple vendor interfaces. Though attempts are under way to make this easier—largely in the form of discovery layer technologies—the perfect solution remains elusive, as demonstrated in the timeline of the evolution of discovery and access technologies in figure 7.1. For the foreseeable future, library research requires skill and, regardless, will always require some level of information-literacy competency.

The issue, then, is how best to help patrons who prefer to learn for themselves or for whom interacting directly with library staff is difficult or inconvenient. One piece of the answer is to give patrons the ability to locate answers independently. Libraries have been trying to do this for several decades, but it is only recently that software systems have been developed making it easy to offer a robust knowledge base grounded in user needs. In

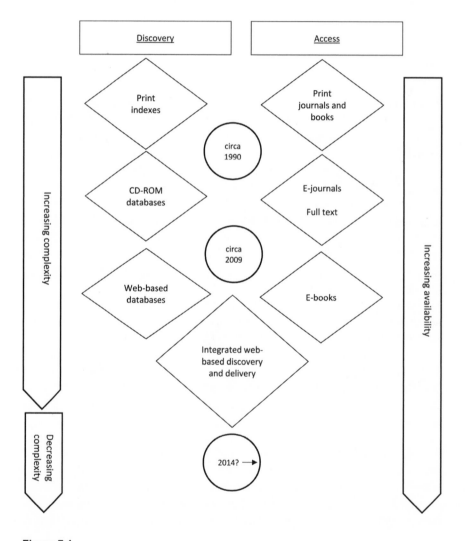

Figure 7.1.

addition, these tools usually present librarians with information to help us understand those needs.

LITERATURE REVIEW

Computers and libraries have been entangled from the start. Though accounts differ, arguably the first full-scale use of computer systems in a library was the Montclair (New Jersey) Public Library's automated circulation system using IBM equipment, unveiled in 1942.[4] The use of computers for library functions such as catalog production, circulation, serials management, and acquisitions grew throughout the 1960s and 1970s.[5] With the advent of the IBM PC in 1981, microcomputers became a widely accepted tool for office applications[6] and librarians began wholeheartedly considering the possibilities for reference services. Much of the literature surrounding this topic focused on expert systems, an application of artificial intelligence intended to replicate human reasoning.

Examples of experiments in using expert system technology for reference applications abound; a review of the literature leaves one with a sense of the breathless excitement of the period. Regrettably, a thorough review of the literature is a topic for another publication, and the authors have limited themselves to several illustrative examples.

In 1986, there was a boom in library publications regarding expert systems. Samuel Waters, then the associate director of the National Agricultural Library, published an article describing Answerman, "a project to develop a microcomputer-based expert system that will help users obtain answers to ready reference questions."[7] In this article, Waters explained that Answerman pointed "users to reference books likely to answer specific kinds of questions . . . linked to external programs providing online access to databases of bibliographic citations and to full-text files that can furnish the answer to a question."[8]

College and Research Libraries published an article in 1986 titled "Robot at the Reference Desk?" This article by Karen F. Smith described an experimental expert system program developed to deliver assistance with federal documents reference questions.[9] At the same time, PLEXUS came into being. This information referral system, initially limited to gardening topics, was a grant-funded project initiated by the University of London's Central Information Service, and several publications from the time cover its development and assessment outcomes.[10] A 1989 special issue of *The Reference Librarian* titled "Expert Systems in Reference Services" included articles regarding projects, project assessment, and possibilities for using expert systems in libraries.[11]

By the end of the 1980s, a discussion had emerged about the difficulty in trying to *replace* library reference functions with artificial intelligence, and toward *assisting* librarians and patrons in discovering answers. In a 1988 review of the research on libraries and expert systems, Patricia F. Anderson noted that "when it comes to information problem solving and search strategies in manual or online systems, librarians are the experts. Unfortunately, as difficult as it is to search for information, it has been even more difficult to analyze the process by which results are achieved."[12]

With the shift to more manageable goals for library systems came a slow change in vocabulary, from the broader term *expert system* to the more specific *knowledge base*, which referred to an "assembly of all of the information and knowledge of a specific field of interest."[13] In this context, a frequently asked questions (FAQ) file represented one type of knowledge base, whether machine or human readable.

It was not until the mid-1990s that the literature reflected any interest in FAQs per se. This is no surprise, given the advent of the World Wide Web and the excitement surrounding this new means of sharing information. Though the term is not specifically used, in 1992 Eloisa Borah provided a review of several FAQ-type projects with the admonishment, "Isn't it about time that librarians assume the role of primary architects of the tools of information's future?"[14]

In another early example of FAQ research, in 1996 Ohio State University librarians John Stalker and Marjorie Murfin published the results of their research into the success of a web-based FAQ developed for library users. In this study, the authors asked students reference questions and observed their success in finding answers using the FAQ, coming to the conclusion that, though their results demonstrated only moderate success, the concept was worthy of investigation.[15]

Much of the recent literature about FAQs has been limited to case studies. For example, a 2007 article by Karen Anello and Brett Bonfield covers their experiences in managing a multi-library business FAQ.[16] With over nineteen business libraries participating worldwide, maintenance, scope, and other project-management issues were key to the success of the tool. For example, "the editorial decision was made that the FAQ would not replace any information sources for patrons, or even supplement them: it would simply guide patrons to the resources that would most likely meet their needs."[17] The FAQ in this article utilized an Oracle database with middleware connecting the data to a web-based search interface, which is to say that it was a major undertaking.

In 2009, Sherri Jones, Jessica Kayongo, and John Scofield published an article describing their process of building a database-driven, searchable FAQ. The article focuses on the technical aspects of the project, which involved mining three thousand questions from e-mail and chat reference transcripts. In addition, the authors reviewed 112 ARL institutions, finding that 54 percent had FAQs, and 29 percent were linked from the library home page. Most were browsable—only 13 percent were searchable and 10 percent both searchable and browsable.[18]

In 2009, Kate Shaw and Amanda Spink published a meta-analysis of library virtual reference services literature to create a common set of best practices.[19] Of note is that after reviewing virtual reference services generally, the authors came to the conclusion that an FAQ database is the most cost-effective option for libraries, as well as the preferred mode of patrons, stating that "allowing patrons to use self-service can reduce staff numbers required for a chat or e-mail VR service, and reduce the number of repetitive or straightforward operational questions handled by staff."[20]

Finally, a 2013 article by Christy R. Stevens[21] provided historical context surrounding desk-centric reference and its associated costs. The author stated that in her institution, online reference transactions were beginning to "make up an increasingly larger percentage of total reference transactions."[22] She argued that answers retrieved from an FAQ, while not representing an immediate patron-librarian interaction, were examples of important and effective reference work, and thus should be viewed alongside other statistics when evaluating reference services.

These articles have made important contributions to the profession by allowing libraries to build on each other's experiences and explore new directions. The profession now needs more evidence-based recommendations, both exploration using mixed-iterative methodologies, and rigorous research into user needs and the success of FAQ systems in meeting them.

BACKGROUND

As noted in the introduction, the emphasis of this chapter is on implementing and optimizing library FAQs using knowledge-base technologies. The emphasis will be on services meant for library patrons, though certainly library staff also will make frequent use of the content within. Entries in the FAQ are referred to as question/answer (QA) pairs.

This chapter uses examples from Boise State University Albertsons Library. Boise State University is a public university with (as of 2014) approximately 22,500 students, 40 percent of whom attend school part-time. The university offers ninety-five baccalaureate, seventy-eight masters, and eight doctorate programs in a broad range of disciplines. The College of Social Sciences and Public Affairs and the College of Health Sciences have the highest undergraduate enrollments. The College of Education's Educational Technology Department offers by far the largest graduate program on campus, with 474 students enrolled during the 2012/2013 academic year.

Albertsons Library is the only campus library and serves the entire university community. The library prides itself on a strong public service and outreach program, and each of the approximately twenty-five librarians liaises closely with one or more campus departments. In support of this strong service commitment, the Reference and Instruction Unit has built and sustained a frequently asked questions knowledge base using LibAnswers. The library began using LibAnswers in 2009 as a replacement for an internal Wiki-based FAQ. During the busiest times of the academic calendar over 450 patron queries are matched with answers each month.

PLANNING AND POLICY

Selecting a system from which to administer an FAQ is an important first step if you have the luxury of a budget for the project. While there are a number of knowledge-base-constructed FAQ options on the market, few of them were designed to meet library needs specifically. Those products that have been designed for use in nonlibrary settings generally emphasize version control and editorial flow features over those designed to meet patron needs. Additionally, the added complexity of content-management options can hinder ease of use on the staff side, and are generally unnecessary in a library setting.

Boise State University Albertsons Library has adopted LibAnswers, which will be used to supply examples throughout this chapter.[23] Though the policy and procedural recommendations can be applied to any system, features related to metadata and use reports will vary. A rating rubric, such as the sample in table 7.1, is an efficient way to compare FAQ products. Because some features may be more or less important for a particular library setting, it is recommended that readers work with this rubric as a starting point and modify it to meet individual needs. Remember that while some aspects of a system can be ascertained with a product trial, it is also a good idea to speak with librarians or other customers who have implemented the product.

STAFFING CONSIDERATIONS

When considering how to administer the FAQ, keep in mind what your intent is for this service. While it may seem compelling to assign maintenance to library computing staff, if your FAQ is a core reference service, you may want to consider whether those who work directly with the public will have sufficient input into content, interface, and update frequency. Due to the ease of administering most FAQ systems on the library market, the authors recommend recruiting a reference librarian to administer the FAQ, perhaps with

Table 7.1.

	Rating	Importance Factor	Score
Costs			
Software price: *Annual or one-time? Updates included?*			
Hosting: *In house versus vendor*			
Product and installation support: *Additional cost? Responsiveness*			
Ease of use for library administrator			
Technical skill requirements			
Implementation: *Support/Difficulty/Time*			
Management: *Easy to update?*			
Other tools and features			
User interface			
Customization options			
Searchability			
Browsing options			
Discoverability			
Search engine intelligence			
Categories or topics			
Other metadata options			
Reporting and Statistics			
Query data			
Use data			
Other statistics and reporting options			

backup support from staff or a team. Firsthand knowledge of patron needs and of using the FAQ to search for information will complement use and query data in making informed decisions about the service.

Albertsons Library has found it beneficial to assign a single individual ownership of the FAQ system, with a backup librarian, who is trained to update or add entries if needed. In addition, all library staff are encouraged to make suggestions and identify errors. There are several reasons for assigning responsibility to one individual. First, it ensures consistent language and streamlines workflow. Further, an individual will tend to take the oversight of an assignment more seriously if outcomes (either positive or negative) will reflect on him or her directly.

A clear sense of the scope of your FAQ up front can save hours of review and editorial work later. While scope may change over time and as user input is collected and analyzed, not having one from the outset invites mission creep. A written policy is also helpful when addressing requests for additions to the FAQ by identifying appropriate content and defining that which is too extraneous or ephemeral for inclusion. Albertsons Library has determined that the purpose of our FAQ is to guide patrons to information that enables them to conduct research projects and answers questions about the library and university. This often requires linking to content created or maintained outside of the library. These include campus resources such as computer labs, testing centers, international student services, and other campus services. Additionally, the FAQ may link to information and services offered by other organizations such as other local libraries or government agencies.

Note that we mention *linking to*, not *duplicating* information from other units. Our experience is that using links with context is an efficient way to meet patron needs. This practice discourages duplication of effort as well as mitigating the risk of the FAQ, including inaccurate or outdated information in QA pairs. In addition, using a link checker (hopefully built into the product) will save time and frustration as the number of QA pairs in the system grows.

While there is a certain appeal to the idea of offering an FAQ with comprehensive information comprised of QA pairs addressing all aspects of the library and every actual or perceived research need, doing so can be detrimental to the user experience. Will patrons be able to find the QA pairs describing how to print in color if they are presented with hundreds of QA entries addressing the minutia of printer driver software? Remember that librarians are expert searchers, while patrons may simply type "printer" and will often review only the first few entries in the results list. If an archive of library documentation is needed, consider separating that function from the public FAQ.

Transferability is also worth considering. QA pairs should be specific enough to be applicable, yet general enough to be useful to a larger audience. The exact balance may shift over time and with the setting—for example, one entry about equipment available for check-out may be enough for a library with only a few items that circulate, while another library may need to address iPads separately from VHS players. In addition, particular equipment may become more or less important to your user base, thus warranting a greater or lesser degree of granularity in the QA pairs about these materials.

Out-of-date or inaccurate information is frustrating to patrons, which can hurt the library's reputation. Every QA pair must be reviewed regularly and updated as necessary. Keeping this in mind while writing and selecting QA pairs can mitigate this process—for example, ephemeral or often-changing information could be left out, instead offering a telephone number and e-mail address. Library hours are posted in one place on the Albertsons Library website, and not duplicated in the FAQ. In addition, to ensure currency and accuracy of QA pairs, the librarian who administers the Albertsons Library FAQ keeps a spreadsheet of all QA pairs, and logs the date of each item as it is reviewed, along with notes about the content or other considerations. Often, entries are referred to other units for consultation and, at times, may be pulled from public view until verified.

DISCOVERABILITY AND ACCESS

Of course a library FAQ that is full of on-target QA pairs that are easy to understand and apply will do your patrons no good if they are unable to locate the right answer for their question. There are two major reasons that this might be so. First, an overpopulated FAQ containing unused or overlapping QA pairs will have the same effect that English ivy has on a garden— the multitude of QA pairs chokes out those that are most relevant to the user. The second reason that patrons may fail to locate an existing QA is that patrons use keywords, spelling, or search syntax that do not yield the desired result.

As with many things, it is easier to identify problems with discovery than it is to fix them. A QA pair may be sparsely used because nobody wants (or needs) to look at it or it may be difficult to locate. Further, in the case that the QA pair holds little interest to the majority of library patrons, it may be of great value to the few individuals who do need the information. Identifying overlap in QA pairs is straightforward if the FAQ has a hands-on administrator, but figuring out how to word a question so that a patron knows to select it from a list, even if it's addressing her query from a broader viewpoint, is a bit trickier. In addition, finding the balance between breadth and detail is unique to each organization and will change over time. This overlaps somewhat with the consideration of transferability outlined in the previous section, but with the added dimension of discoverability. In the case of search failures that can be attributed to the query itself, it is important to determine which of these can be corrected by refining the text of the QA pair or, if your FAQ system allows, by adding metadata to the entry.

IDENTIFYING AND MEETING PATRON NEEDS

The good news is that the information necessary to make these evaluations is captured by many systems in the form of use and query data. Such data can be harvested for topics to consider for inclusion as well as to identify patterns in patron search behavior. By glimpsing into the minds of our patrons, library staff can identify possible improvements to the FAQ. Even in cases where a remedy to a failed search is not as apparent, such as those queries better conducted in the library catalog or an article database, the information is beneficial.

Query data are a rich and continuously updated source of information about what questions your patrons seek to answer. Needs will change or shift for a variety of reasons, including but not limited to coursework and curriculum (true for school and academic libraries, but often also true in a public library setting); changing technologies and their adoption and importance to your user base; and other generational or cultural factors. At Albertsons Library, the authors have observed that needs can change quickly and that data should be reviewed on a regular basis (every one to three months).

Query data are also useful for identifying changes to search vocabulary. This is important because while library professionals have long observed that library jargon is a problem for patrons,[24] colloquial language is a moving target. Observing vocabulary and making changes to metadata and/or QA language based on query data increases query success—the ratio of searches resulting in a direct match to abandoned queries and repeated attempts.

The left column of table 7.2 contains the text of several queries (search strings typed into the Albertsons Library FAQ search box) that did not result in a patron selecting a QA pair. The right column notes an action that the administrator has assigned for this query. The first two in the list are queries for which a QA pair should be added to the FAQ. As you might imagine, "How can I address loud people in the library?" is a question that reveals conflicting user needs. Some patrons wish for a quiet library, while others require spaces to study and work on projects in groups. One way to deal with this grievance collectively is to create a QA pair explaining which parts of the library are designated for each purpose. The query may additionally identify a need for a QA pair clarifying how to report concerns and complaints to the library staff. The second of these entries, "Craap," is an example of changing patron needs. Albertsons Library has recently begun teaching the CRAAP Test[25] (the title uses an acronym for currency, relevance, authority, accuracy, and purpose) as part of the university's recently revised core curriculum.

The remaining two queries shown in table 7.2 make evident a need to enhance discoverability. The first, "end note" is a common misspelling of the EndNote citation software. While LibAnswers does not have a spelling correction feature, it does have a "keywords" feature. Keywords are used by the KB search engine to retrieve results, but do not display to the user. This makes keywords ideal for adding frequent misspellings such as "end note" for "endnote." The last query in the list, "cash machine" is labeled "enhance metadata" because an existing entry about ATM was not retrieved by this search query. Keywords will address this issue, or the question itself could be

Table 7.2.

Query	Action
How can I address loud people in the library?	Add QA
Craap	Add QA
End note	Common misspelling. Enhance metadata for existing QA pair
Cash machine	Enhance metadata for existing QA pair

rewritten to include the words "cash machine." This spreadsheet can then be used by the FAQ manager to keep track of changes and record progress.

There are several ways to improve the discoverability of a QA pair in a LibAnswers FAQ. First, the question and/or answer can be rewritten to speak to a new aspect of the topic, or to include verbiage based on user vocabulary. Second, keywords can be added to an entry. As described in the preceding paragraph, these keywords are used to enhance searchability but do not show in the public view. In addition to common misspellings, keywords are useful for vernacular phrases such as "rent a book."

Topical categories can be used to make it easy for patrons to browse QA pairs. These terms are used to create groupings of QA pairs. Users can then browse relevant entries by selecting the category term from a tag cloud (as shown in figure 7.2) or pop-up box. Topics are most helpful if they employ controlled vocabulary, which is to say that the FAQ manager should create topics and assign QA pairs to them. Otherwise, the FAQ may end up with a topic called "borrowing," another called "access services," and entries assigned to one or both of these, or perhaps neither.

As with the QA pairs themselves, categories should be large enough to be meaningful, yet small enough not to overwhelm. Decisions about this can be based on the number of QA pairs assigned to a category, but should also take into account query data and QA pair use. For example, the category "Boise State & Idaho materials" was based largely on query data, which established the frequency of patron searches in this area. The category "printing" was based both on patron queries and the fact that our collection of QA pairs related to library computing grew large enough to be cumbersome. Questions can be assigned to more than one label, but doing so can create some unwieldy categories. So long as the number of categories is pruned to the most useful, it is preferable to differentiate one from the other.

As previously mentioned, QA-pair-use statistics are useful for identifying patron needs. Unlike query data, these data show us what patrons actually decided to click on and view. While we cannot know whether an individual read the QA or found it useful without other assessment modalities such as a

FREQUENTLY ASKED QUESTIONS

Find an Answer / Send a Question   Popular | Featured

| Type your question here! | **Ask Us** |

Or browse a topic: › **about the library** – › Boise State & Idaho materials – › borrowing – › campus – › computing – › ebooks – › equipment – › password & login help – › printing – › **research/finding things**

Figure 7.2.

survey, use data demonstrate that patrons found the title of the QA pair to be on target enough to look further. Figure 7.3 illustrates use data for the Albertsons Library FAQ, which can be generated for all topics (shown) or for an individual topic category.

These aggregated data can be misleading, however, since some QA pairs have been available to users for longer than others. Monthly use statistics shown in table 7.3 should be used to determine recent QA pair use. Finally, total use over time can be part of the total evaluation of your FAQ service success.

Table 7.3.

Question: How much does a community library card cost annually?				
October 2011	November 2011	December 2011	January 2012	February 2012
20	23	21	19	27

CONCLUSION

Returning to the question of whether library FAQs offer the balance of simplicity and necessary complexity required by our patrons, the authors posit that the answer is held in the relationship between patron and information

Figure 7.3.

professional, mediated by the system. The tools are available to meet user needs, and we draw closer to this moving target by being attentive to the data we have describing these needs. By taking accountability for delivering easy access to the information that our patrons seek, based on how they actually search, we are in a sense collaborating to maximize the value of their library service. Though perfection, defined as matching every query with the perfect answer, is an unlikely target, creating a bridge connecting patrons to their information needs is a realistic and worthwhile aim.

NOTES

1. International Federation of Library Associations and Institutions, "Code of Information for Librarians and Other Information Workers (Short Version)," last modified December 10, 2012, accessed October 2, 2013, www.ifla.org/publications/ifla-code-of-ethics-for-librarians-and-other-information-workers-short-version.

2. Scott Kennedy, "Farewell to the Reference Librarian," *Journal of Library Administration* 51, no. 4 (2011): 322.

3. Boise State University, Albertsons Library, "Libqual Results," accessed September 12, 2013, http://library.boisestate.edu/about/LibQUAL/index.php.

4. Norman Stevens, "Library Equipment," in *Encyclopedia of Library History*, ed. Wayne A. Wiegand and G. Davis Donald Jr. (New York: Garland, 1994), 362–63.

5. Frederick G. Kilgour, "History of Library Computerization," *Journal of Library Automation* 3, no. 3 (1970): 220–25.

6. M. Mitchell Waldrop, "Origins of Personal Computing," *Scientific American* 285, no. 6 (2001): 90.

7. Samuel T. Waters, "Answerman, the Expert Information Specialist: An Expert System for Retrieval of Information from Library Reference Books," *Information Technology and Libraries* 5, no. 3 (1986): 204.

8. Ibid.

9. Karen F. Smith, "Robot at the Reference Desk?," *College & Research Libraries* 47, no. 5 (1986): 486–90.

10. Alina Vickery, "A Reference and Referral System Using Expert System Techniques," *Journal of Documentation* 43, no. 1 (1987): 1–23; Alina Vickery and Helen Brooks, "Plexus—the Expert System for Referral," *Information Processing and Management* 23, no. 2 (1987): 99–117; Alina Vickery and Helen Brooks, "Expert Systems and Their Applications in LIS," *Online Review* 11, no. 3 (1987): 149–65.

11. Christine Roysdon and Howard White, eds., "Expert Systems in Reference Services," Special Issue, *The Reference Librarian*, no. 23 (1989).

12. Patricia F. Anderson, "Expert Systems, Expertise, and the Library and Information Professions," *Library and Information Science Research* 10, no. 4 (1988): 381.

13. Jay Aronson, "Expert Systems," in *Encyclopedia of Information Systems*, ed. Hossein Bidgoli (Boston: Academic Press, 2003), 277.

14. Eloisa Gomez Borah, "Beyond Navigation: Librarians as Architects of Information Tools," *Research Strategies* 10, no. 3 (1992): 139.

15. John Stalker and Marjorie Murfin, "Frequently Asked Questions: An Effective Way to Store and Retrieve Reference Information?," *Reference Services Review* 24, no. 4 (1996): 31–40.

16. Karen Anello and Brett Bonfield, "Providing Reference Service in Our Sleep: Using a FAQ Database to Guide Users to the Right Sources," *Reference & User Services Quarterly* 46, no. 3 (2007): 28–33.

17. Ibid., 29.

18. Sherri Jones, Jessica Kayongo, and John Scofield, "Ask Us Anytime: Creating a Searchable FAQ Using E-mail and Chat Reference Transcripts," *Internet Reference Services Quarterly* 14, no. 3/4 (2009): 67–81.

19. Kate Shaw and Amanda Spink, "University Library Virtual Reference Services: Best Practices and Continuous Improvement," *Australian Academic & Research Libraries* 40, no. 3 (2009): 192–205.

20. Ibid., 200.

21. Christy R. Stevens, "Reference Reviewed and Re-Envisioned: Revamping Librarian and Desk-Centric Services with LibstARs and LibAnswers," *Journal of Academic Librarianship* 39, no. 2 (2013): 202–14.

22. Ibid., 203.

23. Springshare, "LibAnswers with LibChat," accessed October 18, 2013, www.springshare.com/libanswers.

24. Diane Klare and Kendall Hobbs, "Digital Ethnography: Library Web Page Redesign Among Digital Natives," *Journal of Electronic Resources Librarianship* 23, no. 2 (2011): 105.

25. Meriam Library, California State University at Chico, "Evaluating Information—applying the CRAAP Test," accessed December 10, 2013, www.csuchico.edu/lins/handouts/eval_websites.pdf.

BIBLIOGRAPHY

Anderson, Patricia F. "Expert Systems, Expertise, and the Library and Information Professions." *Library and Information Science Research* 10, no. 4 (1988): 367–88.

Anello, Karen, and Brett Bonfield. "Providing Reference Service in Our Sleep: Using a FAQ Database to Guide Users to the Right Sources." *Reference & User Services Quarterly* 46, no. 3 (2007): 28–33.

Aronson, Jay. "Expert Systems." In *Encyclopedia of Information Systems*, edited by Hossein Bidgoli, 277–89. Amsterdam, Boston: Academic Press, 2003.

Boise State University, Albertsons Library. "Libqual Results." Accessed September 12, 2013. http://library.boisestate.edu/about/LibQUAL/index.php.

Borah, Eloisa Gomez. "Beyond Navigation: Librarians as Architects of Information Tools." *Research Strategies* 10, no. 3 (1992): 138–42.

International Federation of Library Associations and Institutions. "Code of Information for Librarians and Other Information Workers (Short Version)." Last modified December 10, 2012. Accessed October 2, 2013. www.ifla.org/publications/ifla-code-of-ethics-for-librarians-and-other-information-workers-short-version.

Jones, Sherri, Jessica Kayongo, and John Scofield. "Ask Us Anytime: Creating a Searchable FAQ Using E-mail and Chat Reference Transcripts." *Internet Reference Services Quarterly* 14, no. 3/4 (2009): 67–81.

Kennedy, Scott. "Farewell to the Reference Librarian." *Journal of Library Administration* 51, no. 4 (2011): 322.

Kilgour, Frederick G. "History of Library Computerization." *Journal of Library Automation* 3, no. 3 (1970): 218–29.

Klare, Diane, and Kendall Hobbs. "Digital Ethnography: Library Web Page Redesign Among Digital Natives." *Journal of Electronic Resources Librarianship* 23, no. 2 (2011): 97–110.

Meriam Library, California State University at Chico. "Evaluating Information—applying the CRAAP Test." Accessed December 10, 2013. www.csuchico.edu/lins/handouts/eval_websites.pdf.

Roysdon, Christine, and Howard White, eds. "Expert Systems in Reference Services." Special Issue, *The Reference Librarian*, no. 23 (1989).

Shaw, Kate, and Amanda Spink. "University Library Virtual Reference Services: Best Practices and Continuous Improvement." *Australian Academic & Research Libraries* 40, no. 3 (2009): 192–205.

Smith, Karen F. "Robot at the Reference Desk?" *College & Research Libraries* 47, no. 5 (1986): 486–90.

Stalker, John, and Marjorie Murfin. "Frequently Asked Questions: An Effective Way to Store and Retrieve Reference Information?" *Reference Services Review* 24, no. 4 (1996): 31–40.

Stevens, Christy R. "Reference Reviewed and Re-Envisioned: Revamping Librarian and Desk-Centric Services with LibstARs and LibAnswers." *Journal of Academic Librarianship* 39, no. 2 (2013): 202.

Stevens, Norman. "Library Equipment." In *Encyclopedia of Library History*, edited by Wayne A. Wiegand and G. Davis Donald Jr., 358–63. New York: Garland, 1994.

Vickery, Alina. "A Reference and Referral System Using Expert System Techniques." *Journal of Documentation* 43, no. 1 (1987): 1–23.

Vickery, Alina, and Helen Brooks. "Expert Systems and Their Applications in LIS." *Online Review* 11, no. 3 (1987): 149–65.

———. "Plexus—the Expert System for Referral." *Information Processing and Management* 23, no. 2 (1987): 99–117.

Waldrop, M. Mitchell. "Origins of Personal Computing." *Scientific American* 285, no. 6 (2001): 84.

Waters, Samuel T. "Answerman, the Expert Information Specialist: An Expert System for Retrieval of Information from Library Reference Books." *Information Technology and Libraries* 5, no. 3 (1986): 204.

Part IV

Assessment: Does Reference Make a Difference?

Chapter Eight

Transforming Reference Services

More Than Meets the Eye

Kawanna Bright, Consuella Askew, and Lori Driver

The nature of reference services has dramatically changed over the past twenty-five years. Historically, the core of reference services centered around a librarian positioned at a service desk waiting to assist users in the pursuit of bibliographic materials, and in later years, in the classroom providing library instructional services as well. The advent of technology has forced librarians to rethink these services and their delivery methods in order to remain relevant to the present generation. Over the last two decades, modes of information delivery and access have changed drastically since the inception of the Internet and World Wide Web; as Kathryn Crowe states, "While WHAT reference librarians do is not so different—we still assist users in finding and evaluating information, offer instruction in using resources, and select materials—HOW we do it, however, and the tools and resources we use have changed dramatically."[1]

Today, librarians can still be found at the desk, but also roving the library and the campus, creating online tutorials, on social media, or providing virtual reference services. The ability to access information whenever and wherever enables information users to find what they need without mediated services, which seems to be their preference. This is evidenced by the decreasing reference transactions that have been reported in the last decade or so. Despite this downward trend for reference transactions, the number of virtual reference transactions is reportedly increasing as libraries utilize modes of delivery that are convenient and preferred by their users. E-mail, chat, and text comprise the core of most virtual reference services offered by libraries, while social networking tools such as Facebook, Twitter, YouTube, and blogs offer additional user-interaction opportunities for reference librarians.

Library instruction in the classroom has also changed over the years, morphing from lecture-style bibliographic instruction to information-literacy instruction focusing on creating collaborative learning environments enabling students to gather, analyze, synthesize, and assess information for lifelong learning. The emphasis on information-literacy instruction along with the changes wrought by technology has created the need for librarians to find avenues other than the library and classroom to provide reference services. However, as librarians become more innovative in their approaches to service delivery, they must also demonstrate their impact on their users for the purposes of funding and institutional accountability. The intent of this chapter is to explore the current direction of reference services and the methods of assessment being implemented to measure their impact and success.

REFERENCE SERVICE DELIVERY MODELS: DESK OR NO DESK?

Since the late nineteenth century, reference service delivery has centered on a physical desk.[2] Early reports from the St. Louis Public Library described the desk as the "place where the library assistant answered questions" and by the late 1890s the term *information desk* was popularly used to describe the reference service desk.[3] Throughout the centuries, reference service delivery has expanded in tandem with emerging communication technologies, facilitating a slow but steady movement from concentrating on a fixed physical place to that of a more mobile and virtual one. The changing service expectations of users seeking more ubiquitous and self-directed services have not dissuaded librarians from continuing to serve at the desk. Although usage of reference services is decreasing, as reported by library members of the Association of Research Libraries (ARL) and illustrated by the Academic Library Survey, few libraries have taken action to eliminate the reference desk. This reticence to take such action has been attributed to librarians' strong sense of identity based on the service desk, which Arndt describes as "a powerful symbol of librarianship and library service" that also provides the basis of their values concerning the interpersonal interactions that the desk symbolizes.[4] Service trends reported by the Association of Research Libraries (ARL) indicate that ARL libraries have experienced a 65 percent decrease in reference transactions from 1991 to 2011.[5] Not only have the number of transactions decreased, but also deeper explorations into the nature of these transactions have indicated that an inordinate number are information and directional. In recognition of this changing need for reference services at the desk, reference department managers began to question the necessity of having their most valuable resources—the librarians—at the reference desk, which led to the introduction of the tiered reference model.

The development of tiered and consultation service models can be viewed as a compromise between keeping the desk staffed while allowing librarians the ability to accomplish more professional-level work. As opposed to having librarians at the desk answering predominantly directional questions, like "Where's the bathroom?," these models allow librarians more time for instruction, collection development, and other specialized library work. The tiered model was popularized at the Brandeis University library and is frequently noted in the literature as the premier effort of this service type.[6] The Brandeis model, as it is also known, used paraprofessional staff and graduate assistants to staff the reference desk and provide reference triage.[7] This first level interaction handled the informational and directional questions only, referring patrons to the reference librarians for one-on-one consultations to address more complex queries. Other libraries have experimented with using well-trained students to cover the majority of service hours at the reference desk with success.[8]

As far back as 1876, forward-thinking librarians such as Samuel S. Green called for alternative methods of service delivery. In one of his classic publications regarding patron-librarian relations, Green addressed both roaming and tiered reference services.[9] Green asserted, "One of the best means of making a library popular is to mingle freely with its users, and help them in every way."[10] Further along in the article, he suggested using "one of the most accomplished persons in the corps of your assistants" in place of a librarian to aid users to pick out books.[11] More than a century has passed and roaming, or roving, services are being successfully employed in a number of academic and public libraries with the aid of mobile technologies, such as cell phones and tablets.[12] The use of technology has empowered reference librarians to move away from reference "as place" services and enabled them to provide focused service at the point of need.

In response to the instant-gratification expectation of millennials who have grown up with the Internet and Google, and the librarians' need to remain relevant to new and future generations of users, the provision of virtual reference services has increased. Failure to adopt new methods and technologies for providing reference services may lead the modern world to perceive libraries as obsolete, warns Ronald Martin Solorzano.[13] Fred D. Barnhart and Jeannette E. Pierce predict that the "trend toward mobile learning in higher education" will lead to "new types of learning, research, and instruction,"[14] prompting librarians to get on board and expand their complement of reference services to include not only e-mail, but also other delivery methods such as chat, text, video chat, and integration into course-management systems such as Blackboard.

As the delivery methods have changed, so have the corollary assessment methods to capture meaningful data for service improvement. The tick sheet, the most widely used, traditional method of tracking reference transactions that occur at the desk, continues to exist as a primary method of capturing quantitative usage data to illustrate the level of question complexity, type of query (information /reference/technology), and trends in hourly usage. However, new statistical analytics systems produced by companies such as Google and SpringShare have afforded reference librarians with electronic options to easily capture, track, analyze, and report usage statistics. In addition to the quantitative data, qualitative transaction data are also being collected. The advantage of most mediums for virtual reference service is the ability to track and record verbatim the reference transaction, such as chat transcripts and online queries via a reference management system like LibAnswers. The information collected from these systems can provide constructive data leading to enhancements in information-literacy programs, way-finding in the library, and also librarian performance.

Yet usage statistics illustrate only a small part of the impact of reference services on user behavior. As Pali U. Kuruppu suggests, what remains to be discovered and revealed is how and to what extent our users are benefitting from reference services.[15] Libraries continue to grapple with these questions by employing both quantitative and qualitative research methods (mixed methods) in attempts to correlate service impact with user behavior, effective service delivery, and management practices.[16] Assessment tools such as LibQUAL+, and programs such as StatsQUAL, developed by the ARL, are widely known examples of the aforementioned efforts. Over the last ten years, the LibQUAL+ instrument has become the foremost tool used to assess service quality in all types of libraries. The StatsQUAL instrument, which focuses on illustrating the academic library's contribution to teaching and learning, measures an aspect of reference services that can occur at the desk, as well as in the classroom.[17]

Individual libraries are also seeking new ways to use data to describe their service value. Susan M. Ryan investigated the cost effectiveness of using professional librarians staffing the reference desk at the Stetson University library by analyzing transaction data.[18] A subsequent study conducted by Ryan and Debbi Dinkins examined the use of paraprofessionals at the reference desk by tracking the number of referrals to librarians.[19] In her first study, Ryan found that the cost of staffing the reference desk with professional librarians exceeded the need for services, since only a small amount of reference transactions were found to require the expertise of a librarian and could easily be addressed by well-trained paraprofessional staff. Further, she determined that the cost of each transaction, regardless of query type (i.e., informational, directional, reference, etc.), number of resources used to respond, or length of time to address, was $7.09. While these results are specific to one library, they are still meaningful.

David W. Harless and Frank R. Allen used the contingent valuation method to ascertain the economic value that patrons place on reference service provided at the desk in academic libraries.[20] Their study determined the dollar amount the faculty and students of the Virginia Commonwealth University (VCU) were willing to pay for reference services. The findings revealed that students were willing to pay $5.59 per semester to maintain the current hours of the reference desk, while faculty were willing to pay $45.76 per year. Again, while not generalizable, the results indicate the value that the VCU community—particularly their faculty—placed on the service offered by their reference librarians. If this study were replicated in other academic library settings with the same results, it has potential as an effective advocacy tool for library administrators.

Librarians across the globe continue to explore ways to find measures that will yield data that more closely describe the impact of their services on the individual user and on society at large. Yet, for the most part, these efforts have been limited to individual libraries and therefore are not generalizable to the broader spectrum of libraries and their respective user communities. However, as Roswitha Poll determined, it is possible to develop a standard for quantifying impact assessment that will allow for some uniformity.[21] As evidenced by the professional literature, there are very few standardized instruments in existence, such as LibQUAL+, that yield results that can be generalized across libraries and library types. Typically libraries implement assessment methods that are tailored to yield information that is pertinent to their particular community. In recognition of the aforementioned, a consensus to the question "desk or no desk?" in reference services will continue to remain elusive in the library profession.

PROVIDING REFERENCE SERVICES WITH INSTRUCTIONAL INTENT

While the "desk or no desk" question continues to be debated, another question related to reference services also looms: whether reference services should focus on providing information or instruction. Academic libraries are now seen as having a role in supporting the teaching missions of their institutions.[22] Reference librarians, in particular, have the most impact in contributing this support, through their interactions with students via reference services.[23] However, the history of reference services shows that the idea of offering instruction during the reference interaction was not and is not always the goal.

A review of the literature shows a range of views concerning the role of instruction in reference services. Some librarians argue that reference services are distinct from instruction services, and were not or should not be related.[24] Others view the reference desk as better suited for quick, informational interactions, and engaging in instructional interactions actually diminished the services offered.[25] A third perspective presents reference and instruction as "intimately connected,"[26] complementary activities with the potential to educate patrons.[27] Though the debate still continues, many have begun to see teaching as a major goal of reference services, and it is not uncommon for teaching and instruction to be included in the standards for provision of reference services.[28] The Reference and User Services Association (RUSA) provides one example of such within the searching section of their *Guidelines for Behavioral Performance of Reference and Information Services Providers*, which details the opportunities for teaching patrons about the search process during the reference interaction.[29]

No matter what side of the debate one is on, research has shown that instruction is taking place during reference interactions, both in person and virtually.[30] However, many librarians may not realize they are instructing as they assist patrons. Most libraries are also not assessing their reference transactions with the idea of measuring whether instruction has taken place, or the quality of that instruction. It is the suggestion of the chapter authors that one important step for libraries toward producing data to their institutions that shows their impact on student learning is to provide reference services with instructional intent.

The idea of instructional intent is that the reference query is addressed with the goal of teaching patrons how to find the answer for themselves, rather than simply giving them the answer. Depending on the mode of communication, or the venue where services are being offered, instructional intent can mean different things, but the main requirement for providing reference with instructional intent is preparation. Preparation entails making sure that reference services have learning outcomes in place, just as bibliographic instruction typically does. Susan Avery and David Ward discuss this idea of applying learning standards and outcomes to reference services, and the relation to assessment of reference services.[31] Guidelines used for e-mail service at the Dr. Martin Luther King Jr. Library in San José, California, call for the balancing of facts and instruction in the answers sent to patrons.[32] Along with standards, it is important for librarians to consider what teaching in a reference interaction would actually look like. Though many have raised the idea of instruction as part of the reference transaction, descriptions of what this would look like did not occur immediately.[33] As the research continues, descriptions of teaching opportunities that can occur during reference interactions are beginning to appear, and can be used as guides for other librarians.[34]

The reference interview plays a role in whether the librarian is prepared to provide instruction while at the desk. The reference interview has not historically been seen as a teaching tool, but it has the potential to serve an instructional role in reference.[35] David Ward looked at the idea of applying Bloom's taxonomy to the reference interview as a way of enhancing learning outcomes and found that the taxonomy could be used to direct the reference interview toward information-literacy-specific outcomes.[36] Kristin Partlo also emphasized using modeling, visualizations, and note taking as methods that can be included in part of the reference interview and used to teach students during reference consultations.[37] Lisa A. Ellis introduced the idea of using a "topic development exercise" that could be administered in both the physical and virtual environments as part of the reference interview, as a means of helping patrons to figure out what they already, need to, or want to know.[38]

Knowing about instructional methods that are conducive to reference work can aid librarians in their quest to impart instruction during reference interactions. In their comparison of teaching at the reference desk versus through chat reference, Christina M. Desai and Stephanie J. Graves found that there were five types of instruction taking place: modeling, resource suggestion, terms suggestion, leading, and lessons.[39] In their review of chat transcripts, Megan Oakleaf and Amy VanScoy identified eight instructional strategies that were and could be used in the provision of chat reference.[40] It is obvious from these studies that librarians are already using instructional techniques as part of their reference services in both physical and virtual settings. For those concerned about translating instructional methods into the online environment, Ellis indicates that techniques for teaching online can be applied to the virtual reference environment, including the use of examples.[41] The next step, then, will be to knowingly implement these techniques while providing reference services.

Technology plays a key role in helping librarians offer reference with instructional intent. With traditional reference desk services, librarians are able to use technology, such as dual monitors, to give patrons a way to follow along as searches are demonstrated. Installing dual monitors at a reference desk is a cost-effective way to improve the reference interaction for both the patron and the librarian. Another option for the desk is the use of iPads, which would allow patrons not only to follow along with searches, but also to get the hands-on experience of performing a search. A study conducted at the University of the Pacific indicates that iPads can be successfully used at the reference desk as a way to support learning for patrons with research questions.[42]

In virtual reference, canned messages, co-browsing, ready-made tutorials, and screencast software have all offered librarians options for administering instruction throughout the reference process. Trying to write out difficult and detailed instructions for patrons who may struggle with following those typed instructions has been identified as one of the drawbacks of chat reference.[43] Canned messages cut down on the amount of time that it takes for librarians to type out lengthy instructions for patrons and can also be used with e-mail reference, as long as they are written with instructional intent.[44] Co-browsing, where the librarian is able to share their screen with the patron or take over the patron's screen, is another way for librarians to provide instruction during the virtual interaction.[45] If available, it is seen to be an effective reference interaction instructional technique.[46]

Both ready-made tutorials and screencasting software offer librarians options when co-browsing is not available. Ready-made tutorials that show patrons how to complete basic library tasks can be sent to patrons to provide continued instruction both during and after the transaction. Screencasting software that allows librarians to create quick videos on the fly has enabled librarians' almost instantaneous ability to create instructional videos as needed. Free and low-cost options for creating screencasts are available and can be used in tandem with ready-made tutorials to make the chat interaction more interactive than relying on typing out instructions.[47] It is also noted that screencast videos can also be useful for in-person reference interactions, as it can leave students with visual "notes" that they can refer back to after they leave the desk.[48]

Assessment of instruction within reference services offers a different challenge for libraries. As noted earlier, the evaluation of reference services looks at a number of elements, but whether or not instruction took place during the interaction is not normally considered. Virtual reference tends to be the easier venue for analysis, as services often have an assessment method built in with chat transcripts, and the ability to save e-mail exchanges, allowing librarians to review the interactions and determine whether instruction occurred.[49] But appraisal of instruction during a face-to-face interaction requires other methods be considered. Some methods that have been used in the past and have the potential for assessing instruction include unobtrusive testing, observational studies, and surveys.

One popular unobtrusive method of assessing reference services is the secret- or mystery-shopper technique. The business world has been using this technique for a number of years, and most see it as a cost-effective and ideal way to see what real customers experience when they use a service.[50] Most libraries employing the secret-shopper process for assessing reference services center their investigation on the quality of customer service throughout the reference interaction, or whether the correct answer was given to the patron.[51] Even though the usual intent of secret shopping is to look at service quality control, it is a technique that can easily be modified to assess not only whether instruction was offered during the interaction, but also the quality of that instruction. Candice Benjes-Small and Elizabeth Kocevar-Weidinger offer suggestions for successful secret shopping, including setting goals, establishing model behaviors, and designing an effective shopping instrument. These approaches can easily be used to develop a secret-shopper program aimed at assessing instruction.[52] Secret shopping can also be used multiple times to provide continuous feedback, especially to determine if any changes put into place were effective and improved the service.[53]

The more obtrusive methods of surveys and observational studies have already been applied to the assessment of instruction within reference services. Surveys administered to either patrons, librarians, or both can be used to determine if instruction took place in the reference transaction, and depending on how the survey is designed, what type of instruction took place. Denise D. Green and Janis K. Peach developed a survey based on the Wisconsin-Ohio Reference Evaluation Program (WOREP), and their research suggests that their survey is a viable option for evaluating teaching at the reference desk.[54] Gillian S. Gremmels and Karen Shostrom Lehmann followed up with a survey of their own designed not only to ascertain if teaching had occurred, but also to look at what was taught and whether the student learned what the librarian had intended for them to learn.[55] Heather Empey reported on a modified questionnaire used at the University of Northern British Columbia that included a section for recording the type of instruction used during a reference transaction.[56] Surveys can also be used to evaluate virtual reference services, determining whether instruction was offered and the quality of that instruction.[57] These studies show that surveys and questionnaires can easily be created or modified to allow libraries to assess the type and the quality of instruction being given in reference services at the desk. The major drawbacks of using survey forms involve the amount of time it can take to collect the data, and the possibility of human error in recording the information.[58] However, careful planning during the creation of the survey can help to eliminate the risk of human error, and online options, such as LibAnswers and Qualtrics, can make it easier and faster to record the transaction data.

Observational studies allow for review of the reference transaction by a third party who is not involved in the transaction, making it more objective. Observation is normally one of the techniques suggested for assessment of user behavior or for appraising library staff behavior and communication skills.[59] Observational studies can be adapted to look at instruction simply by designating instruction or information-literacy teaching techniques as a particular behavior to be monitored. The drawback to this type of evaluation is the potential for bias and the possibility that either librarians or patrons will change their behavior since they know they are being observed. Bicknell and others suggest that one way to combat issues related to bias and validity is to use more than one type of assessment to improve the overall results.[60]

It is possible for librarians to also collect reference statistics in a way that records whether instruction was a part of the interaction with the patron. For those libraries using technology to record their statistics, such as LibAnswers, categories of questions could be defined in such a way as to offer an option for indicating that instruction took place, or a separate category could be created. For those looking for a traditional tick-mark system, the READ Scale offers a way to assess a number of aspects related to reference service provision, such as whether or not teaching was included.[61] As we continue to develop methods for assessing the quality of instruction provided through our reference services, it is important to keep in mind the connection this assessment will have to the university as a whole.

PROMOTION OF REFERENCE SERVICES AS OUTREACH

A final, but important component of reference services to be discussed in this chapter is outreach. Toni M. Carter and Priscilla Seaman note that libraries use outreach for various reasons: to reach out to users, encourage use of the library and its resources, and to promote a positive image of the library.[62] Many library organizations are creating new positions with titles such as "User Experience Librarian" or "User Engagement Librarian," or adding responsibilities that focus specifically on efforts to engage users with the library and its resources to existing positions.[63] Further, Carter and Seaman identified two categories of outreach: (a) services and (b) the promotion of services.[64] This section will concentrate on the service category since reference services is the primary concern. Using Carter and Seaman's definition, *services* for the purposes of this chapter is defined as "assistance with research or finding information and the resources available at a library."[65] While outreach in academic libraries has many forms, it is often built around a commitment to instruction.[66] Should the number of reference transactions continue to decline, reference librarians will need to balance their outreach efforts between their instruction and reference services.

Typical reference services as outreach have included subject-liaison programs, orientation and instruction sessions, embedded librarians, and roaming services. Technology has allowed reference librarians to expand their reach by employing virtual methods to engage with users via social networking tools and mobile applications such as Twitter, Facebook, Foursquare, and Scvngr. These technologies allow librarians to inform, instruct, and interact with their users on a global scale. The subject-liaison program serves as a gateway to the library and its resources for university faculty and students. In this model, library subject or discipline specialists work closely with faculty and students within the disciplines with the intent of forging collaborative partnerships within the teaching process while promoting library services and resources.[67] The embedded and roaming librarian operates with the same goals as the subject liaison, but these roles often require the librarian to be outside the library. Embedded librarians are most likely to be found in the classroom with their classroom faculty counterparts. On the other hand, roaming librarians are most likely to be seen in areas or buildings where there is a high population of students. Whether embedded or roaming, the intention of each is to bring reference and/or instruction services to where the users are and at their point of need. Secondary to this is the enhanced visibility of library services and resources and the engagement of users.

As more library resources have transitioned to an online environment, so have our users. To accommodate users' new information-seeking behavior, librarians have been incorporating new technologies to evolve their services and delivery methods. As a result, virtual reference services (VRS) have become a standard part of the complement of services. Mu et al. characterize VRS as being "more commonly associated with synchronous communication via the internet," which includes chat, texting, and video chat.[68] Social networking tools, such as Facebook, Twitter, YouTube, and blogs, are also being employed as outreach tools. These mobile-enabled applications provide real-time delivery of information to users outside of the confines of the web. Additionally, beyond the one-way delivery of information, social networking tools such as Facebook and blogs allow for continued interactivity and archiving capabilities.

There is little literature to be found that focuses solely on methods of assessing outreach activities. This may be the result of the notion that outreach is not an integral component of reference service and therefore not treated as such. Lee A. Vulcovich et al. note that while the usefulness of social network tools is not lost on librarians, the ability to evaluate their impact is difficult and leads one to question whether or not it is worth the effort.[69] In doing so, they were able to apply usage data provided by these tools to assess the use and significance of their virtual products. They discovered their Facebook page—their primary social media tool—was experiencing a decline in posts, reducing its effectiveness as an outreach tool and thus prompting them to consider moving away from using Facebook as a principal tool for their marketing efforts. They were also able to determine that interconnecting information delivered on multiple social networking tools intensified the effect of the message. Despite the dearth of literature addressing the assessment of virtual services, future assessment efforts should keep in mind that quantity does not equate to quality, nor does in-person service guarantee quality.

CONCLUSION

Despite the desk or no desk conundrum, reference services continue to revolve around the needs of the user through both in-person and virtual interactions. The reference desk has been a central fixture in reference services for more than a century, but changes in how users seek information, along with the advent of new technology, have forced librarians to reconsider the prominent placement of the reference desk. Assessment of reference offerings has furnished evidence that a change in how, when, and where services are provided is necessary. Libraries must continually develop new ways to reach and work with their patrons, while still providing the high level of assistance that is demanded of them. In an era of growing accountability, libraries must be able to demonstrate their impact on user behavior and performance. Providing reference services with instructional intent, whether on the desk or not, offers librarians the means to identify and provide measurable and demonstrable outcomes to their parent institution. Through a willingness to continuously assess, change, and promote, reference services can be transformed to meet the challenges of shifting user needs.

NOTES

1. Kathryn M. Crowe, "Collaborative Leadership: A Model for Reference Services," *The Reference Librarian* 39, no. 81 (2003): 60.

2. Dennis B. Miles, "Shall We Get Rid of the Reference Desk?," *Reference & User Services Quarterly* 52, no. 4 (2013): 323.

3. Ibid., 320.

4. Miles, "Shall We Get Rid," 321; Theresa S. Arndt, "Reference Service Without the Desk," *Reference Services Review* 38, no. 1 (2010): 74.

5. Association of Research Libraries, "Service Trends in ARL Libraries, 1991–2011," *Statistical Trends*, accessed April 18, 2014, www.arl.org/focus-areas/statistics-assessment/statistical-trends.

6. David A. Tyckoson, "Issues and Trends in the Management of Reference: A Historical Perspective," *Journal of Library Administration* 51, no. 3 (2011): 263.

7. Ibid.

8. Megan S. Mitchell et al., "Paradigm Shift in Reference Services at the Oberlin College Library: A Case Study," *Journal of Library Administration* 51, no. 4 (2011): 359–74; Christy R. Stevens, "Reference Reviewed and Re-envisioned: Revamping Librarian and Desk-Centric Services with LibStARs and LibAnswers," *The Journal of Academic Librarianship* 39, no. 2 (2013): 202–14.

9. David S. Pena and Samuel S. Green, "Personal Relations Between Librarians and Readers," *Journal of Access Services* 4, no. 1–2 (2008): 157–67.

10. Ibid., 164.

11. Ibid.

12. Katherine Penner, "Mobile Technologies and Roving Reference," *Public Services Quarterly* 7, no. 1–2 (2011): 27; Barbara Pitney and Nancy Slote, "Going Mobile: The KCLS Roving Reference Model," *Public Libraries* 46, no. 1 (2007): 54–68; Fiona May, "Roving Reference, iPad-Style," *The Idaho Librarian* 61, no. 2 (2011), http://theidaholibrarian.wordpress.com/2011/11/23/roving-reference-ipad-style; Katharine Widdows, "Mobile

Technology for Mobile Staff: Roving Enquiry Support," *Multimedia Information & Technology* 37, no. 2 (2011): 12–15.

13. Ronald M. Solorzano, "Adding Value at the Desk: How Technology and User Expectations Are Changing Reference Work," *The Reference Librarian* 54, no. 2 (2013): 100.

14. Fred D. Barnhart and Jeannette E. Pierce, "Becoming Mobile: Reference in the Ubiquitous Library," *Journal of Library Administration* 51, no. 3 (2011): 279.

15. Pali U. Kuruppu, "Evaluation of Reference Services—a Review," *The Journal of Academic Librarianship* 33, no. 3 (2007): 376.

16. Carol Tenopir, "Beyond Usage: Measuring Library Outcomes and Value," *Library Management* 33, no. 1–2 (2012): 5–13.

17. Association of Research Libraries, "StatsQUAL," accessed February 14, 2014, www.arl.org/focus-areas/statistics-assessment/statsqual.

18. Susan M. Ryan, "Reference Transaction Analysis: The Cost-Effectiveness of Staffing a Traditional Academic Reference Desk," *The Journal of Academic Librarianship* 24, no. 5 (2008): 389–99.

19. Debbi Dinkins and Susan M. Ryan, "Measuring Referrals: The Use of Paraprofessionals at the Reference Desk," *The Journal of Academic Librarianship* 36, no. 4 (2010): 279–86.

20. David W. Harless and Frank R. Allen, "Using the Contingent Valuation Method to Measure Patron Benefits of Reference Desk Service in an Academic Library," *College & Research Libraries* 60, no. 1 (1999): 56–69.

21. Roswitha Poll, "Can We Quantify the Library's Influence? Creating an ISO Standard for Impact Assessment," *Performance Measurement and Metrics* 13, no. 2 (2012): 121–30.

22. James K. Elmborg, "Teaching at the Desk: Toward a Reference Pedagogy," *portal: Libraries and the Academy* 2, no. 3 (2002): 455.

23. Megan Oakleaf and Amy VanScoy, "Instructional Strategies for Digital Reference: Methods to Facilitate Student Learning," *Reference & User Services Quarterly* 49, no. 4 (2010): 380.

24. Anita R. Schiller, "Reference Service: Instruction or Information," *The Library Quarterly* 35, no. 1 (1965): 53.

25. Ibid., 54.

26. Mary Reichel, "Bibliographic Instruction and the Reference Desk," *The Journal of Academic Librarianship* 9, no. 1 (1983): 10.

27. Susan Avery and David Ward, "Reference Is My Classroom: Setting Instructional Goals for Academic Library Reference Services," *Internet Reference Services Quarterly* 15, no. 1 (2010): 35.

28. Elmborg, "Teaching at the Desk," 456.

29. Reference and User Services Association, "Guidelines for Behavioral Performance of Reference and Information Service Providers," accessed April 18, 2014, www.ala.org/rusa/resources/ guidelines/guidelinesbehavioral.

30. Christina M. Desai and Stephanie J. Graves, "Cyberspace or Face-to-Face: The Teachable Moment and Changing Reference Mediums," *Reference & User Services Quarterly* 47, no. 3 (2008): 254; Oakleaf and VanScoy, "Instructional Strategies," 381.

31. Avery and Ward, "Reference Is My Classroom," 36.

32. Lauren Miranda Gilbert, Mengxiong Liu, and Toby Matoush, "Assessing Digital Reference and Online Instructional Services in an Integrated Public/University Library," *The Reference Librarian* 46, no. 95–96 (2006): 153.

33. Beth S. Woodard, "One-on-One Instruction: From the Reference Desk to Online Chat," *Reference & User Services Quarterly* 44, no. 3 (2005): 203.

34. Desai and Graves, "Cyberspace or Face-to-Face," 242.

35. Kristin Partlo, "The Pedagogical Data Reference Interview," *IASSIST Quarterly* 33/34, no. 4 (2009): 6.

36. David Ward, "Expanding the Reference Vocabulary: A Methodology for Applying Bloom's Taxonomy to Increase Instruction in the Reference Interview," *Reference Services Review* 39, no. 1 (2011): 178.

37. Partlo, "Pedagogical Data Reference Interview," 9.

38. Lisa A. Ellis, "Approaches to Teaching Through Digital Reference," *Reference Services Review* 32, no. 2 (2004): 114.

39. Desai and Graves, "Cyberspace or Face-to-Face," 249.

40. Oakleaf and VanScoy, "Instructional Strategies," 382.

41. Ellis, "Approaches to Teaching," 109.

42. Michelle M. Maloney and Veronica A. Wells, "iPads to Enhance User Engagement During Reference Interactions," *Library Technology Reports* 48, no. 8 (2012): 15.

43. Allison Carr and Pearl Ly, "'More Than Words': Screencasting as a Reference Tool," *Reference Services Review* 37, no. 4 (2009): 410; Kate Gronemyer and Anne-Marie Deitering, "'I Don't Think It's Harder, Just That It's Different'," *Reference Services Review* 37: no. 4 (2009): 428.

44. Buff Hirko and Mary Bucher Ross, *Virtual Reference Training: The Complete Guide to Providing Anytime, Anywhere Answers* (Chicago: American Library Association, 2004), EBSCO ebook, 13; Joseph E. Straw, "Using Canned Messages in Virtual Reference Communication," *Internet Reference Services Quarterly* 11, no. 1 (2006): 40; Martha Portree et al., "Overcoming Transactional Distance: Instructional Intent in an E-mail Reference Service," *Reference & User Services Quarterly* 48, no. 2 (2008): 149.

45. Stephanie J. Graves and Christina M. Desai, "Instruction via Chat Reference: Does Co-Browse Help?," *Reference Services Review* 34, no. 3 (2006): 340; Hirko and Ross, *Virtual Reference Training*, 15; Woodard, "One-on-One Instruction," 207.

46. Daniel Beck, "The Role of Information Literacy in the Provision of Virtual Reference Services at the Enquiry Desk," *Journal of Information Literacy* 4, no. 2 (2010): 92; Graves and Desai, "Instruction Via Chat Reference," 355.

47. Carr and Ly, "'More Than Words,'" 410.

48. Ibid., 415.

49. Hirko and Ross, *Virtual Reference Training*, 15; Avery and Ward, "Reference Is My Classroom," 39.

50. Jan Clark, "How Do Others See Us? Mystery Visiting in Service Evaluation," *Library + Information Update* 4, no. 12 (2005): 36; Jan Mattsson, "Strategic Insights from Mystery Shopping in B2B Relationships," *Journal of Strategic Marketing* 20, no. 4 (2012): 313.

51. Candice Benjes-Small and Elizabeth Kocevar-Weidinger, "Secrets to Successful Mystery Shopping: A Case Study," *College & Research Libraries News* 72, no. 5 (2011): 274; Elaina Norlin, "Reference Evaluation: A Three-Step Approach—Surveys, Unobtrusive Observations, and Focus Groups," *College & Research Libraries* 61, no. 6 (2000): 547; Philip Calvert, "It's a Mystery: Mystery Shopping in New Zealand's Public Libraries," *Library Review* 54, no. 1 (2005): 24.

52. Benjes-Small and Kocevar-Weidinger, "Secrets to Successful Mystery Shopping," 274–75.

53. Elizabeth Kocevar-Weidinger et al., "Why and How to Mystery Shop Your Reference Desk," *Reference Services Review* 38, no. 1 (2010): 30.

54. Denise D. Green and Janis K. Peach, "Assessment of Reference Instruction as a Teaching and Learning Activity: An Experiment at the University of Illinois-Springfield," *College & Research Libraries News* 64, no. 4 (2003): 258.

55. Gillian S. Gremmels and Karen Shostrom Lehmann, "Assessment of Student Learning from Reference Service, "*College & Research Libraries* 68, no. 6 (2007): 490.

56. Heather Empey, "Transaction Analysis of Interactions at the Reference Desk of a Small Academic Library," *Partnership: the Canadian Journal of Library and Information Practice and Research* 5, no. 2 (2010): 3.

57. Gilbert, Liu, and Matoush, "Assessing Digital Reference," 154.

58. Ibid.

59. Tracy Bicknell, "Focusing on Quality Reference Service," *Journal of Academic Librarianship* 20, no. 2 (1994): 78–79.

60. Ibid., 79; Gilbert, Liu, and Matoush, "Assessing Digital Reference," 154.

61. Bella Karr Gerlich and G. Lynn Berard, "Introducing the READ Scale: Qualitative Statistics for Academic Reference Services," *Georgia Library Quarterly* 43, no. 4 (2007): 7.

62. Toni M. Carter and Priscilla Seaman, "The Management and Support of Outreach in Academic Libraries," *Reference & User Services Quarterly* 51, no. 2 (2011): 164.

63. Melissa Dennis, "Creating an Outreach Librarian at the University of Mississippi," *Mississippi Libraries* 74, no. 2 (2010): 31–33; Karen Okamoto and Mark Aaron Polger, "Off to Market We Go: A Content Analysis of Marketing and Promotion Skills in Academic Librarian Job Ads," *Library Leadership & Management* 26, no. 2 (2012): 1–20; Melissa Dennis, "Outreach Initiatives in Academic Libraries, 2009–2011," *Reference Services Review* 40, no. 3 (2012): 368–83.

64. Carter and Seaman, "Management and Support of Outreach," 164.

65. Ibid.

66. Corey M. Johnson, Sarah K. McCord, and Scott Walter, "Instructional Outreach Across the Curriculum: Enhancing the Liaison Role at a Research University," *Reference Librarian* 39, no. 82 (2003): 19–37.

67. Rebakah Kilzer, "Reference as Service, Reference as Place: A View of Reference in the Academic Library," *The Reference Librarian* 52, no. 4 (2011): 294.

68. Xiangming Mu et al., "A Survey and Empirical Study of Virtual Reference Service in Academic Libraries," *The Journal of Academic Librarianship* 37, no. 2: 120.

69. Lee A. Vulcovich et al., "Is the Time and Effort Worth It? One Library's Evaluation of Using Social Networking Tools for Outreach," *Medical Reference Services Quarterly* 32, no. 1 (2013): 13.

BIBLIOGRAPHY

Arndt, Theresa S. "Reference Service Without the Desk." *Reference Services Review* 38, no. 1 (2010): 71–80.

Association of Research Libraries. "Service Trends in ARL Libraries, 1991–2011." *Statistical Trends.* Accessed April 18, 2014. www.arl.org/focus-areas/statistics-assessment/statistical-trends.

———. "Statsqual." Accessed February 14, 2014. www.arl.org/focus-areas/statistics-assessment/statsqual.

Avery, Susan, and David Ward. "Reference Is My Classroom: Setting Instructional Goals for Academic Library Reference Services." *Internet Reference Services Quarterly* 15, no. 1 (2010): 35–51.

Barnhart, Fred D., and Jeannette E. Pierce. "Becoming Mobile: Reference in the Ubiquitous Library." *Journal of Library Administration* 51, no. 3 (2011): 279–90.

Beck, Daniel. "The Role of Information Literacy in the Provision of Virtual Reference Services at the Enquiry Desk." *Journal of Information Literacy* 4, no. 2 (2010): 91–94.

Benjes-Small, Candice, and Elizabeth Kocevar-Weidinger. "Secrets to Successful Mystery Shopping: A Case Study." *College & Research Libraries News* 72, no. 5 (2011): 274–76, 287.

Bicknell, Tracy. "Focusing on Quality Reference Service." *Journal of Academic Librarianship* 20, no. 2 (1994): 77–81.

Calvert, Philip. "It's a Mystery: Mystery Shopping in New Zealand's Public Libraries." *Library Review* 54, no. 1 (2005): 24–35.

Carr, Allison, and Pearl Ly. "'More Than Words:' Screencasting as a Reference Tool." *Reference Services Review* 37, no. 4 (2009): 408–20.

Carter, Toni M., and Priscilla Seaman. "The Management and Support of Outreach in Academic Libraries." *Reference & User Services Quarterly* 51, no. 2 (2011): 163–71.

Clark, Jan. "How Do Others See Us? Mystery Visiting in Service Evaluation." *Library + Information Update* 4, no. 12 (2005): 36–37.

Crowe, Kathryn M. "Collaborative Leadership: A Model for Reference Services." *The Reference Librarian* 39, no. 81 (2003): 59–69.

Dennis, Melissa. "Creating an Outreach Librarian at the University of Mississippi." *Mississippi Libraries* 74, no. 2 (2010): 31–33.

————. "Outreach Initiatives in Academic Libraries, 2009–2011." *Reference Services Review* 40, no. 3 (2012): 368–83.

Desai, Christina M., and Stephanie J. Graves. "Cyberspace or Face-to-Face: The Teachable Moment and Changing Reference Mediums." *Reference & User Services Quarterly* 47, no. 3 (2008): 242–55.

Dinkins, Debbi, and Susan M. Ryan. "Measuring Referrals: The Use of Paraprofessionals at the Reference Desk." *Journal of Academic Librarianship* 36, no. 4 (2010): 279–86.

Ellis, Lisa A. "Approaches to Teaching through Digital Reference." *Reference Services Review* 32, no. 2 (2004): 103–19.

Elmborg, James K. "Teaching at the Desk: Toward a Reference Pedagogy." *portal: Libraries and the Academy* 2, no. 3 (2002): 455.

Empey, Heather. "Transaction Analysis of Interactions at the Reference Desk of a Small Academic Library." *Partnership: The Canadian Journal of Library & Information Practice & Research* 5, no. 2 (2010): 1–17.

Gerlich, Bella Karr, and G. L. Berard. "Introducing the READ Scale: Qualitative Statistics for Academic Reference Services." *Georgia Library Quarterly* 43, no. 4 (2007): 7–13.

Gilbert, Lauren Miranda, Mengxiong Liu, and Toby Matoush. "Assessing Digital Reference and Online Instructional Services in an Integrated Public/University Library." *The Reference Librarian* 46, no. 95–96 (2006): 149–72.

Graves, Stephanie J., and Christina M. Desai. "Instruction via Chat Reference: Does Co-Browse Help?" *Reference Services Review* 34, no. 3 (2006): 340–57.

Green, Denise D., and Janis K. Peach. "Assessment of Reference Instruction as a Teaching and Learning Activity." *College & Research Libraries News* 64, no. 4 (2003): 256–58.

Gremmels, Gillian S., and Karen Shostrom Lehmann. "Assessment of Student Learning from Reference Service." *College & Research Libraries* 68, no. 6 (2007): 488–501.

Gronemyer, Kate, and Anne-Marie Deitering. "'I Don't Think It's Harder, Just That It's Different.'" *Reference Services Review* 37, no. 4 (2009): 421–34.

Harless, David W., and Frank R. Allen. "Using the Contingent Valuation Method to Measure Patron Benefits of Reference Desk Service in an Academic Library." *College & Research Libraries* 60, no. 1 (1999): 56.

Hirko, Buff, and Mary Bucher Ross. *Virtual Reference Training: The Complete Guide to Providing Anytime, Anywhere Answers.* Chicago: American Library Association, 2004. EBSCO e-book.

Johnson, Corey M., Sarah K. McCord, and Scott Walter. "Instructional Outreach Across the Curriculum: Enhancing the Liaison Role at a Research University." *Reference Librarian* 39, no. 82 (2003): 19–37.

Kilzer, Rebekah. "Reference as Service, Reference as Place: A View of Reference in the Academic Library." *Reference Librarian* 52, no. 4 (2011): 291–99.

Kocevar-Weidinger, Elizabeth, Candice Benjes-Small, Eric Ackermann, and Virginia R. Kinman. "Why and How to Mystery Shop Your Reference Desk." *Reference Services Review* 38, no. 1 (2010): 28–43.

Kuruppu, Pali U. "Evaluation of Reference Services—a Review." *Journal of Academic Librarianship* 33, no. 3 (2007): 368–81.

Maloney, Michelle M., and Veronica A. Wells. "iPads to Enhance User Engagement During Reference Interactions." *Library Technology Reports* 48, no. 8 (2012): 11–16.

Mattsson, Jan. "Strategic Insights from Mystery Shopping in B2B Relationships." *Journal of Strategic Marketing* 20, no. 4 (2012): 313–22.

May, Fiona. "Roving Reference, iPad-Style." *The Idaho Librarian* 61, no. 2 (2011): 14. http://theidaholibrarian.wordpress.com/2011/11/23/roving-reference-ipad-style.

Miles, Dennis B. "Shall We Get Rid of the Reference Desk?" *Reference & User Services Quarterly* 52, no. 4 (2013): 320–33.

Mitchell, Megan S., Cynthia H. Comer, Jennifer M. Starkey, and Eboni A. Francis. "Paradigm Shift in Reference Services at the Oberlin College Library: A Case Study." *Journal of Library Administration* 51, no. 4 (2011): 359–74.

Mu, Xiangming, Alexandra Dimitroff, Jeanette Jordan, and Natalie Burclaff. "A Survey and Empirical Study of Virtual Reference Service in Academic Libraries." *The Journal of Academic Librarianship* 37, no. 2: 120–29.

Norlin, Elaina. "Reference Evaluation: A Three-Step Approach—Surveys, Unobtrusive Observations, and Focus Groups." *College & Research Libraries* 61, no. 6 (2000): 546–53.

Oakleaf, Megan, and Amy VanScoy. "Instructional Strategies for Digital Reference: Methods to Facilitate Student Learning." *Reference & User Services Quarterly* 49, no. 4 (2010): 380–90.

Okamoto, Karen, and Mark Aaron Polger. "Off to Market We Go: A Content Analysis of Marketing and Promotion Skills in Academic Librarian Job Ads." *Library Leadership & Management* 26, no. 2 (2012): 1–20.

Partlo, Kristin. "The Pedagogical Data Reference Interview." *IASSIST Quarterly* 33/34, no. 4 (2009): 6–10.

Pena, David S., and Samuel S. Green. "Personal Relations Between Librarians and Readers." *Journal of Access Services* 4, no. 1–2 (2008): 157.

Penner, Katherine. "Mobile Technologies and Roving Reference." *Public Services Quarterly* 7, no. 1–2 (2011): 27–33.

Pitney, Barbara, and Nancy Slote. "Going Mobile: The KCLS Roving Reference Model." *Public Libraries* 46, no. 1 (2007): 54–68.

Poll, Roswitha. "Can We Quantify the Library's Influence? Creating an ISO Standard for Impact Assessment." *Performance Measurement and Metrics* 13, no. 2 (2012): 121–30.

Portree, Martha, R. S. Evans, Tina M. Adams, and John J. Doherty. "Overcoming Transactional Distance: Instructional Intent in an E-Mail Reference Service." *Reference & User Services Quarterly* 48, no. 2 (2008): 142–52.

Reference and User Services Association. "Guidelines for Behavioral Performance of Reference and Information Service Providers." Accessed April 18, 2014. www.ala.org/rusa/resources/guidelines/guidelinesbehavioral.

Reichel, Mary. "Bibliographic Instruction and the Reference Desk." *Journal of Academic Librarianship* 9, no. 1 (1983): 9–10.

Ryan, Susan M. "Reference Transactions Analysis: The Cost-Effectiveness of Staffing a Traditional Academic Reference Desk." *Journal of Academic Librarianship* 34, no. 5 (2008): 389–99.

Schiller, Anita R. "Reference Service: Instruction or Information." *The Library Quarterly* 35, no. 1 (1965): 52–60.

Solorzano, Ronald Martin. "Adding Value at the Desk: How Technology and User Expectations are Changing Reference Work." *Reference Librarian* 54, no. 2 (2013): 89–102.

Stevens, Christy R. "Reference Reviewed and Re-envisioned: Revamping Librarian and Desk-Centric Services with LibStARs and LibAnswers." *Journal of Academic Librarianship* 39, no. 2 (2013): 202–14.

Straw, Joseph E., and Christopher N. Cox. "Using Canned Messages in Virtual Reference Communication." *Internet Reference Services Quarterly* 11, no. 1 (2006): 39–49.

Tenopir, Carol. "Beyond Usage: Measuring Library Outcomes and Value." *Library Management* 33, no. 1–2 (2012): 5–13.

Tyckoson, David A. "Issues and Trends in the Management of Reference Services: A Historical Perspective." *Journal of Library Administration* 51, no. 3 (2011): 259–78.

Vulcovich, Lee A., Valerie S. Gordon, Nicole Mitchell, and Lisa A. Ennis. "Is the Time and Effort Worth It? One Library's Evaluation of Using Social Networking Tools for Outreach." *Medical Reference Services Quarterly* 32, no. 1 (2013): 12–25.

Ward, David. "Expanding the Reference Vocabulary: A Methodology for Applying Bloom's Taxonomy to Increase Instruction in the Reference Interview." *Reference Services Review* 39, no. 1 (2011): 167–80.

Widdows, Katharine. "Mobile Technology for Mobile Staff: Roving Enquiry Support." *Multimedia Information & Technology* 37, no. 2 (2011): 12–15.

Woodard, Beth S. "One-on-One Instruction: From the Reference Desk to Online Chat." *Reference & User Services Quarterly* 44, no. 3 (2005): 203–9.

Chapter Nine

Dialogic Mapping

*Evolving Reference into an Instructional Support for
Graduate Research*

Corinne Laverty and Elizabeth A. Lee

The present research arose out of a librarian's use of visual mapping as a method to address students' need to find context at the start of their research journey. As students explained their research query at the reference desk, I, the librarian, used a visual map to record the conversation around students' research topics. This enabled me to analyze complex topics and their inter-relationships so that I could better understand the types of resources that would be helpful. Throughout this process, students elaborated and defined relationships between concepts that we recorded on the map. The external representation of unfamiliar ideas allowed the student and I to identify connections between ideas and their relationship to resources. These experiences led to the research described in this chapter. Visual maps are known to support learning, but the systematic use of them during a reference conference is infrequent.

Students usually develop a research focus through discussion with faculty members who supervise their theses or dissertations. A meta-analysis of graduate student search behavior confirms that they begin research on the web and consult their faculty advisors before seeking further assistance.[1] This initiated a collaborative approach in which an academic librarian and a professor at a faculty of education decided to examine how visual maps and collaborative dialogue could extend student thinking when students were first narrowing their topic. Previous experiences of both the librarian and professor confirmed that graduate students in education often struggle with formulating research questions, searching the research literature, and developing coherent research proposals. The previous educational experience of some students has not equipped them to meet these demands as the field of education accepts students from many different disciplines with varied educational experiences.

THE CURRENT PARADOX OF REFERENCE SERVICES

A decade ago, Cheryl LaGuardia alerted us to a paradigm shift in reference question complexity stating that reference questions were becoming "more complex, more time-consuming, and larger in scope."[2] One reason for this increasing complexity is access to the online information environment, where information tools and their interfaces are constantly changing.[3] The technical demands of using and managing online resources also increases users' need for support.[4] We know that traditional face-to-face reference transactions are decreasing. Reference transactions are information consultations in which library staff recommend, interpret, evaluate, and/or use information resources to help others to meet particular information needs.[5] For example, numbers in American research libraries dropped by 65 percent from 1991 to 2011.[6] In an e-mail message in September 2013, the Canadian Association of Research Libraries reported a 28.5 percent decline over the past decade from 2001 to 2011.[7] It is not surprising that easy remote access to full-text databases, e-books, and discovery tools, in conjunction with extensive web resources, have contributed to the steady decline of reference questions in academic institutions.

However, reference services are also evolving in ways that are unanticipated. Could we have predicted that making enormous amounts of information accessible to students would result in diminishing research capabilities? Current research[8] has exposed a range of shortcomings in student search behavior that underscores the need to develop information-literacy competencies that include strategic selection of research tools determined by the information need rather than the simplest search portal at hand. A compelling study from Project Information Literacy revealed that students graduating into the workforce attempt to solve information problems on the job using superficial research strategies.[9] Students who have spent their postsecondary years searching Google and equivalent library search platforms may have little experience with a range of research tools.

Graduate students face more significant challenges. Lack of experience with discipline-specific information tools coupled with the expectation of automatic location of resources using a "discovery" layer poses problems for complex research tasks. A discovery tool simultaneously searches an institution's library catalog and journal articles for metadata and online full text and returns results in a single interface. LaGuardia confirms that library discovery search platforms that mimic Google's simple interface reaffirm the need for reference and information instruction.[10] These interfaces enable the simultaneous searching of much of the full text of online academic resources held by an institution. In practice, discovery layers provide only superficial searching because they do not expose the underlying information structures from which the materials have been harvested. We cannot know what is missing nor are we prompted to think systematically through the choices that offer alternate perspectives to our query. It is paradoxical that in an age of ubiquitous information, research is harder than ever.[11] Researching a topic is about more than finding a few articles based on the nearest match to search terms. For students to become critical readers of information, we need to teach them how to seek information written from multiple perspectives. Reference transactions offer one method for attending to this issue.

In academic communities, keeping up with changing information tools is a daunting task, but it falls within the purview of the reference librarian. Reference librarians possess a broad view of the resource landscape and know how information is constructed, packaged, and disseminated. This knowledge gives a huge advantage in designing search strategies. If we think aloud while working with students, we can demonstrate how complex questions require the sifting and compilation of various forms and types of information. John Fritch and Scott Mandernack describe this as a multifaceted mini-instruction session where librarians help to:

> develop the topic idea, lay out the structure of information (catalogs, indexes, Web sites . . . etc.), explain and differentiate between types of information, provide an overview of general search strategies, demonstrate the use of a particular database, explain the interface, lead users in their search, direct them to where they can retrieve the materials found, and guide them in presenting their information clearly and appropriately.[12]

Reference librarians might think of themselves as conduits to the many channels of information that are invisible to most—the specialized databases and rare collections that provide detailed information and cannot be retrieved without plunging into deeper and deeper layers of knowledge. Initial information searches scan surface documents, but as learning about a subject intensifies, the search changes; terms, word combinations, perspective shifts, and research approaches change as learning happens. Anne M. Fields discusses these types of questions as "ill-structured problems . . . with indefinite starting points, multiple and arguable solutions, and unclear maps for finding one's way through information."[13] Fields also notes that research involves strengths in two domains: subject knowledge and information-literacy knowledge.[14] Subject domain expertise includes a knowledge base that is highly structured and well organized, and information-literacy domain knowledge involves the ability to distinguish patterns of information needs.

A shared feature of expertise in both domains is the ability to categorize problems and identify relationships between concepts and subconcepts. Novice researchers are at a disadvantage on both fronts because they are only developing their understanding of the area of research while having to search for literature on it at the same time.

A study of graduate students' search behavior indicates that their strategies are both random and organized.[15] They are random during the initial stages of research when they are isolating a topic focus, looking for background information, and determining an overall search strategy. It is at this point, when students are trying to find context in both their subject and information-literacy domains, that reference help can be especially useful. In a meta-analysis, Amy Catalano notes that graduate students overrate their searching abilities, especially in basic search skills.[16] The research by Alison Head and Michael Eisenberg reveals that students graduate from their first degree with a common set of research challenges around finding context within their topic area.[17] We suggest that new graduate students bring the same research deficiencies as they enter a Master's-level program. The first step of finding context occurs when students are gathering background information and tapping into complex information landscapes, which students find to be the most difficult part of the research process.[18] Selecting and narrowing a topic is part of "big picture context" and finding and accessing relevant information is part of "information-gathering context."[19] Given the amount of information accessible to students, it is surprising that this poses the greatest challenge. Identifying starting points and background information mirrors the first step in a reference transaction.[20] To find context in terms of developing a topic, librarians need to help students develop deeper understanding of research extant in the field. This involves teaching students how to locate and analyze information that will contribute to their understanding. As students establish context, they are better able to refine their research focus. The two areas are complementary and symbiotic and as such should be addressed during a reference consultation.

Various systems that visually represent information, such as graphic organizers, flow charts, and concept maps, have demonstrated their benefit in supporting learning. Concept maps represent ideas in multiple ways with images as well as words, illustrating the conceptual links that underpin complex topics and serving as "a scaffold to help organize knowledge and structure it."[21] At the postgraduate level, David Hay investigated concept mapping as an instructional tool and as a method to assess the quality of learning.[22] Concept mapping allows for "the sharing of 'expert' knowledge and understanding among teachers and learners.[23] When individuals are asked to draw maps on the same topic at different stages of learning, changes in learning can be made visible.[24] In this study, we used a free form of visual mapping rather than a traditional concept map, which has a hierarchical structure and requires formal naming of relationships. Our purpose was to focus on the representation of ideas through spontaneous conversation as it would take place during a reference consultation.

Collaborative dialogue allows individuals to engage in reciprocal meaning-making through a directed discussion of a topic that can result in the co-construction of knowledge. The dialogue can extend and clarify ideas and may enhance an understanding of the inter-relationships among them through an extended focused discussion.[25] This reiterative process encourages the revision of ideas. Thinking aloud, in which individuals speak aloud the thoughts going through their mind while engaging in a task, allows access to their working memory, that is, what they are thinking about at that moment.[26] This technique has been used extensively in research about problem solving through the analysis of verbal protocols. The collaborative construction of a concept map results in a map that shows the underlying structure of a topic and deeper understanding of the topic by the participants.[27] The co-construction of a concept map leads to a cognitively productive interaction among group members.[28]

METHODOLOGY FOR THE STUDY ON DIALOGIC MAPPING

Our study proposed that collaborative dialogue and visual mapping recasts reference transactions into academic conversations. Graduate students typically take a research-methods course early on in their program with a final assignment of writing a thesis proposal. The researchers, a librarian-faculty team in a faculty of education, theorized that the co-construction of a visual map would enhance the initial conceptualization of the research topic and help focus the literature review. Drawing on these approaches we investigated the following research question: How does collaborative dialogue between a graduate student and a librarian-faculty team extend student thinking while the student constructs a visual map of his or her thesis topic?

Five graduate students in education (four females and one male) participated in the study. The second author was the thesis supervisor for these students. All had completed their course work in a Master's program but were at different stages in developing their thesis proposal at the time of data collection. Each graduate student was individually audio- and videotaped while constructing a map of their research topic. Students were asked to independently draw a visual map of their research topic while thinking aloud to explain their ideas to us. We then began a dialogue in which we prompted each student to explain and expand the map through questioning and commenting on the map. These prompts led to a variety of additions and changes being made to the map in response to the dialogue. Videotaping recorded the dynamic evolution of the map. Videotape coding is an iterative process of analysis to develop and refine a coding scheme[29] that enables analysis of the effects of the dialogue on the conceptualization of the research topic. After the mapping experience, students were asked to respond by e-mail to a short survey on the value of the mapping exercise.

Analysis and Interpretation of the Visual Maps

Analysis of the data involved multiple stages:

1. The audio component of the sessions was transcribed verbatim.
2. The video was viewed and every change to the map was annotated in the transcript.
3. For each change, the dialogue was examined for possible prompts that triggered the change. These were identified, defined, and coded. Resulting categories were "clarifying" and "knowledge prompts."
4. Conversations about the research journey were identified and categorized according to the stage within the research process. These were later grouped into three categories: (1) questions, (2) research methods and design, and (3) information gathering and evaluation as part of the literature review.
5. Prompts that triggered a change on the map relating to a specific aspect of the research journey were identified.
6. Initial student maps were compared to maps resulting from dialogue with the researchers.
7. Students were surveyed for their feedback on the value of the mapping exercise.

Table 9.1.   Examples of Clarifying and Knowledge Prompts

Examples of Clarifying Prompts	*Examples of Knowledge Prompts*
What are your research questions?	Offering advice on more specific things:
What is the context for this study?	Is X also one of your research questions?
What is a suitable research method?	Would knowing more about X help with
What do you know about this research method?	the context of the study?
	Did you think of gathering data on . . . ?
What terms are used to identify . . . ?	Did you think of connecting . . . ?
How does concept X relate to concept Y?	Did you think of including X in the
What is the relationship between . . . ?	literature review?
How will you include this in the literature review?	Did you think of gathering information or data on this aspect?
What other types of information do you need for the literature review?	You need to include X in the ethical review process.
How will you order sections in the literature review?	Did you think of comparing information from other disciplines?

After reading and coding transcripts individually for prompts, we developed definitions for the two main types. Clarifying prompts occurred when researchers asked questions to unravel the verbal description or visual representation given by the student. Knowledge prompts occurred when researchers offered information to students to extend their thinking or analysis. Examples of the two types are presented in table 9.1. These are similar to questions raised during a traditional reference interview; however, they extend the discussion beyond sources and location of information to include research design and methods.

Figure 9.1 provides a picture of student A's independent map and figure 9.2 provides a map following the dialogue.

Student A's research topic was "Application of Word Prediction Software for Learning Disabled Students." She initially created a map with eight key topics, three subtopics, and five links connecting topics. She added an additional new fifteen topics, twenty-six new subtopics, and eight new links during the dialogue. Examples of prompts leading to a change on the co-constructed map follow.

1. In response to a clarifying prompt, "Will you be evaluating the software too?," during the collaborative dialogue, student A added two subtopics—"software criteria" and "evaluation"—above Word Q, the name of the software program to be used in the study.
2. In response to the clarifying prompt, "Is there anything in your broad research question that you don't have?," student A replied, "How the writing process happens," and the researcher further prompted, "So . . . something on the writing process," and student A added "writing process for average students" underneath the topic heading "Cognitive Load Theory."
3. In response to a knowledge prompt, "You'd have to give a historical trajectory as to why you're investigating this," student A added two subtopics: "previous approaches" and "historical context."
4. A knowledge prompt about the need for defining the term *learning disabilities* resulted in student A adding Canadian/U.S./UK with a note to compare definitions.

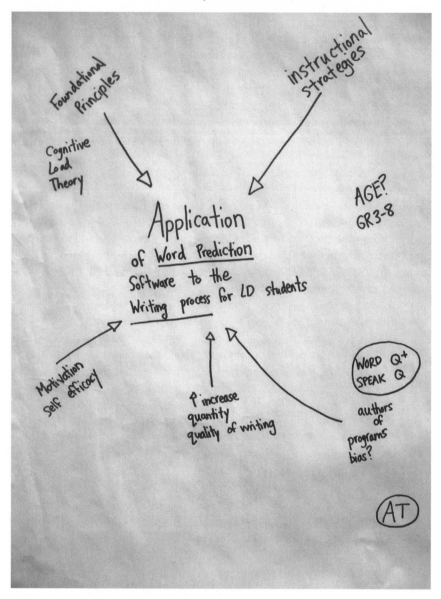

Figure 9.1.   Student's independent map

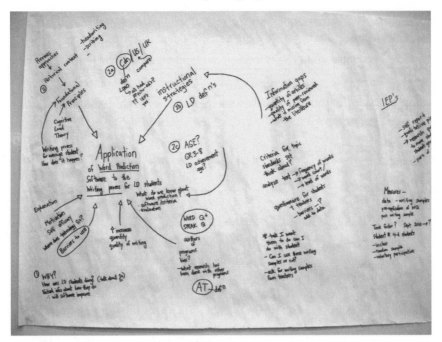

Figure 9.2. Map following the dialogue

The increased number of topics and subtopics on the co-constructed map reveals a deeper understanding of the research problem and its interrelationships. Differences between individual and collaboratively constructed maps in terms of numbers of key topics, subtopics, and links resulting from the conversation are presented in table 9.2.

Table 9.2. Key Topics, Subtopics, and Links in the Visual Maps

| Student | Individual Map | | | Collaborative Map | | |
	Key Topics	Subtopics	Links	New Key Topics	New Subtopics	New Links
Student A	8	3	5	15	26	8
Student B	4	2	0	6	19	8
Student C	4	11	15	9	23	32
Student D	5	3	9	13	15	12
Student E	8	0	2	7	10	3

Table 9.3 shows the number and type of prompts from the researchers leading to a change on the map over the course of each hour-long session. Clarifying prompts accounted for 37 percent and knowledge prompts accounted for 63 percent of the total. Not all changes to the visual map were in response to a prompt, as some were self-generated by the student. As this

was a dialogue, some prompts involved several exchanges between the researchers and student before a change in the visual map occurred.

Table 9.3.   Number and Type of Researcher Prompts

Student	Clarifying Prompts	Knowledge Prompts
Student A	16	16
Student B	6	8
Student C	3	14
Student D	3	8
Student E	5	11
Total	33 (37%)	57 (63%)

Stages of the research process or journey were defined following the outline in an introductory research-methods text: research purpose—research question—study design—resource selection—evaluation of resources—literature review.[30] Table 9.4 shows the number of times a change was made to the map that addressed a specific component of the research journey in response to either a clarifying or knowledge prompt. It was difficult to code a piece of extended dialogue as focusing on a single aspect of the research process. For that reason, we collapsed the categories into the following three areas: discussion around the research purpose and questions (Q), research design and methods (M), and aspects of the literature review (LR) that included potential sources of information. Prompts made by the researchers that elicited changes on the map relating to the research journey are included in table 9.4.

Table 9.4.   Prompts That Triggered Changes to the Map Involving the Research Journey

Student	Research Journey: Clarifying Prompts			Research Journey: Knowledge Prompts			Research Journey Totals		
Student A	0Q	6M	10LR	1Q	7M	8LR	1Q	13M	18LR
Student B	3Q	3M	0LR	0Q	4M	4LR	3Q	7M	4LR
Student C	2Q	0M	1LR	3Q	8M	3LR	5Q	8M	4LR
Student D	0Q	2M	1LR	1Q	4M	3LR	1Q	6M	4LR
Student E	0Q	3M	2LR	3Q	8M	0LR	3Q	11M	2LR
Total	5Q	14M	14LR	8Q	31M	18LR	13Q (14%)	45M (50%)	32LR (36%)

Abbreviations: Q: research purpose and questions—M: research design and method—LR: literature review and sources.

Changes to the map were broadly matched to stages of the research journey. Study design and methods accounted for 50 percent of changes, 36 percent related to the literature review and identification of information, and 14 percent pertained to research purpose and study questions. Traditional reference work does not usually focus on research design and methods. The standard definition of *reference transactions* emphasizes finding, managing, and evaluating information sources.[31] It may not occur to librarians that discussion around research methods is appropriate in the context of a reference query. Librarians who engage in research themselves can share their understanding of study design and how it informs the information-seeking process. Time constraints also pose a barrier to extending a reference interview to include more in-depth conversations about methodology.

To gauge students' perception of the mapping process, we asked the following question: Did the process of having a dialogue with us help? Table 9.5 shows student responses.

Table 9.5. Student Responses on the Usefulness of the Collaborative Dialogue

Student	Student responses to the question: Did the process of having a dialogue with us help?
Student A	Thinking through the possible research questions out loud. Answering the questions posed to me from both of you was helpful in forcing me to be concise, something I struggle with often in my thought processes. Demystified the [literature review] process and made it seem attainable rather than a mammoth task!
Student B	In response to how the exercise helped: The aspects of talking about each of my subtitles [subtopics].
Student C	The part that helped me most was the dialogue. For students headed to university, I think it helps prepare them to be more successful at independent learning and for other students it helps them understand concepts more thoroughly. The part of the dialogue that helped me the most was the persistent questioning about issues against which I had dug my heels. . . . I think it'll be important for me to be able to justify the choices I have made and to help me anticipate questions in the future.
Student D	Discussing the topic, and justifying what is needed for research was helpful. The visualization helped me to group major concepts, and finally create an outline of how the research should feed into my literature review. Articulating my research plans was helpful . . . to see what ideas I had a grasp on, and which needed further research. It also helped in generating new search criteria to find literature I had previously had trouble finding.
Student E	Having an opportunity to reflect and map out with professors (critical friends) the understandings which were foundational to my research was much needed at this point in my research. Yes this session was helpful because I could see how the ideas fit together. . . . Time was spent reviewing the purpose, method etc. . . . I will take the concept map and

look at the research questions to further refine my ideas and understandings. Just explaining my ideas out loud to someone else helped me to clarify things. Explaining them to two academics who understand the research process was very helpful to force me to choose my research focus question and to tie the question/method/data analysis together. Critical questions from other academics really forced me to hone my thinking and to move my research forward. This dialogue would be helpful at key points throughout the research. I can see the benefit in meeting with your supervisor or another academic on a regular basis. This would hold me accountable and help me to keep learning and growing.

Students found the exercise useful, especially the free-form dialogue, think-alouds, and visual documentation. It is interesting to note that student B used a later version of the map as part of his thesis defense to present his research findings.

DISCUSSION AND IMPLICATIONS FOR REFERENCE PRACTICE

This study provides evidence that collaborative dialogue between graduate education students and a librarian-faculty team helped to extend student thinking. "Clarifying" and "knowledge prompts" were the two categories that triggered students to make additions to their map. Knowledge prompts accounted for 63 percent of the prompts, supporting the idea that the faculty-librarian team brought both subject and information-literacy domain expertise to the conversation, and this contributed to the students' generation of new ideas. The resulting maps included more key topics, subtopics, and interconnections between ideas than the student's initial map. This change reflects a deepening and an elaboration of the conceptualization of the research topic.

Survey results indicated that students found the questioning and think-aloud process useful in focusing ideas from different perspectives. The visualization helped to group, articulate, and develop new ideas. We surmise that the visual record allows students to find the "big picture context" by reducing the cognitive load inherent in verbal conversations. Student E captures this process when she notes that the exercise helped her see how "the ideas fit together" and "tie the question/method/data analysis together" (table 9.5).

Study findings have implications for reference and instructional services:

a. Visualization assists shared understanding and development of research ideas and the research process. Seeing relationships on paper reveals connections, gaps, and themes.

b. Dialogue where students are equal partners in the conversation provides a constructivist approach to learning, allowing for the free flow of questions and ideas.

c. Students may need to target the research design as much, if not more than, finding information sources. Research design is a new area for them. Discussion about methods helped to sculpt the research questions and narrow the sources for the literature review. Librarians can explore methods during a reference consultation by prompting for study population, the type of data that will be collected, and how to identify scholarly literature that uses similar research approaches. Research-methods databases, handbooks, and textbooks that describe qualitative and quantitative techniques should also be included in the conversation.

d. Librarians should explore the subject domain of the topic as much as the information resources through questioning and clarification. Both areas are critical for finding context during the research process.

e. Visual maps provide evidence of the value of the reference process as well as a clear record for the student of the scope of their topic. This record is also important in order to demonstrate the impact of reference service and the overall accountability of academic libraries.

f. Mapping can be used during formal instructional sessions as a means of capturing the evolving understanding of the topic and research strategies. This approach has been adopted in our introductory research methods course for graduate education students. Students are asked to map their existing research process at the start of a two-hour class. This includes the starting point for finding information resources and tactics they follow when they encounter barriers. Students then redraw the process at the end of the class to integrate changes they will consider for the future. This may include strategies for gathering gray literature, government documents, nongovernmental organizations, open-access materials, and related research in other fields.

Typical reference transactions jump quickly to the search for resources without helping students find the context they need for their research. Discussions that allow students to further articulate their questions are a productive way to broaden the evidence that students consider during this process. Increased discussions also position reference interactions as "a dialogue of equals wherein the librarian assumes the more empowering role of partner as opposed to information guru," as suggested by John Doherty.[32] Specific questions, such as the prompts we identified, can trigger the elaboration and generation of new ideas. In our study, examples of clarifying prompts include:

- What is missing from the literature?
- What information gaps have you come across?
- How will you bring these ideas together in the literature review?
- How are these ideas related?
- Should this be one of your research questions?
- Will you be able to get access to the data/population you want?
- Will you look for information that offers international perspectives?
- What type of analysis will you use with your data?
- What definition will you use for these concepts?

Examples of knowledge prompts include:

- Would knowing more about x help with the context of the study?
- Did you think of gathering data on . . . ?
- Did you think of connecting . . . ?
- Did you think of including x in the literature review?

James K. Elmborg theorizes that categories of questions could be used to structure the reference transaction, which he refers to as an "academic conference."[33] These questions are not about locating information, but are about self-reflection on what students understand of their topic. Our study confirms that specific prompts help students to unravel their topics. Dialogue plus visualization allows students to further unpack the research process so they are aware of their decisions and choices. This practice reduces the compelling desire to find information before the purpose for the information is fully understood. "Slow research" makes for a clearer focus and a more equitable exchange between librarians and students. Engaging in collaborative consultation is a powerful opportunity for students to articulate and co-construct their ideas, providing context in both subject and information-literacy domains.

NOTES

1. Amy Catalano, "Patterns of Graduate Students' Information Seeking Behavior: A Meta-synthesis of the Literature," *Journal of Documentation* 69, no. 2 (2013): 243, doi:10.1108/00220411311300066.

2. Cheryl LaGuardia, "The Future of Reference: Get Real!," *Reference Services Review* 31, no. 1 (2003): 40, doi:10.1108/00907320310460898.

3. Steven Deineh, Julie Middlemas, and Patrichia Morrison, "A New Service Model for the Reference Desk: The Student Research Center," *Library Philosophy and Practice*, paper 554 (2011): 3, http://digitalcommons.unl.edu/libphilprac/554.

4. Jack O'Gorman and Barry Trott, "What Will Become of Reference in Academic and Public Libraries?," *Journal of Library Administration* 49, no. 4 (2009): 334, doi:10.1080/01930820902832421.

5. American Library Association, Reference and User Services Association, "Definitions of Reference," accessed February 10, 2014, www.ala.org/rusa/resources/guidelines/definitionsreference.

6. American Research Libraries, *Service Trends in ARL Libraries 1991–2011* (Washington: American Research Libraries, 2011), www.arl.org/storage/documents/service-trends.pdf.

7. Canadian Association of Research Libraries, e-mail communication October 2013.

8. Centre for Information Behaviour and the Evaluation of Research (CIBER), *Information Behaviour of the Researcher of the Future: The Literature on Young People and Their Information Behaviour* (London: University College London, 2008); Lynda M. Duke and Andrew D. Asher, *College Libraries and Student Culture: What We Now Know* (Chicago: American Library Association, 2012); Alison J. Head and Michael B. Eisenberg, *Lessons Learned: How College Students Seek Information in the Digital Age* (Seattle: University of Washington, Project Information Literacy, 2009b), http://projectinfolit.org/pdfs/PIL_Fall2009_finalv_YR1_12_2009v2.pdf; Arthur Taylor, "A Study of the Information Search Behavior of the Millennial Generation," *Information Research* 17, no. 1 (2012), http://informationr.net/ir/17-1/paper508.html.

9. Alison J. Head, *Learning Curve: How College Graduates Solve Information Problems Once They Join the Workplace* (Seattle: University of Washington, Project Information Literacy, 2012): 3, http://projectinfolit.org/pdfs/PIL_fall2012_workplaceStudy_FullReport_Revised.pdf.

10. Cheryl LaGuardia, "Library Instruction in the Digital Age," *Journal of Library Administration* 51, no. 3 (2011): 302, doi:10.1080/01930826.2011.556948.

11. Alison J. Head and Michael B. Eisenberg, *Finding Context: What Today's College Students Say about Conducting Research in the Digital Age* (Seattle: University of Washington, Project Information Literacy, 2009a), 2, http://projectinfolit.org/pdfs/PIL_ProgressReport_2_2009.pdf.

12. John W. Fritch and Scott B. Mandernack, "The Emerging Reference Paradigm: A Vision of Reference Services in a Complex Information Environment," *Library Trends* 50, no. 2 (2001): 294–95.

13. Anne M. Fields, "Ill-Structured Problems and the Reference Consultation," *Reference Services Review* 34, no. 3 (2006): 405, doi: 10.1108/00907320610701554.

14. Ibid., 411.

15. Carole George et al., "Scholarly Use of Information: Graduate Students' Information Seeking Behaviour," *Information Research* 11, no. 4 (2006): 12.

16. Catalano, "Patterns of Graduate Students' Information Seeking Behavior," 266.

17. Head and Eisenberg, *Finding Context*, 4.

18. Ibid., 5.

19. Ibid., 6–9.

20. Fritch and Mandernack, "Emerging Reference Paradigm," 294–95.

21. Joseph D. Novak and Alberto J Cañas, "The Theory Underlying Concept Maps and How to Construct and Use Them," *Technical Report IHMC CmapTools 2006-01* (Florida Institute for Human and Machine Cognition, 2008), doi: 7.http://cmap.ihmc.us/Publications/ResearchPapers/TheoryUnderlyingConceptMaps.pdf.

22. David B. Hay, "Using Concept Maps to Measure Deep, Surface and NonLearning Outcomes," *Studies in Higher Education* 32, no. 1 (2007): 52, doi:10.1080/03075070601099432.

23. David Hay, Ian Kinchin, and Simon Lygo-Baker, "Making Learning Visible: The Role of Concept Mapping in Higher Education," *Studies in Higher Education* 33, no. 3 (2008): 295, doi:10.1080/03075070802049251.

24. Hay, "Using Concept Maps," 52.

25. Anna O. Soter, "The Use of Discussion as a Pedagogical Tool in the University Context," *Talking About Teaching*, 2 (2007): 40, http://hdl.handle.net/1811/34607.

26. Peter Afflerbach, "Verbal Reports and Protocol Analysis," in *Handbook of Reading Research Vol. III*, ed. Michael L Kamil, Peter B. Mosenthal, P. David Pearson, and Rebecca Barr (Mahwah, NJ: Lawrence Erlbaum, 2000), 171–72.

27. Olusola O. Adesope and John C. Nesbit, "A Systematic Review of Research on Collaborative Learning with Concept Maps," in *Handbook of Research on Collaborative Learning*

Using Concept Mapping, ed. Patricia Lupion Torres and Rita de Cássia Veiga Marriott (Hershey, PA: Information Science Reference, 2010), 243.

28. Josianne Basque and Béatrice Pudelko, "Intersubjective Meaning—Mapping in Dyads Using Object-Typed Concept Mapping," in *Handbook of Research on Collaborative Learning Using Concept Mapping,* ed. Patricia Lupion Torres and Rita de Cássia Veiga Marriott (Hershey, PA: Information Science Reference, 2010), 192.

29. Alan H. Schoenfeld, "On Paradigms and Methods: What Do You Do When the Ones You Know Don't Do What You Want Them To? Issues in the Analysis of Data in the Form of Videotapes," *Journal of the Learning Sciences* 2, no. 2 (1992): 189–90, doi:10.1207/s15327809jls0202_3.

30. Bruce L. Berg, *Qualitative Research Methods for the Social Sciences,* 4th ed. (Boston: Allyn and Bacon, 2001), 19.

31. American Library Association, Reference and User Services Association, "Definitions of Reference."

32. John J. Doherty, "Reference Interview or Reference Dialogue," *Internet Reference Services Quarterly* 11, no. 3 (2006): 107, doi:10.1300/J136v11n03_07.

33. James K. Elmborg, "Teaching at the Desk: Toward a Reference Pedagogy," *portal: Libraries and the Academy* 2, no. 3 (2002): 460, doi:10.1353/pla.2002.0050.

BIBLIOGRAPHY

Adesope, Olusola O., and John C. Nesbit. "A Systematic Review of Research on Collaborative Learning with Concept Maps." In *Handbook of Research on Collaborative Learning Using Concept Mapping,* edited by Patricia Lupion Torres and Rita de Cássia Veiga Marriott, 238–51. Hershey, PA: Information Science Reference, 2010.

Afflerbach, Peter. "Verbal Reports and Protocol Analysis." In *Handbook of Reading Research Vol. III,* edited by Michael L Kamil, Peter B. Mosenthal, P. David Pearson, and Rebecca Barr, 163–79. Mahwah, NJ: Lawrence Erlbaum, 2000.

American Library Association, Reference and User Services Association. "Definitions of Reference." Accessed February 10, 2014. www.ala.org/rusa/resources/guidelines/definitionsreference.

American Research Libraries. *Service Trends in ARL Libraries 1991-2011.* Washington, DC: American Research Libraries, 2008. www.arl.org/storage/documents/service- trends.pdf.

Basque, Josianne, and Béatrice Pudelko. "Intersubjective Meaning—Mapping in Dyads Using Object-Typed Concept Mapping." In *Handbook of Research on Collaborative Learning Using Concept Mapping,* edited by Patricia Lupion Torres and Rita de Cássia Veiga Marriott, 180–206. Hershey, PA: Information Science Reference, 2010.

Berg, Bruce L. *Qualitative Research Methods for the Social Sciences.* 4th ed. Boston, MA: Allyn and Bacon, 2001.

Canadian Association of Research Libraries. E-mail communication October 3, 2013, stating the percentage decrease of reference questions between 2002 and 2011 at academic research libraries in Canada.

Catalano, Amy. "Patterns of Graduate Students' Information Seeking Behavior: A Meta-synthesis of the Literature." *Journal of Documentation* 69, no. 2 (2013): 243–74. doi:10.1108/00220411311300066.

Centre for Information Behavior and the Evaluation of Research. *Information Behaviour of the Researcher of the Future: The Literature on Young People and Their Information Behaviour.* London: University College London, 2008.

Deineh, Steven, Julie Middlemas, and Patrichia Morrison. "A New Service Model for the Reference Desk: The Student Research Center." *Library Philosophy and Practice.* Paper 554 (2011). http://digitalcommons.unl.edu/libphilprac/554.

Doherty, John J. "Reference Interview or Reference Dialogue." *Internet Reference Services Quarterly* 11, no. 3 (2006): 97–109. doi:10.1300/J136v11n03_07.

Duke, Lynda M., and Andrew D. Asher. *College Libraries and Student Culture: What We Now Know.* Chicago: American Library Association, 2012.

Elmborg, James K. "Teaching at the Desk: Toward a Reference Pedagogy." *portal: Libraries and the Academy* 2, no. 3 (2002): 455–64. doi:10.1353/pla.2002.0050.

Fields, Anne M. "Ill-Structured Problems and the Reference Consultation." *Reference Services Review* 34, no. 3 (2006): 405–20. doi: 10.1108/00907320610701554.

Fritch, John W., and Scott B. Mandernack. "The Emerging Reference Paradigm: A Vision of Reference Services in a Complex Information Environment." *Library Trends* 50, no. 2 (2001): 286–305.

George, Carole, Alice Bright, Terry Hurlbert, Erika C. Linke, Gloriana St. Clair, and Joan Stein. "Scholarly Use of Information: Graduate Students' Information Seeking Behaviour." *Information Research* 11, no. 4 (2006): 1–14. http://InformationR.net/ir/11-4/paper272.html.

Hay, David B. "Using Concept Maps to Measure Deep, Surface and Non-learning Outcomes." *Studies in Higher Education* 32, no. 1 (2007): 39–57. doi:10.1080/03075070601099432.

Hay, David, Ian Kinchin, and Simon Lygo-Baker. "Making Learning Visible: The Role of Concept Mapping in Higher Education." *Studies in Higher Education* 33, no. 3 (2008): 295–311. doi:10.1080/03075070802049251.

Head, Alison J. *Learning Curve: How College Graduates Solve Information Problems Once They Join the Workplace.* Seattle: University of Washington, Project Information Literacy, 2012. http://projectinfolit.org/pdfs/PIL_fall2012_workplaceStudy_FullReport_Revised.pdf.

Head, Alison J., and Michael B. Eisenberg. *Finding Context: What Today's College Students Say about Conducting Research in the Digital Age.* Seattle: University of Washington, Project Information Literacy, 2009a. http://projectinfolit.org/pdfs/PIL_ProgressReport_2_2009.pdf.

———. *Lessons Learned: How College Students Seek Information in the Digital Age.* Seattle: University of Washington, Project Information Literacy, 2009b. http://projectinfolit.org/pdfs/PIL_Fall2009_finalv_YR1_12_2009v2.pdf.

LaGuardia, Cheryl. "Library Instruction in the Digital Age." *Journal of Library Administration* 51, no. 3 (2011): 301–8. doi:10.1080/01930826.2011.556948.

———. "The Future of Reference: Get Real!" *Reference Services Review* 31, no. 1 (2003): 39–42. doi:10.1108/00907320310460898.

Novak, Joseph D., and Alberto J. Cañas. "The Theory Underlying Concept Maps and How to Construct and Use Them." *Technical Report IHMC CmapTools 2006-01.* Pensacola, FL: Florida Institute for Human and Machine Cognition, 2008. http://cmap.ihmc.us/Publications/ResearchPapers/TheoryUnderlyingConceptMaps.pdf.

O'Gorman, Jack, and Barry Trott. "What Will Become of Reference in Academic and Public Libraries?" *Journal of Library Administration* 49, no. 4 (2009): 327–39. doi:10.1080/01930820902832421.

Schoenfeld, Alan H. "On Paradigms and Methods: What Do You Do When the Ones You Know Don't Do What You Want Them To? Issues in the Analysis of Data in the Form of Videotapes." *Journal of the Learning Sciences* 2, no. 2 (1992): 179–214. doi:10.1207/s15327809jls0202_3.

Soter, Anna O. "The Use of Discussion as a Pedagogical Tool in the University Context." *Talking about Teaching* 2 (2007): 30–43. http://hdl.handle.net/1811/34607.

Taylor, Arthur. "A Study of the Information Search Behavior of the Millennial Generation." *Information Research* 17, no. 1 (2012). http://informationr.net/ir/17-1/paper508.html.

Chapter Ten

Does the Reference Desk Still Matter?

Assessing the Desk Paradigm at the University of Washington Libraries

Deb Raftus and Kathleen Collins

The University of Washington (UW) comprises three campuses and several off-campus facilities and is the largest comprehensive research institution in the Pacific Northwest. UW's Seattle campus, its largest, has thirteen libraries, which serve 43,000 students and 4,300 faculty and host over 5 million annual visits to library facilities and 9 million separate visits to the libraries' websites.[1] With the increasing availability of research content online, a significant portion of UW's faculty, graduate students, and undergraduates now privilege desktop delivery of content over physical visits to library buildings for their research.[2] A growing shift toward remote access is similarly evident in reference services—one-fifth of questions in 2011 came in via e-mail and chat.[3] It is logical, then, to ask: Are librarians with advanced degrees making their most effective contribution to the scholarly community by staffing walk-up reference desks, where annual statistics show a steep decline in business? To address this question, the Reference Desk Services Task Force (hereafter "the task force") was established in winter 2011 to assess services at the three Seattle campus libraries that still maintained stand-alone reference desks: the main research library, Suzzallo-Allen; the Odegaard Undergraduate Library; and the Engineering Library.

REVIEWING THE LITERATURE

In completing its charge, the task force trod a well-followed path; the questions of *how* and even *whether* to staff a physical reference desk are hardly

153

new ones. Traditionally, libraries have used a "just-in-case" model, staffing reference desks with professional librarians in anticipation of the occasional in-depth research question requiring such expertise.[4] As early as 1977, however, a study concluded that 80 percent of the questions asked at the reference desk could be answered by trained nonprofessionals.[5] More recently, similar studies found that the majority of questions asked at the reference desk could be answered without extensive research knowledge.[6]

Some argue that freeing librarians from answering directional and low-level reference questions at a desk will give them more time to pursue high-impact professional-level activities, such as teaching, curriculum mapping, and in-depth research consultations.[7] Since collaborations with faculty and partnerships with campus teaching and learning programs, writing centers, and computer labs provide opportunities to meet students when and where they need help, librarians' time could be better spent conducting outreach to their departments and establishing such partnerships.[8]

Many libraries have experimented with offering in-person help beyond the physical service desk, employing a referral and consultation model, virtual reference services, a roving-around model, or a blended model incorporating multiple services.[9] Reference librarians are expanding their scope through outreach to become embedded field librarians. Given budget pressures in the new century, a 65 percent decline in reference statistics in Association of Research Libraries (ARL) member libraries over the last twenty years,[10] and the by-now well-documented disinclination of students to seek research help from staffed reference service points,[11] some libraries have completely eliminated their reference desks, while an argument has been advanced to do away with face-to-face reference services entirely.[12]

ASSESSING THE REFERENCE DESK PARADIGM AT UW

The literature makes clear that, for many librarians, the reference desk carries an emotional and symbolic weight, serving as an emblem not only of reference service, but also of librarianship itself. Thus, taking away the desk devalues the reference librarian and removes the most prominent public representative of the profession. The powerful symbolism embodied in the reference desk has even been used as a justification for keeping it, and institutions that have moved away from a traditional reference desk describe the change as a "paradigm shift."[13] As Steven J. Bell explains, "Some reference librarians are so attached to the idea of the desk that they will likely refuse to even discuss the possibility of exploring alternative service delivery models. But talk about it we must."[14] The totemic power of the reference desk was brought home to the task force when one member repeatedly experienced librarians shouting, "Save the reference desk!" as they passed by her office door.

To invite staff input and open up a conversation about the reference desk paradigm, the task force developed a survey to determine the value reference staff placed on the reference desk and the role they believed it played. The survey included fifteen multiple-choice, short answer, and ratings scale questions covering staff demographics, work history, and feelings on and ideas about reference desk services. Thirty-five respondents completed the survey. Over a third of the respondents indicated they had more than twenty years of reference desk experience, while most had at least eleven years of experience and participated in other reference services, like chat and consultations, in addition to desk hours. Most indicated that the reference desk was important to them personally. Interestingly, when asked whether changes should or should not be made to the reference desk, respondents showed an even split in opinion (figure 10.1). Further responses were more nuanced, with the overall impression indicating that, although the majority of reference staff vehemently opposed doing away with in-person reference services altogether, some might support merging reference with other service points or ceding desk time to trained students.

Comments reiterated the split feelings among staff: In answer to one open question, "One thing I would keep about the reference desk is . . ." one

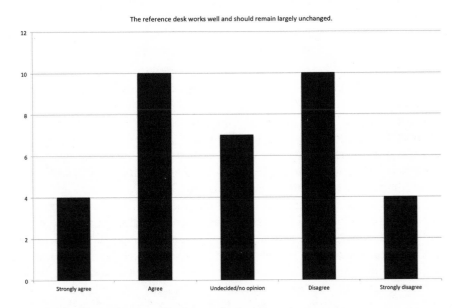

Figure 10.1. Staff responses to survey question: "The reference desk works well and should remain largely unchanged."

librarian wrote simply, "the reference desk." Several respondents expressed variations on the statement that "Reference is why I became a librarian," even as some acknowledged that walk-up desks were no longer the central service they once had been, "an antiquated mode of service delivery that is no longer relevant to the majority of students and faculty that make up our academic community."

As with many surveys of this nature, the results were inconclusive. What did emerge is that staff continued to value the walk-up reference desk for its opportunities for personal, one-on-one interaction and connections with students, "the chance to humanize the library/research experience for all who come here for help." Some respondents argued that, with proper training and a willingness to help people, students could successfully staff a reference desk. Others, however, clearly expressed the importance they placed on the desk as symbol and safety net: "If we get rid of the reference desk, we are telling our patrons in a very dramatic way that reference is not important, nor are librarians. If anyone can sit at a desk and answer any type of question, then really why do we need librarians?"

Based on the strong reactions in the survey, the task force knew it would need to communicate openly and regularly about the work of assessing reference services, and that we would need clear and unquestionable data about what was—and was not—going on at the Seattle campus reference desks, in order to begin to break down strong staff resistance to changing what so many saw as an essential service and a cornerstone of their professional identity.

CAPTURING QUESTION DATA

Statistics at the UW Libraries mirrored national trends: over the last decade, there was a steep drop-off in the number of reference queries, even with the exponential growth of e-mail and chat reference services factored in.[15] Meanwhile, anecdotal evidence suggested that "ready reference" inquiries, now easily answered by readily available online sources, were less frequent, while the proportion of questions requiring construction of an answer or counseling on a search strategy had increased. The UW Libraries had tried variations on the traditional staffed reference desk model by experimenting with roving reference, on-call reference, and various configurations of e-mail and chat reference services; co-locating reference service points with circulation desks or with campus IT help desks; and holding office hours in academic departments. Some of these experiments had been abandoned, but a number had taken hold. However, many of these services were offered *in addition to* physical reference desks rather than as alternatives, with the effect of placing yet more time demands on subject-liaison librarians, who were also increasingly drawn into teaching and outreach efforts. The Seattle campus employs a liaison model of librarianship; subject librarians serve their academic departments with reference services, teaching and learning partnerships, outreach and marketing, and guidance on other relevant issues, such as scholarly communication. The charge of the task force made clear that the most pressing question was whether it was an effective use of the libraries' most specialized personnel to staff a general walk-up reference desk. Unwilling to rely on anecdotal evidence, the task force sought an assessment method that would not simply count but also document the complexity of reference questions.

Although the UW Libraries collects user query statistics at all service points during four one-week sampling periods each year, this existing data was not sufficiently granular, since it merely *counted* reference questions [16] and gave no other context. The task force wanted data documenting the range and type of questions received at the Suzzallo, Odegaard, and Engineering reference desks, and in discerning whether there were consistent patterns in the times of the day and time of the academic quarter when types of questions clustered—information not available in UW Libraries' statistical samples.

Since the libraries already used Compendium Library Services' Desk Tracker, a cloud-based subscription statistical system, to track not just user queries but also instruction sessions and some research consultations, the task force chose Desk Tracker to collect data on every question received at the three reference desks for an entire eleven-week academic quarter. A simple Desk Tracker form used quick-pick radio buttons to facilitate quick recording (figure 10.2).

While the task force's initial intention had been to develop a coding system based on the "Type of Question" and "Time Spent" categories of the question form, a continuing scan of professional literature turned up Dr. Bella Karr Gerlich's Reference Effort Assessment Data (READ) Scale. The READ Scale attempts to assess the effort, knowledge, and skill required to answer a reference question—information that has not been systematically recorded in other question-tallying methods. [17] The scale consists of six levels of effort, from 1 (least amount of effort, no specialized knowledge or skill required) to 6 (most time and effort expended, requiring substantial specialized knowledge and research). Coding reference questions received at UW Seattle's reference desks according to this scale would add a needed dimension to question data by including a judgment on the knowledge necessary to answer the majority of questions logged at the desks—and thus, perhaps, help to determine the optimal level of staffing needed at those desks.

The READ Scale is intended for use by individual librarians to record effort at the time questions are answered. Since the task force decided to use the READ Scale to code question data only after the Desk Tracker form had

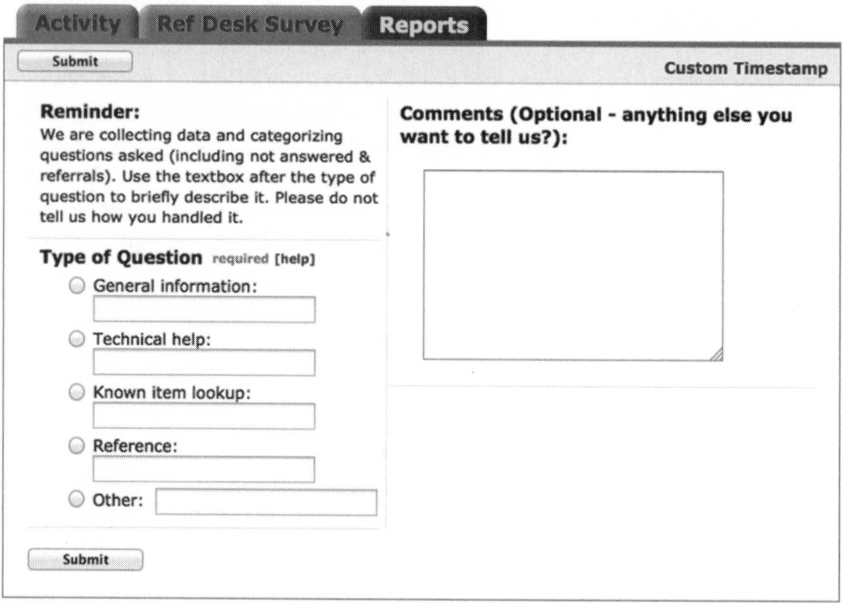
Activity | Ref Desk Survey | Reports

Submit

Custom Timestamp

Reminder:
We are collecting data and categorizing questions asked (including not answered & referrals). Use the textbox after the type of question to briefly describe it. Please do not tell us how you handled it.

Type of Question required [help]

- General information:
- Technical help:
- Known item lookup:
- Reference:
- Other:

Comments (Optional - anything else you want to tell us?):

Submit

Figure 10.2. Form for recording questions at the reference desks

been in use for several weeks, it was decided to test whether it could be applied by one coder to analyze transactions after the fact. A graduate student assistant with data-analysis experience was assigned to the task. With guidance from the task force, she developed a detailed coding system defining sample questions for the form's five categories and then mapped those examples to READ Scale code ranges. To test the consistency of the coding guidelines, the data coder consulted with a task force member on a representative sample of twenty-five questions.

Because the initial question data from spring 2011 applied READ Scale codes in this manner, for comparative purposes the task force repeated the study for another eleven weeks during fall 2011 quarter, once again recording every question asked at the three reference desks. In fall, however, staff themselves were asked to assign READ codes to the questions as part of the recording process. Discrepancies in the spring and fall quarter data were expected because of the different coding methods; however, although more effort codes clustered in the lower nonreference (1–2) and fewer in the lower-level reference (3–4) categories during the fall quarter, the higher proportion of orientation-type questions from new students and the research rhythm of the academic year more than likely account for a significant proportion of this difference.

As in other studies applying the READ Scale at service points,[18] the majority of questions (over 70 percent) recorded during the two-quarter sampling period fell into the 1–2 categories of effort, while 27.5 percent of questions were in the lower 3–4 range of reference effort. Only a small fraction of questions fell into the 5–6 range, where subject librarians are most often necessary. While this pattern, illustrated in tables 10.1 and 10.2, held true for all three service points, the Suzzallo reference desk, as would be expected from UW's flagship research library, recorded the highest overall number of questions (70 percent of the total questions) and also an overall higher number of questions in the 5–6 effort range. Suzzallo, however, also recorded slightly higher percentages of questions in the "nonreference" (1–2 range) categories, perhaps because the desk is located on the main floor of a complicated three-wing library building and, thus, patrons require considerable way-finding assistance.

Significantly, even during the heaviest traffic time of the quarters at UW Libraries' busiest reference desk, staff fielded an average of 8.5 total questions per hour, and only slightly more than one-third of those inquiries were reference questions, as opposed to directional, policy, or technology ones (figure 10.3).

APPLYING THE DATA

While it had been obvious for some time that the majority of questions asked at University of Washington Libraries' reference desks were not research-level questions, the very small proportion of inquiries requiring true expertise did come as a surprise. Although many reference staff had been skeptical of the task force's charge at the outset of the study, the question data gathered over two quarters began to convince staff that changes were necessary. The

Table 10.1. Question Percentages by READ Code, Spring 2011 (Rounded to Nearest 0.1 Percent)

	1	2	3	4	5	6	% of Total Questions
Engineering	43.4%	18.0%	29.3%	8.6%	0.6%	0.0%	**11.6%** (801)
Odegaard	42.7%	18.5%	28.4%	8.6%	1.7%	0.0%	**20.8%** (1,432)
Suzzallo	35.8%	28.4%	28.9%	6.3%	0.5%	0.0%	**67.5%** (4,647)
All Desks	**36.4%**	**26.5%**	**28.2%**	**7.6%**	**1.3%**	**0.0%**	**100%** (6,880)

Table 10.2. Question Percentages by READ Code, Fall 2011 (Rounded to Nearest 0.1 Percent)

	1	2	3	4	5	6	% of Total Questions
Engineering	47.0%	30.0%	16.2%	4.0%	1.8%	0.2%	12.5% (940)
Odegaard	46.4%	27.6%	15.9%	7.0%	2.9%	0.2%	15.3% (1,148)
Suzzallo	50.6%	29.0%	13.9%	5.0%	1.2%	0.2%	72.1% (5,409)
All Desks	**49.5%**	**28.9%**	**14.1%**	**5.2%**	**1.5%**	**0.2%**	**100%** (7,497)

READ Scale, contextualized by the actual questions themselves, provided a clear and true representation of desk activity. Armed with actual data and an archive of the questions asked rather than mere anecdote, the task force was equipped to argue for some different staffing models and approaches to reference services.

Engineering Library Reference Desk

Although the lowest number of reference questions was recorded at the Engineering Library, even questions at READ Scale levels 3 and 4 often require the use of specialized collections like standards, technical reports, and patent and trademark information. Thus, the engineering librarians judged that it was still important to maintain an active help presence. However, the question data collected over two quarters was used to justify merging the circulation desk and the reference desk into a single service point. Reference librarians and trained students from the UW Information School's Master of Library and Information Science (MLIS) program now work at a sit-down desk located behind the single service desk, where they are available to be called into transactions that require their expertise, but can otherwise concentrate on other liaison, committee, and managerial work.

Odegaard Undergraduate Library Reference Desk

In the Odegaard Library, the question statistics added support for a move that some had already been advocating. Even as the data was being analyzed, Odegaard was planning a major building renovation for the 2012–2013 budget year. Because the entire first floor of the three-story building would be closed during the renovation project, it was necessary to consolidate services located on the first floor into a central service point during construction. The

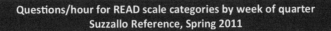

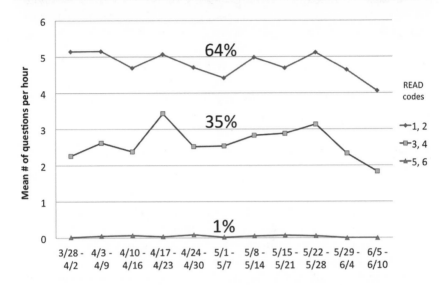

Figure 10.3. Questions per hour by week of quarter, Suzzallo Reference, spring 2011

reference desk, which had been co-located with the second-floor Learning Commons help desk run by UW's Information Technology department, closed to make room for the information desk, formerly located on the first floor. Odegaard's reference librarians spent a transitional year holding "office hours" in a second-floor room, where question statistics dropped dramatically, but most of the questions fielded actually required research resources.

When the renovation ended, Odegaard's research help service relocated to the prominent new Odegaard Writing and Research Center (OWRC) space on the first floor. The reference question data and the upcoming renovation were the perfect chance to change the service model to one of closer collaboration with a writing center that had formerly been run on a shoestring in an out-of-the-way third-floor room of the library building.

The OWRC functions primarily by appointment, although walk-in writing and research help are offered on an as-available basis. The research help service is staffed by seven librarians and four graduate assistants. Odegaard's subject librarians (who handle many of the social science disciplines for the UW Seattle campus) advertise their assigned OWRC research help hours as "office hours" on their subject pages. While the collaboration between library and writing center is not an original idea[19] and both departments are still feeling the way toward wholehearted partnership, it is the hope to expand the scope of research services by cross-training peer writing tutors to engage in a sort of "viral reference." This plan makes sense when one considers the lopsided numbers—there are now seventy-five student peer tutors who offer writing experience in dozens of disciplines and the librarians anticipate doubling last year's 11,751 tutoring sessions in the coming academic year—far more than the reference staff could manage alone.[20] The same Desk Tracker form the task force devised for collecting READ Scale statistics is currently being used in the OWRC to gather comparative data in order to assess the impact of the new service model on the nature of the research help interactions taking place there.

Suzzallo Reference Desk

The Suzzallo-Allen Libraries comprise a labyrinthine maze of collections and spaces, spanning three buildings and five floors. Due to the confusing nature of the buildings and the quantity of questions received at the reference desk, librarians concluded that a desk must be maintained precisely where it is currently located—in the middle of the complex, nearest the elevators, central staircase, computers, printers, and reference collection. Because Suzzallo logged thousands of reference-level questions during the sampling period, it was decided that the desk should be staffed full time by trained reference personnel: a mix of librarians, staff, and graduate MLIS students. However, the question data initiated a shift in Suzzallo's staffing model; formerly staffed primarily by librarians, the desk is now chiefly staffed by paraprofessional staff and trained graduate students.

Two years after this shift, one big obstacle still stands in the way of its complete success: fall quarter. Graduate student appointments begin at the start of the quarter, and thus new hires are at the beginning of their training during this crucial time and therefore are not yet competent to staff the desk alone. Until the training of new graduate student specialists is completed every fall, librarians are required to work more hours than envisioned to cover desk hours and to staff weekend shifts. However, the Suzzallo Reference and Research Services division regards itself as analogous to a "teaching hospital" for library school students. While the mentoring and training shown these future librarians benefits the division in subsequent quarters as they assume more hours on the desk, on chat reference, and in the classroom, it is also in service to them and to the profession and thus an appropriate use of librarians' time and expertise. Therefore, fall quarter requires the division to use a slightly different staffing model, even though consequently librarians have less time for outreach activities when the reference and instruction load is at its peak.

CHARTING FUTURE DIRECTIONS

As user needs and habits change, the UW Libraries will conduct further assessments of reference services and staffing models, continuing to take occasional quarter-long snapshots of questions coded with the READ Scale to compare that question data against the 2011 benchmark. Further, the task force recommended that the libraries conduct a similar study of other reference services, notably chat and e-mail reference, which in 2011 accounted for over 20 percent of total reference traffic. Since these services were excluded from the initial study of the UW Seattle's physical reference desks, using the READ Scale to once again answer the question, "Is this the most effective use of librarians' time?," is a natural extension of work already begun.

At UW Libraries, the reference service paradigm is in the process of shifting from the sacred tradition of librarians staffing a desk "just in case" to striving toward more intentional and profound collaborations with faculty, students, and student support services. However, the manner in which we now do so attempts to conserve librarians' skills for use where they are truly necessary. In making this change, we had to push past subjective impressions by gathering and assessing the data necessary to check those impressions; and then apply solutions while mindful that local climate and user needs dictate individual, rather than cookie-cutter, solutions.

University of Washington Libraries still remains dedicated to providing face-to-face, on-demand research help, especially since brand-new data indicates that students who consult with a librarian report greater ability to find needed information, complete course work, and achieve academic success.[21] In realizing that such valuable consultation with librarians did not have to take place at the reference desk, we have begun at last to "separate the service from the symbol."[22]

NOTES

The authors gratefully acknowledge the contributions of the other members of the UW Libraries Reference Desk Services Task Force: Grace Chung, Julie Cook, Nancy Huling (chair), Terry Jankowski, Lisa Oberg, and Margarete Walden.

1. University of Washington Libraries, "Libraries Fact Sheet," accessed October 10, 2013, www.lib.washington.edu/assessment/stats/facts.

2. University of Washington Libraries, *2010 Triennial Survey Report to Libraries Council*, 2010, accessed October 10, 2013, https://digital.lib.washington.edu/dspace/handle/1773/19833; UW Libraries, "Triennial Survey," accessed October 10, 2013, www.lib.washington.edu/assessment/surveys/triennial.

3. UW Libraries, "Libraries Fact Sheet."

4. Irene M. Lubker et al., "Refocusing Reference Services outside the Library Building," *Medical Reference Services Quarterly* 29 (2010): 218–28.

5. Jeffrey W. St. Clair, Rao Aluri, and Maureen Pastine, "Staffing the Reference Desk: Professionals or Nonprofessionals?," *Journal of Academic Librarianship* 3, no. 3 (July 1977): 149–53.

6. Scott Carlson, "Are Reference Desks Dying Out?," *The Reference Librarian* 48 (June 2007): 28; Bella Karr Gerlich and Edward Whatley, "Using the READ Scale for Staffing Strategies," *Library Leadership & Management* 23, no. 1 (January 2009): 26–30.

7. Marianne Stowell Bracke et al., "Finding Information in a New Landscape," *College & Research Libraries* 68, no. 3 (May 2007): 248–67.

8. Marianne Ryan and Julie Garrison, "What Do We Do Now?," *Reference & User Services Quarterly* 51, no. 1 (Fall 2011): 12–14; Caroline Cason Barratt, Phoebe Acheson, and Emily Luken, "Reference Models in the Electronic Library," *Reference Services Review* 38 (2010): 44–56; Susan Miller and Nancy Murillo, "Why Don't Students Ask Librarians for Help?," in *College Libraries and Student Culture*, ed. Lynda M. Duke and Andrew D. Asher (Chicago: ALA Editions, 2011), 49–70; Bracke et al., "Finding Information."

9. Sarah Watstein and Steven J. Bell, "Is There a Future for the Reference Desk?," *The Reference Librarian* 49, no. 1 (2008): 1–20; Eric Novotny, *Assessing Reference and User Services in a Digital Age* (Binghamton, NY: Haworth Information Press, 2006); Christy R. Stevens, "Reference Reviewed and Re-envisioned," *Journal of Academic Librarianship* 39, no. 2 (March 2013): 202–14.

10. Martha Kyrillidou, "Research Library Trends," *Research Library Issues*, no. 280 (September 2012): 20–27.

11. Nancy Fried Foster and Susan Gibbons, *Studying Students* (Chicago: Association of College and Research Libraries, 2007); Andrew D. Asher, Lynda M. Duke, and David Green, "Ethnographic Research in Illinois Academic Libraries," in *College Libraries and Student Culture*, 1–14 (Chicago: ALA Editions, 2011); Alison J. Head and Mike Eisenberg, *Lessons Learned: How College Students Seek Information in the Digital Age* (Seattle: Information School, University of Washington, 2009).

12. Lynda M. Duke, "Transformative Changes in Thinking, Services, and Programs," in *College Libraries and Student Culture*, 145–47 (Chicago: ALA Editions, 2011); Sara Davidson and Susan Mikkelsen, "Desk Bound No More," *The Reference Librarian* 50 (2009): 346–55; Jerry D. Campbell, "Clinging to Traditional Reference Services," *Reference & User Services Quarterly* 39, no. 3 (2000): 223–27.

13. Stephanie J. Schulte, "Eliminating Traditional Reference Services in an Academic Health Sciences Library: A Case Study," *Journal of the Medical Library Association* 99, no. 4 (October 2011): 273–79.

14. Watstein and Bell, "Is There a Future?"

15. UW Libraries, "Selected Library Statistics by Campus," accessed October 10, 2013, www.lib.washington.edu/assessment/stats/default; UW Libraries, "Libraries Fact Sheet." Over five years, recorded queries dropped by 50 percent.

16. UW Libraries uses the ARL definition of a reference question: "An information contact that involves the knowledge, use, recommendations, interpretation, or instruction in the use of one or more information sources by a member of the library staff." Queries that do not fit this definition are recorded as "nonreference."

17. Bella Karr Gerlich and G. Lynn Berard, "Testing the Viability of the READ Scale," *College & Research Libraries* 71, no. 2 (2010): 116–37.

18. Gerlich and Berard, "Testing the Viability;" Gerlich and Whatley, "Using the READ Scale for Staffing Strategies."

19. See, for example, James K Elmborg and Sheril Hook, *Centers for Learning* (Chicago: Association of College and Research Libraries, 2005); Elise Ferer, "Working Together," *Reference Services Review* 40, no. 4 (2012): 543–57.

20. Odegaard Writing and Research Center, *2012–2013 Annual Report*, July 2013.

21. Steve Hiller, "University of Washington Libraries Triennial Survey 2013: UWS Undergrads' Consultation with a Librarian and Abilities," unpublished graph, September 2013.

22. Steven J. Bell, "Who Needs a Reference Desk?," *Library Issues: Briefings for Faculty and Administrators* 27, no. 6 (2007): 5.

BIBLIOGRAPHY

Asher, Andrew D., Lynda M. Duke, and David Green. "Ethnographic Research in Illinois Academic Libraries: The ERIAL Project." In *College Libraries and Student Culture: What We Now Know*, 1–14. Chicago: ALA Editions, 2011.

Barratt, Caroline Cason, Phoebe Acheson, and Emily Luken. "Reference Models in the Electronic Library: The Miller Learning Center at the University of Georgia." *Reference Services Review* 38 (2010): 44–56.

Bell, Steven J. "Who Needs a Reference Desk." *Library Issues: Briefings for Faculty and Administrators* 27, no. 6 (2007): 1–4.

Bracke, Marianne Stowell, Michael Brewer, Robyn Huff-Eibl, Daniel R. Lee, Robert Mitchell, and Michael Ray. "Finding Information in a New Landscape: Developing New Service and Staffing Models for Mediated Information Services." *College & Research Libraries* 68, no. 3 (May 2007): 248–67.

Campbell, Jerry D. "Clinging to Traditional Reference Services: An Open Invitation to Libref.com." *Reference & User Services Quarterly* 39, no. 3 (2000): 223–27.

Carlson, Scott. "Are Reference Desks Dying Out?," *The Reference Librarian* 48 (June 2007): 25–30.

Davidson, Sara, and Susan Mikkelsen. "Desk Bound No More: Reference Services at a New Research University Library." *The Reference Librarian* 50 (October 5, 2009): 346–55.

Duke, Lynda M. "Transformative Changes in Thinking, Services, and Programs." In *College Libraries and Student Culture: What We Now Know*, 143–60. Chicago: ALA Editions, 2011.

Elmborg, James K., and Sheril Hook. *Centers for Learning: Writing Centers and Libraries in Collaboration*. Chicago: Association of College and Research Libraries, 2005.

Ferer, Elise. "Working Together: Library and Writing Center Collaboration." *Reference Services Review* 40, no. 4 (2012): 543–57.

Foster, Nancy Fried, and Susan Gibbons. *Studying Students: The Undergraduate Research Project at the University of Rochester*. Chicago: Association of College and Research Libraries, 2007.

Gerlich, Bella Karr, and Edward Whatley. "Using the READ Scale for Staffing Strategies: The Georgia College and State University Experience." *Library Leadership & Management* 23, no. 1 (January 2009): 26–30.

Gerlich, Bella Karr, and G. Lynn Berard. "Testing the Viability of the READ Scale (Reference Effort Assessment Data)©: Qualitative Statistics for Academic Reference Services." *College & Research Libraries* 71, no. 2 (March 1, 2010): 116–37.

Head, Alison J., and Mike Eisenberg. *Lessons Learned: How College Students Seek Information in the Digital Age*. Seattle: Information School, University of Washington, 2009.

Hiller, Steve. "University of Washington Libraries Triennial Survey 2013: UWS Undergrads' Consultation with a Librarian and Abilities." Unpublished graph, September 2013.

Kyrillidou, Martha. "Research Library Trends: A Historical Picture of Services, Resources, and Spending." *Research Library Issues*, no. 280 (September 2012): 20–27.

Lubker, Irene M., Margaret E. Henderson, Catharine S. Canevari, and Barbara A. Wright. "Refocusing Reference Services Outside the Library Building: One Library's Experience." *Medical Reference Services Quarterly* 29 (July 28, 2010): 218–28.

Miller, Susan, and Nancy Murillo. "Why Don't Students Ask Librarians for Help? Undergraduate Help-Seeking Behavior in Three Academic Libraries." In *College Libraries and Student Culture: What We Now Know*, edited by Lynda M. Duke and Andrew D. Asher, 49–70. Chicago: ALA Editions, 2011.

Novotny, Eric. *Assessing Reference and User Services in a Digital Age*. Binghamton, NY: Haworth Information Press, 2006.

Odegaard Writing and Research Center. *2012–2013 Annual Report*. July, 2013.

Ryan, Marianne, and Julie Garrison. "What Do We Do Now?: A Case for Abandoning Yesterday and Making the Future." *Reference & User Services Quarterly* 51, no. 1 (Fall 2011): 12–14.

Schulte, Stephanie J. "Eliminating Traditional Reference Services in an Academic Health Sciences Library: A Case Study." *Journal of the Medical Library Association* 99, no. 4 (October 2011): 273–79.

St. Clair, Jeffrey W., Rao Aluri, and Maureen Pastine. "Staffing the Reference Desk: Professionals or Nonprofessionals?" *Journal of Academic Librarianship* 3, no. 3 (July 1977): 149–53.

Stevens, Christy R. "Reference Reviewed and Re-envisioned: Revamping Librarian and Desk-Centric Services with LibStARs and LibAnswers." *Journal of Academic Librarianship* 39, no. 2 (March 2013): 202–14.

University of Washington Libraries. *2010 Triennial Survey Report to Libraries Council.* 2010. Accessed October 10, 2013. https://digital.lib.washington.edu/dspace/handle/1773/19833.

——. "Libraries Fact Sheet." Accessed October 10, 2013. www.lib.washington.edu/assessment/stats/facts.

——. "Selected Library Statistics by Campus." Accessed October 10, 2013. www.lib.washington.edu/assessment/stats/default.

——. "Triennial Survey." Accessed October 10, 2013. www.lib.washington.edu/assessment/surveys/triennial.

Watstein, Sarah, and Steven J. Bell. "Is There a Future for the Reference Desk? A Point-Counterpoint Discussion." *The Reference Librarian* 49, no. 1 (2008): 1–20.

Part V

Professional Competencies: Skills for a New Generation

Chapter Eleven

From Ready Reference to Research Conversations

The Role of Instruction in Academic Reference Service

Melanie Maksin

In the twentieth-century academic library, visitors to the reference desk were typically greeted by a generalist reference librarian and rows of "ready reference" titles: dictionaries, encyclopedias, and other useful volumes that presented *facts*. In today's academic library, when patrons arrive at the reference desk (if the library still has a reference desk) they might encounter a subject-specialist librarian, a paraprofessional, or a trained student employee. They might even bypass the library altogether, in favor of sending a research query by e-mail or conducting an online chat with a librarian. In the twenty-first-century academic library, where print encyclopedias gather dust, patrons seldom ask librarians for facts; they've already skimmed a relevant *Wikipedia* article for those.[1]

In many academic libraries, the ready reference paradigm is being replaced by what can be thought of as "research conversations." Research conversations can complement and reinforce information-literacy instruction, or even provide this instruction in the absence of course-integrated workshops or a programmatic approach to information literacy. Rather than facing each other across the reference desk, the librarian and the patron might work side by side, at the desk or elsewhere, to uncover relevant resources and collections, talk through thorny research queries, and evaluate sources. Reference services might encompass everything from support for citation management and plagiarism prevention to assistance with technological tools that allow researchers to create and disseminate scholarship. Unlike ready reference transactions, in which a librarian delivers facts and sources to the patron, research conversations are an exchange between librarian and patron, with the librarian providing personalized, in-depth instruction in sources and strategies while honoring the knowledge, experience, and learning preferences of the patron. Reference interactions are changing, and librarians must hone the skills required to meet patrons' evolving needs.

This chapter first considers instructional reference through the lens of historical and contemporary debates about the purpose and praxis of academic reference services. The move toward research conversations is situated within developments in library instruction and trends in higher education more broadly. Finally, a rationale for the interweaving of reference and instruction is paired with recommendations for one-on-one approaches to research conversations and suggestions for building an instructional reference program at the institutional level.

INFORMATION VERSUS INSTRUCTION: ONE OF LIBRARIANSHIP'S GREAT DEBATES

The proposal that reference service might fulfill or advance an instructional imperative is not a neutral one. The professional literature reveals a long history of debates about the appropriateness of blending instruction with reference service, even in academic libraries. In these debates, reference service is conceived as either a vehicle for the delivery of information or a venue for instruction in resources and research skills. Although the information-delivery model is adequate for ready reference interactions, instructional reference holds many possibilities for the in-depth research consultations that are increasingly prevalent in academic libraries.

In the information-versus-instruction dispute, differing conceptions of professional praxis emerge. Among those who argue that instruction is a vital component of reference service, Samuel S. Green's 1876 article, "Personal Relations Between Librarians and Readers," is a touchstone.[2] David Tyckoson notes that this is the first published essay that provides a framework for reference service—and that Green's framework emphasizes both the instructional and interpersonal dimensions of reference.[3] Proponents of the idea that reference is primarily information delivery look to Anita Schiller's forceful articulation, in 1965, of the ways in which information and instruction are "opposing and often inimical views" that, "when incorporated within reference service, often reduce overall effectiveness of this service."[4] Later theories of reference suggest that there are distinct levels of service that librarians might offer patrons, often described as conservative, moderate, or liberal[5] (or minimum, middling, and maximum[6]). At the conservative/minimum end of the spectrum, usually favored in academic or school libraries, the librarian focuses on instructing the patron to answer his/her own query, while at the liberal/maximum end, preferred in special libraries, the librarian performs the search and delivers information to the patron.[7]

Questions of professional training and identity also factor into the debate about the function of reference service. Are librarians teachers? Frances L. Hopkins argues that the bibliographic scholars of the late nineteenth and early twentieth centuries were intimately connected to academic disciplines, and thus better equipped to offer instruction in library research; although graduates of "the clerically oriented library schools" were suited to the "ad hoc information service" at the reference desk, they lacked "the competence or status to teach research methods."[8] Other authors, like Hannelore B. Rader, regard the full suite of services that reference librarians provide—not just their work at the desk, but the tours they lead, the development of guides and pathfinders, their evaluation of how library spaces are used, and so on— as part of the teaching function of reference, because all of these activities require assessment of users' needs and a familiarity with teaching methodologies and learning styles.[9] For tenure-track academic librarians, reference service is often considered teaching, even if, as Denise D. Green and Janis K. Peach show, reference is "an under-documented teaching activity" that is challenging to assess in terms of teaching and student learning.[10]

Whether or not librarians are seen as or identify with teachers, some assert that by privileging instruction over information, librarians have "minimized their role as trained professionals."[11] In this view, librarians should mediate "between the individual and the frightening amount of information out there," and reference service that "inflict[s] instruction on those who don't want it" is irresponsible and "no way to earn respect."[12] While some have claimed that creating self-sufficient researchers will be the end of reference as we know it,[13] others maintain that the only way to keep up is to reenvision our professional identity and make the work of reference librarians relevant to the contemporary academic community. James K. Elmborg, in his 2002 article that proposes a true pedagogy of reference, calls on reference librarians "to oppose vigorously the notion that power and professionalism depend on maintaining special skills that librarians withhold from patrons or students."[14] For Elmborg, information delivery and fact-finding are secondary to "impart[ing] our knowledge and competence to our students," because "in educational institutions, the way to be seen as a professional is to teach."[15] This echoes earlier scholars who believed that the academic library must become a "teaching library"—more than "a support service," but an organization "which is itself actively and directly involved in implementing the mission of higher education."[16] The teaching library and the teaching librarian offer alternatives to the notion of the librarian as gatekeeper to information.

The clash between the informational and instructional models of reference service is also seen in differing views of the desired outcomes for reference interactions. Some authors begin with the premise that the ideal end result of a reference question is a correct answer[17] or maintain that integrating instruction and reference is like "teaching students how to be librarians," whether they want to be or not.[18] Jim Rettig suggests that reference service must be flexible enough to accommodate "dependence when individuals are not comfortable with independence" while allowing patrons the opportunity for in-depth instruction, if they desire it.[19] Other authors maintain that empowerment is the ultimate goal, and that this outcome is not at the expense of high-quality service; as Elmborg writes, answering a student's question "without teaching the student how we answered it or why we answered it as we did" leads to "a dependence in that student that undermines rather than strengthens the learning process."[20]

THE RISE OF INFORMATION LITERACY AND IMPLICATIONS FOR ACADEMIC REFERENCE

As generations of practitioners debated the future of reference services and the role, if any, that instruction should play in such a vision, information literacy came into its own. In 2000, the Association of College and Research Libraries (ACRL) adopted the *Information Literacy Competency Standards for Higher Education*. These standards, undergoing revision at the time of this writing, have provided a framework by which librarians, faculty, and even accrediting agencies like the Middle States Commission on Higher Education can assess student learning.[21] Although information literacy is often rebranded for specific institutional contexts, commitment to research education for patrons is widespread in academic libraries. At some institutions, information literacy is thoroughly embedded into the curriculum, with for-credit, semester-long courses, often taught by a librarian with faculty status. Elsewhere, information literacy isn't a stand alone course, but woven systematically throughout the library's instructional offerings, through mandatory sessions in a required course or scaffolded instruction within a discipline or established curricular sequence. Even at institutions without a formalized information literacy program, instruction librarians might incorporate information literacy concepts, including how to evaluate sources and reflect critically on the context in which information is produced, into one-shot sessions. This activity related to instruction and information literacy drives several important trends in academic reference services.

While traditional reference desks have seen declining numbers of transactions, some argue that the questions that do come to the desk, or to related services like chat reference, are more complex. One explanation for greater sophistication in reference questions, put forth by Steven Deineh, Julie Middlemas, and Patricia Morrison, is that patrons, with the vast Internet available to them, arrive at the library having already explored a topic, and maybe even having identified potential sources, before turning to the library "when they are truly stumped."[22] Another explanation is that the greater emphasis on library instruction, whether it occurs in a programmatic way across the curriculum or only reaches certain courses and students, generates higher demand for in-depth research assistance. Gerald Burke, Carol Anne Germain, and Xu Lijuan found that as instruction increases, so do substantive reference interactions; even when "students come away from [information literacy] courses empowered, they will still seek additional assistance from reference librarians" to build on and synthesize what they've learned in the classroom.[23] Students' expectations of reference services are informed by their exposure to library instruction and by their own experiences as researchers.

The centrality of instruction in academic libraries is not just reflected in reference interactions, but in changing job descriptions as well. Numerous studies of job advertisements have shown that the number of academic reference librarian positions that include instruction rose steadily throughout the last decades of the twentieth century. For example, Beverly P. Lynch and Kimberley Robles Smith analyzed 220 job advertisements published in *College & Research Libraries News* between 1973 and 1998 and determined that, while no ads in 1973 highlighted instruction as a responsibility for a reference librarian, by the 1990s, all of the reference postings mentioned instruction.[24] This is still the case in the twenty-first century; indeed, it is challenging to find an academic reference librarian position that does not feature instruction as an essential duty. The prevalence of instruction in reference librarian job descriptions also aligns with Laura Saunders's recent survey of employers and current reference librarians, in which more than 90 percent of survey participants identified "comfort with instruction" as one of the top five competencies for reference librarians.[25]

As more reference librarians take on instructional responsibilities, and as information-literacy education reaches more students, the already-hazy line between reference and instruction in academic libraries continues to blur.

PARALLELS TO HIGHER EDUCATION

The growing emphasis on instruction and information literacy in academic libraries is not the only factor that influences the changing landscape of reference service. Academic libraries must keep pace with and further the missions of their institutions in order to remain relevant. Therefore, changes in academic library services, including the move toward more in-depth, personalized, instructive reference assistance, should be considered within the context of pedagogical and cultural trends in higher education more broadly.

The study of teaching and learning is undergoing a renaissance. Many institutions have created centers for teaching and learning to assist faculty with the development of student-centered teaching practices and to encourage the crossing of disciplinary boundaries to explore new pedagogies. While these centers might have different organizational structures or go by different names, the types of programming and support provided to faculty are often similar, and resemble Ken Bain's proposal in *What the Best College Teachers Do*:

> Colleges and universities can establish departments or institutes that study and advance university learning, academic entities whose faculty spend their time researching educational issues, thinking about their implications for the university educational enterprise, and helping their colleagues in other departments realize and benefit from the meaning of those studies.[26]

At the heart of this renewed energy around teaching and learning is constructivist pedagogy. In constructivist thought, learners are not passive recipients of information, but active participants who construct their own meaning by building on prior knowledge, interacting with other learners and social groups, and engaging in meaningful learning activities. Constructivist teaching in action, as Alison King explains, consists of "the professor, instead of being the 'sage on the stage,' [functioning] as a 'guide on the side,' facilitating learning in less directive ways."[27] The constructivist classroom, according to Bain, is a "natural critical learning environment," in which students are called to "[confront] intriguing, beautiful, or important problems" through "authentic tasks that will challenge them to grapple with ideas, rethink their assumptions, and examine their mental models of reality."[28] The constructivist methods used by teaching faculty vary, but might include opportunities for hands-on or problem-based learning or assignments that have real-world applications. Some instructors have found that flipping the classroom—usually by sharing video lectures that students watch outside of class—allows students more time and space to interact with both the teacher and their peers. Constructivist methods are concerned with the ways in which individual learners come to understand and construct knowledge, rather than how facts are transmitted from teacher to student.

Concurrent with these developments in the classroom, many institutions have placed greater emphasis on the "student experience." Writing centers, peer tutoring, wellness initiatives, and other campus services provide support for students' intellectual, social, and emotional development. Increased awareness of and sensitivity to disparities among incoming students have led to efforts to address gaps in college preparedness through summer programs and mentoring. Even as technology becomes ever more embedded in students' daily lives, and despite the rise of distance learning and new educational offerings like Massive Open Online Courses (MOOCs) that resemble a vast lecture hall, students continue to value and expect high-touch, personalized services and support.

Academic libraries have responded to these pedagogical and cultural shifts in a variety of ways. At some institutions, librarians have made inroads with teaching and learning centers, or have collaborated with teaching faculty to create assignments that inspire the innovative use of library resources while encouraging the development of real-world research skills. Libraries often seek partnerships with writing centers and other offices around campus to develop student-centered services that support students' individual growth.[29] Alongside these collaborations, a vision of reference services that embraces instruction—and the personalization, constructivism, and active learning that students have come to experience in the classroom—can make students' use of the library less anomalous and more consonant with the rest of their academic lives.

RESEARCH CONVERSATIONS: ONE-ON-ONE APPROACHES

A model for reference services that is focused on student learning, not solely on the delivery of answers, dovetails with the growing emphasis on instruction in academic libraries and with salient trends in higher education.

Research conversations that embrace the instructional potential of reference can reinforce library instruction and serve as "a venue for guided practice" in research methods.[30] This is particularly true when library instruction is intended to "[address] an increasingly diverse body of students in the classroom," as Hua Yi notes, because personalized follow-up consultations build on classroom learning while concentrating on the individual student's needs and any gaps or questions he/she might have.[31] Additionally, even the most robust instructional programs are not without limitations. Library instruction rarely reaches every student; plus, some information-literacy programs focus on particular points in the curriculum (e.g., introductory-level courses or senior capstone projects), without offering instruction at all levels. When library instruction is available, it is not always delivered at the point of need. Furthermore, research is messy, iterative, and idiosyncratic, and a one-size-fits-most one-shot session can only scratch the surface of these challenges.

Research conversations also reinforce students' experiences with constructivist learning and personalized attention outside the library, and can situate the academic library as a partner in broader institutional goals related to student learning. Elmborg asserts that "the reference desk is perhaps the most natural constructivist teaching environment" in academia, as it is "a staging area from which to launch into the multi-voiced, multi-genred array of resources that can be used to create knowledge."[32] Constructivism in reference services encourages the patron to exercise greater agency and to set his or her own goals for learning, and emphasizes the development of transferable skills and new mental models of the research process.[33]

Not every reference interaction lends itself to a research conversation. But in the same way that the notion of the reference interview has given practitioners a model for understanding and framing patrons' information needs, a paradigm that blends reference service with instructional methods and outcomes can inspire new ways of engaging with researchers in academic libraries.

Look for Teachable Moments

A starting point for instructional reference is an awareness of "teachable moments," those contexts in which students are most receptive to synthesizing new information and pushing beyond familiar skills and habits. Because an individual consultation typically occurs at the student's point of need and is focused on a particular research question, the possibility of capturing a teachable moment is perhaps greater in this situation than in the more structured, less personalized environment of the library instruction session. As part of staff training in instructional reference, Susan Avery and David Ward recommend sharing "specific guidance for recognizing teachable moments during the course of a reference interview."[34]

Encourage an Active Partnership

The quest for the teachable moment doesn't require mind reading. Unlike the standard reference interview model, in which the librarian begins with the assumption that the patron requires professional assistance to clarify an information need, a research conversation starts with the premise that the patron and the librarian are equal partners. Before a scheduled consultation, the librarian might ask the patron preliminary questions about his/her research topic, either informally (e.g., by e-mail) or in a more structured way (e.g., an online questionnaire or survey). Knowing more about the patron's experiences and interests opens up the possibility of tying the consultation back to previous research endeavors and encouraging the patron to make connections between familiar resources and methods and his/her current research needs. The librarian might also ask an open-ended question about the patron's expectations for the consultation, as a way of teasing out what the researcher hopes to accomplish. Allowing the patron to shape and direct his or her own desired outcomes gives the patron more agency in the interaction, while also establishing the interaction as a potential site for student learning. Concerns that instructional reference seeks to produce mini-librarians can be put to rest if the patron is actively engaged in the reference process and given the opportunity to articulate his/her goals.

Be the Guide on the Side

During the research conversation itself, reference librarians can learn from King's "guide on the side" concept. Rather than using a reference interaction to perform one's professional prowess or to wield the ACRL *Information Literacy Standards* like a checklist, librarians can serve as research coaches[35] or mentors. Megan Oakleaf and Amy VanScoy have proposed strategies, based on theories of metacognition, constructivism and active learning, and social constructivism, for integrating instruction into digital reference that can also apply to in-person consultations. Their eight recommended methods work well for the guide on the side, as they "allow students to make decisions and take actions while librarians serve as guides who create connections, help students see patterns, ask relevant questions, and encourage reflection."[36] These techniques prompt students to exercise agency ("Catch Them Being Good," "Show, Don't Tell," "Chunk It Up," "Let Them Drive") while the librarian serves as a mentor for understanding confusing library jargon ("Share Secret Knowledge"), making the potential messiness of the research process more transparent ("Think Aloud"), and initiating students into new communities of practice ("Be the Welcome Wagon," "Make Introductions").

Don't Try to "Cover" Everything

Even when the librarian isn't physically the guide on the side, instructional materials can extend the research conversation beyond a one-time interaction. Tutorials, guides, videos, podcasts, FAQs, and other resources that students can access independently as a follow-up to a formal instruction session or as a take-away from a research consultation can be "an equal partner in teaching library use."[37] The creation and availability of well-crafted instructional materials can help librarians with good intentions shift away from the "'just-in-case' mindset" when meeting with patrons, allowing more time for personalized, relevant discussions of research issues.[38]

RESEARCH CONVERSATIONS: AN INSTITUTIONAL FRAMEWORK

In addition to the steps that individual librarians can take to merge instructional practices into their reference interactions, instructional reference services can be supported at the institutional level. The programmatic recommendations below might be implemented by an academic library's reference department or across an institution's library system.

Rethink Spaces and Services

Academic institutions of all sizes have reconfigured reference services and library spaces to adapt to changes in teaching, learning, and research. If the traditional reference desk setup isn't conducive to research conversations, other reference models might be a better fit. Some libraries have merged their reference and circulation desks to provide frontline service, or created dedicated consultation space for in-depth research interactions.[39] Elsewhere, students might schedule an appointment with a librarian or drop in during the librarian's office hours. Some successful research consultation services, like the model introduced at Oberlin College that combines scheduled office appointments with a walk-up reference desk for visibility, are driven by strong faculty support; as awareness of how these appointments can enhance student learning spreads, "more students learn about research appointments from faculty than any other source."[40] Similarly, the office hours idea, as Iris Jastram and Ann Zawistoski note, "resonate[s] with the most prevalent method of one-on-one academic assistance on a college or university campus—faculty office hours," and unlike brief encounters at a public desk or group instruction in the library classroom, office-hour consultations provide the necessary "time and space for researchers to grapple with pressing research needs, to increase their understanding of those needs, and to develop strategies for overcoming these and future research challenges."[41]

Support All Stages of the Research Process

Instructional reference doesn't just provide the opportunity to expand reference services beyond finding answers and presenting patrons with facts; it might even generate ideas for new types of research support unrelated to questions about bibliographic databases, search strategies, or other common reference queries. Because research conversations are largely directed by patrons' needs and desired learning outcomes, these interactions can be flexible enough to accommodate discussions of all stages of the research process. At many institutions, librarians already consult with patrons on technological tools, multimedia components for presentations, the data life cycle, citation management, and other services that support particular user populations' research questions and methods. If public services staff make note of these emerging trends, and directors ensure that staff have the necessary training to address these needs, the academic library can promote a fuller suite of services that are relevant to the current research landscape.

Communicate with Colleagues

Whether instructional reference is woven into an individual librarian's interactions with patrons or implemented as a set of strategies for an entire department or library, communication and ongoing training are essential. While there is overlap in some libraries between reference staff and those who provide library instruction, this is not always the case—and professional librarians are not necessarily the only frontline staff fielding complex questions from patrons. As Hannah Hauxwell notes, "Paraprofessionals often bridge the gap between formal information literacy teaching, such as induction sessions, and individual students' needs."[42] Because of the potential for these staff members "to offer tailored, relevant snippets of information literacy training within the day-to-day business of the library,"[43] fostering knowledge-sharing between these factions is critical to the success of an instructional reference program. Camille McCutcheon and Nancy M. Lambert propose that "all who teach at the reference desk should observe formal instruction sessions (if not teach them)," in order to build familiarity with instructional methods, information-literacy outcomes, and the curricula and assignments that drive students' research needs.[44] Libraries or departments might also create online repositories for instructional materials and make these collections available to all public services staff; these repositories can include instruction session outlines, handouts, and other resources that show what happens in the instruction classroom and how these skills and learning outcomes can be more intentionally connected to and reinforced by reference services.

CONCLUSION: BEYOND READY REFERENCE

Ultimately, research conversations are an alternative to both ready reference and the reference interview. In ready reference transactions and in the traditional concept of the reference interview, the librarian is the gatekeeper to information, who knows which volume to consult and which questions will lead the patron to a clearer articulation of his/her research need. Research conversations, on the other hand, allow the patron to guide the reference interaction. Whether implemented by an individual librarian or approached in a programmatic fashion by an entire department or library, the move toward research conversations reflects changes in information-seeking behaviors and shifts in higher education. Reference service with an instructional component also aligns the academic library more closely with the teaching and learning missions of many institutions of higher education, while providing students with a caliber of support that resonates with other aspects of their academic lives. Rows of once-essential encyclopedias might collect dust in the stacks, but academic libraries can still perform a vital service for their patrons by embracing the instructional possibilities of reference service.

NOTES

1. In their study of undergraduates' use of Wikipedia, Alison J. Head and Michael B. Eisenberg note that students who turn to Wikipedia often do so "in the very beginning of the research process as a precursor to a more in-depth investigation of a topic." See Alison J. Head and Michael B. Eisenberg, "How Today's College Students Use Wikipedia for Course-Related Research," *First Monday* 15, no. 3 (2010), http://firstmonday.org/ojs/index.php/fm/article/view/2830/2476.

2. Samuel S. Green, "Personal Relations Between Librarians and Readers," *Library Journal* 1, no. 2 (1876): 74–81.

3. David Tyckoson, "On the Desirableness of Personal Relations Between Librarians and Readers: The Past and Future of Reference Service," *Reference Services Review* 31, no. 1 (2003): 13, 14.

4. Anita R. Schiller, "Reference Service: Instruction or Information," *Library Quarterly* 35, no. 1 (1965): 53.

5. For definitions of conservative, moderate, and liberal levels of reference service, see James I. Wyer, *Reference Work* (Chicago: American Library Association, 1930).

6. Wyer's levels of reference service were re-envisioned by Samuel Rothstein as minimum/middling/maximum. See Samuel Rothstein, "Reference Service: The New Dimension in Librarianship," in *Reference Services*, ed. Arthur R. Rowland, 35–46 (Hamden, CT: Shoe String, 1964).

7. Hannelore B. Rader, "Reference Services as a Teaching Function," *Library Trends* 29, no. 1 (1980): 96.

8. Frances L. Hopkins, "A Century of Bibliographic Instruction: The Historical Claim to Professional and Academic Legitimacy," *College & Research Libraries* 43, no. 3 (1982): 196.

9. Rader, "Reference Services as a Teaching Function," 100.

10. Denise D. Green and Janis K. Peach, "Assessment of Reference Instruction as a Teaching and Learning Activity," *College & Research Libraries News* 64, no. 4 (2003): 257.

11. Schiller, "Reference Service," 57.

12. Bill Katz, "Long Live Old Reference Services and New Technologies," *Library Trends* 50, no. 2 (2001): 270.

13. C. P. Vincent, "Bibliographic Instruction and the Reference Desk: A Symbiotic Relationship," *Reference Librarian* 10 (Spring 1984): 41.

14. James K. Elmborg, "Teaching at the Desk: Toward a Reference Pedagogy," *portal: Libraries & the Academy* 2, no. 3 (2002): 463.

15. Ibid., 462.

16. Alan E. Guskin, Carla J. Stoffle, and Joseph A. Boissé, "The Academic Library as a Teaching Library: A New Role for the 1980s," *Library Trends* 28 (1979): 283.

17. The interest in accuracy is reflected in the "55 percent rule," a term coined by Peter Hernon and Charles R. McClure to reflect their findings that librarians only answer 50–60 percent of reference questions correctly. See Peter Hernon and Charles R. McClure, "Unobtrusive Reference Testing: The 55 Percent Rule," *Library Journal* 111 (1986): 37–41.

18. Vincent, "Bibliographic Instruction and the Reference Desk," 41.

19. Jim Rettig, "The Convergence of the Twain or Titanic Collision? BI and Reference in the 1990s Sea of Change," *Reference Services Review* 23, no. 1 (1995): 18.

20. Elmborg, "Teaching at the Desk," 459.

21. This standards-based approach to measuring students' research abilities is not without its limitations or critics, many of whom regard the concept of "literacy" and its inherent value judgments as problematic. See James K. Elmborg, "Critical Information Literacy: Implications for Instructional Practice," *Journal of Academic Librarianship* 32, no. 2 (2006): 192–99.

22. Steven Deineh, Julie Middlemas, and Patricia Morrison, "A New Service Model for the Reference Desk: The Student Research Center," *Library Philosophy and Practice* (e-journal), 2011, http://digitalcommons.unl.edu/libphilprac/554.

23. Gerald Burke, Carole Anne German, and Xu Lijuan, "Information Literacy: Bringing a Renaissance to Reference," *portal: Libraries & the Academy* 5, no. 3 (2005): 367.

24. Beverly P. Lynch and Kimberley Robles Smith, "The Changing Nature of Work in Academic Libraries," *College & Research Libraries* 62, no. 5 (2001): 415.

25. Laura Saunders, "Identifying Core Reference Competencies from an Employers' Perspective: Implications for Instruction," *College & Research Libraries* 73, no. 4 (2012): 399.

26. Ken Bain, *What the Best College Teachers Do* (Cambridge, MA: Harvard University Press, 2004), 176.

27. Alison King, "From Sage on the Stage to Guide on the Side," *College Teaching* 41, no. 1 (1993): 30.

28. Bain, *What the Best College Teachers Do*, 17.

29. Elise Ferer has identified many forms of collaboration between libraries and writing centers, including cross-training for staff, shared office hours, and workshops that support students throughout the research, writing, and revising processes. See Elise Ferer, "Working Together: Library and Writing Center Collaboration," *Reference Services Review* 40, no. 4 (2012): 543–57.

30. Gillian S. Gremmels and Karen Shostrom Lehmann, "Assessment of Student Learning from Reference Service," *College & Research Libraries News* 64, no. 4 (2003): 495.

31. Hua Yi, "Individual Consultation Service: An Important Part of an Information Literacy Program," *Reference Services Review* 31, no. 4 (2003): 346.

32. Elmborg, "Teaching at the Desk," 463.

33. For an exploration of constructivist methods in library instruction, see Susan E. Cooperstein and Elizabeth Kocevar-Weidinger, "Beyond Active Learning: A Constructivist Approach to Learning," *Reference Services Review* 32, no. 2 (2004): 141–48.

34. Susan Avery and David Ward, "Reference Is My Classroom: Setting Instruction Goals for Academic Library Reference Services," *Internet Reference Services Quarterly* 15, no. 1 (2010): 47.

35. The librarian-as-coach model is discussed by Melissa Moore, "What's in a Name?" *College & Research Libraries News* 74, no. 3 (2013): 152–53.

36. Megan Oakleaf and Amy VanScoy, "Instructional Strategies for Digital Reference," *Reference & User Services Quarterly* 49, no. 4 (2010): 383.

37. Susan E. Beck and Nancy B. Turner, "On the Fly BI: Reaching and Teaching from the Reference Desk," *Reference Librarian* 34, no. 72 (2001): 90.

38. Ibid.

39. Erin Meyer, Carrie Forbes, and Jennifer Bowers describe the research consultation space at the University of Denver's Penrose Library. See Erin Meyer, Carrie Forbes, and Jennifer Bowers, "The Research Center: Creating an Environment for Interactive Research Consultations," *Reference Services Review* 38, no. 1 (2010): 57–70.

40. Megan S. Mitchell, Cynthia H. Comer, Jennifer M. Starkey, and Eboni A. Francis, "Paradigm Shift in Reference Services at the Oberlin College Library: A Case Study," *Journal of Library Administration* 51, no. 4 (2011): 366.

41. Iris Jastram and Ann Zawistoski, "Personalizing the Library via Research Consultations," in *The Desk and Beyond: Next Generation Reference Services*, ed. Sarah K. Steiner and M. Leslie Madden (Chicago: Association of College and Research Libraries, 2008), 14.

42. Hannah Hauxwell, "Information Literacy at the Service Desk: The Role of Circulations Staff in Promoting Information Literacy," *Journal of Information Literacy* 2, no. 2 (2008).

43. Ibid.

44. Camille McCutcheon and Nancy M. Lambert, "Tales Untold: The Connection Between Instruction and Reference Services," *Research Strategies* 18, no. 3 (2001): 214.

BIBLIOGRAPHY

Avery, Susan, and David Ward. "Reference Is My Classroom: Setting Instructional Goals for Academic Library Reference Services." *Internet Reference Services Quarterly* 15, no. 1 (2010): 35–51.

Bain, Ken. *What the Best College Teachers Do*. Cambridge: Harvard University Press, 2004.

Beck, Susan E., and Nancy B. Turner. "On the Fly BI: Reaching and Teaching from the Reference Desk." *Reference Librarian* 34, no. 72 (2001): 83–96.

Burke, Gerald, Carol Anne Germain, and Xu Lijuan. "Information Literacy: Bringing a Renaissance to Reference." *portal: Libraries & the Academy* 5, no. 3 (2005): 353–70.

Cooperstein, Susan E., and Elizabeth Kocevar-Weidinger. "Beyond Active Learning: A Constructivist Approach to Learning." *Reference Services Review* 32, no. 2 (2004): 141–48.

Deineh, Steven, Julie Middlemas, and Patricia Morrison. "A New Service Model for the Reference Desk: The Student Research Center." *Library Philosophy and Practice* (e-journal), 2011, http://digitalcommons.unl.edu/libphilprac/554.

Elmborg, James K. "Critical Information Literacy: Implications for Instructional Practice." *The Journal of Academic Librarianship* 32, no. 2 (2006): 192–99.

———. "Teaching at the Desk: Toward a Reference Pedagogy." *portal: Libraries & the Academy* 2, no. 3 (2002): 455–64.

Ferer, Elise. "Working Together: Library and Writing Center Collaboration." *Reference Services Review* 40, no. 4 (2012): 543–57.

Green, Denise D., and Janis K. Peach. "Assessment of Reference Instruction as a Teaching and Learning Activity." *College & Research Libraries News* 64, no. 4 (2003): 256–58.

Green, Samuel S. "Personal Relations Between Librarians and Readers." *Library Journal* 1, no. 2 (1876): 74–81.

Gremmels, Gillian S., and Karen Shostrom Lehmann. "Assessment of Student Learning from Reference Service." *College & Research Libraries* 68, no. 6 (2007): 488–502.

Guskin, Alan E., Carla J. Stoffle, and Joseph A. Boissé. "The Academic Library as a Teaching Library: A Role for the 1980s." *Library Trends* 28 (1979): 281–96.

Hauxwell, Hannah. "Information Literacy at the Service Desk: The Role of Circulations Staff in Promoting Information Literacy." *Journal of Information Literacy* 2, no. 2 (2008): 86–93.

Head, Alison J., and Michael B. Eisenberg. "How Today's College Students Use Wikipedia for Course-Related Research." *First Monday* 15, no. 3 (2010), http://firstmonday.org/ojs/index.php/fm/article/view/2830/2476.

Hernon, Peter, and Charles R. McClure. "Unobtrusive Reference Testing: The 55 Percent Rule." *Library Journal* 111 (1986): 37–41.

Hopkins, Frances L. "A Century of Bibliographic Instruction: The Historical Claim to Professional and Academic Legitimacy." *College & Research Libraries* 43, no. 3 (1982): 192–98.

Jastram, Iris, and Ann Zawistoski. "Personalizing the Library Via Research Consultations." In *The Desk and Beyond: Next Generation Reference Services*, edited by Sarah K. Steiner and M. Leslie Madden, 14–24. Chicago: Association of College and Research Libraries, 2008.

Katz, Bill. "Long Live Old Reference Services and New Technologies." *Library Trends* 50, no. 2 (2001): 263–85.

King, Alison. "From Sage on the Stage to Guide on the Side." *College Teaching* 41, no. 1 (1993): 30–35.

Lynch, Beverly P., and Kimberley Robles Smith. "The Changing Nature of Work in Academic Libraries." *College & Research Libraries* 62, no. 5 (2001): 407–20.

McCutcheon, Camille, and Nancy M. Lambert. "Tales Untold: The Connection between Instruction and Reference Services." *Research Strategies* 18, no. 3 (2001): 203–14.

Meyer, Erin, Carrie Forbes, and Jennifer Bowers. "The Research Center: Creating an Environment for Interactive Research Consultations." *Reference Services Review* 38, no. 1 (2010): 57–70.

Mitchell, Megan S., Cynthia H. Comer, Jennifer M. Starkey, and Eboni A. Francis. "Paradigm Shift in Reference Services at the Oberlin College Library: A Case Study." *Journal of Library Administration* 51, no. 4 (2011): 359–74.

Moore, Melissa. "What's in a Name?" *College & Research Libraries News* 74, no. 3 (2013): 152–53.

Oakleaf, Megan, and Amy VanScoy. "Instructional Strategies for Digital Reference." *Reference & User Services Quarterly* 49, no. 4 (2010): 380–90.

Rader, Hannelore B. "Reference Services as a Teaching Function." *Library Trends* 29, no. 1 (1980): 95–103.

Rettig, Jim. "The Convergence of the Twain or Titanic Collision? BI and Reference in the 1990s Sea of Change." *Reference Services Review* 23, no. 1 (1995): 7–20.

Rothstein, Samuel. "Reference Service: The New Dimension in Librarianship." In *Reference Services*, edited by Arthur R. Rowland, 35–46. Hamden, CT: Shoe String, 1964.

Saunders, Laura. "Identifying Core Reference Competencies from an Employers' Perspective: Implications for Instruction." *College & Research Libraries* 73, no. 4 (2012): 390–404.

Schiller, Anita R. "Reference Service: Instruction or Information." *The Library Quarterly* 35, no. 1 (1965): 52–60.

Tyckoson, David. "On the Desirableness of Personal Relations Between Librarians and Readers: The Past and Future of Reference Service." *Reference Services Review* 31, no. 1 (2003): 12–16.

Vincent, C. P. "Bibliographic Instruction and the Reference Desk. A Symbiotic Relationship." *Reference Librarian*, no. 10 (Spring 1984): 39–47.

Wyer, James I. *Reference Work*. Chicago: American Library Association, 1930.

Yi, Hua. "Individual Research Consultation Service: An Important Part of an Information Literacy Program." *Reference Services Review* 31, no. 4 (2003): 342–50.

Chapter Twelve

Necessities of Librarianship

Competencies for a New Generation

Danielle Colbert-Lewis, Jamillah Scott-Branch, and David Rachlin

In 2009, the American Library Association (ALA) approved and adopted the *Core Competencies of Librarianship* as policy. These competencies define the "basic knowledge to be possessed by all persons graduating from an ALA-accredited master's program in library and information studies."[1] The *Core Competencies of Librarianship* allow prospective, new, and current librarians a way to gauge their knowledge and competency level within the profession. This chapter highlights the practical competencies involved in library reference. In 1965, Gordon Moore, co-founder of Intel Corporation, stated that "the number of transistors incorporated in a chip [microprocessor] will approximately double every 24 months."[2] This concept, known as Moore's Law, suggests that new technological advances occur quickly, causing people to try to keep pace with these changes, and this poses a challenge to librarians as they too must keep pace with new innovations.

In order to deliver the best services possible, reference librarians need to keep abreast of emerging technologies while also continuing to provide traditional library services. These new skills fall into the following areas: *core competencies*, the necessary skills required of librarians for professional and "hallmark effectiveness"; *technical competencies*, having experience with various technologies such as metadata, web development, and the ability to work and teach in a technology-rich environment; *professional competencies*, the abilities of librarians to engage in instruction, to develop collections and programs, to market the library, and to assess their services; *personal competencies*, the possession of abilities such as creativity, problem solving, reflection, public speaking, and transformative leadership.[3] This chapter explores the three competencies—technical, professional, and personal—in detail and will explain how these competencies allow librarians to function in the fast-paced and technologically saturated environments of today's libraries.

The core competencies constitute the heart and soul of librarianship as they often overlap with the personal, professional, and technical competencies. As mentioned previously, core competencies represent the necessary skills and hallmarks of effective librarianship.[4] Librarians demonstrate these competencies through their communication with users via customer service, instruction, knowledge of reference sources (including online sources), searching skills, and conducting reference interviews.[5]

Furthermore, the core competencies give a basic overview of the more detailed competencies explored in this chapter. In the *Professional Competencies for Reference and User Services Librarians*, the Reference and User Services Association (RUSA) Task Force on Professional Competencies defines reference and user services librarians as "Librarians that assist, advise, and instruct users in accessing all forms of recorded knowledge. The assistance, advice, and instruction include both direct and indirect service to patrons."[6] This chapter will focus on how competencies are imperative to the daily work of reference librarians.

TECHNICAL COMPETENCIES

An increase in technological advances within libraries has profoundly impacted the work of librarians, the services they provide to patrons, and the spaces available for research and learning. Library professionals experience a conundrum as they have to juggle the challenges of connecting to technology-driven spaces while constantly progressing through the choices available to them for technology procurement. They also have to deal with the plethora of accessible technologies at their disposal. For librarians, the new normal now consists of working in technology-rich environments where they have the expectation of possessing the technological skills required to meet the needs of twenty-first-century learners and researchers. In order to remain professionally relevant, librarians must have a comfort zone in working with current technologies while having a willingness to learn and keep abreast of emerging trends.

Several library organizations and countless authors have offered competencies that established a technological skill as a prerequisite for employment opportunities within libraries. The ALA and its divisions, Reference and User Services Association (RUSA) and Library Information Technology Association (LITA), have established competencies that specify technological knowledge and skills as core competencies for librarians. Sections 4A and 4D (Technological Knowledge and Skills) of ALA's *Core Competences of Librarianship* outline key elements of knowledge and skills librarians must know and demonstrate daily.[7] A few of these skills include the ability to employ the use of "technology and tools consistent with professional ethics and prevailing service norms and applications," and "analyze emerging technologies and innovations in order to recognize and implement relevant technological improvements."[8]

Moreover, in the section titled "Applications of Knowledge, Strategies 2, 3, and 4" of RUSA's *Professional Competencies for Reference and User Services Librarians*, the goals listed recommend that librarians use new knowledge that "integrates use of the latest technologies . . . into every day practice," explore available technologies, and experiment with the newest technologies to meet user needs as strategies for enhancing reference and user service practices.[9] Additionally, under the section "Dissemination of Knowledge, Strategy 3," RUSA recommends that librarians create web pages as a strategy for sharing their expertise.[10] John Heinrichs and Jeen-Su Lim's study, "Emerging Requirements of Computer Related Competencies for Librarians," focused on library and information science graduate students' desired and perceived computer and productivity tool skills required for careers in librarianship, reveals that future librarians recognize the need of improved technology-related skills in the area of database development, web design, and multimedia skills.[11] Furthermore, in the chapter titled "The Library School's Role in Preparing New Librarians for Working with Technology," Diane Neal maintains that:

> At the very minimum, all new librarians should possess skills in computer hardware and software operation and troubleshooting, Web site development, database searching, technology planning, and social software use. If schools do not ensure their graduates possess these core competencies, they are doing their students—and the profession—a disservice.[12]

Similarly, Youngok Choi and Edie Rasmussen's study points out

> that current awareness and appropriate technological skills and experience in digital library environments, knowledge and experience in creation and management of digital information, and metadata are the most required qualifications for digital librarian positions.[13]

Reviewing both the established competencies provided by our professional organizations and the increasing amount of literature on this topic confirms that library professionals must acquire multiple technological skills as a non-negotiable rule for future employment.

Now that we have established that current and upcoming librarians should have multiple technological skills for employment, we will address the importance of the applicability of these skills in today's libraries. Librarians use technology in every aspect of their work at the reference desk, in the classroom, or through outreach efforts. The technological tools available within libraries vary tremendously, but some noticeable features exist when visiting the virtual spaces of libraries. Many libraries have incorporated various ways for users to connect to the library for assistance. It is now common to see a library's presence on social networking sites such as Facebook, Instagram, Twitter, or Google+. Moreover, patrons may find video tutorials created by librarians on YouTube that utilize screen capture software such as Camtasia, Screenflow, or Jing. In fact, it is not unusual for many librarians to have the duty of maintaining social networks for marketing purposes, and creating instructional tutorials they embed into a course-management system. A few of the popular library services established over the last few years include platforms that allow patrons to text questions to the library and receive answers by text messaging, engage in chat via real-time links on a library's web page, and submit questions through Twitter. Additionally, knowledge sharing via subject-specific LibGuides continues to remain a staple of library websites.

Emerging trends in libraries, including Massive Open Online Courses (MOOCs), online videos that support flipped-classroom instruction, and the use of Google+, give more in-depth support to online learners. The interest in and concerns surrounding MOOCs have created much discussion within the library community. Currently librarians seek to determine how to support these courses with open-access content while others have started to create content and teach courses using this medium. The future of MOOCs and their impact remains uncertain, but librarians should definitely consider this a viable new technology for learning. One must note that the development of online instruction tutorials has existed for some time, but information literacy through the flipped-classroom instruction model represents a new and exciting concept. Ilka Datig and Claire Ruswick provide suggestions on how to develop information literacy through the flipped-classroom model.[14] The authors prepared online tutorials and materials for students to review prior to attending class. They then geared their instruction session toward cooperative learning and other student-centered activities as opposed to direct instruction. Datig and Ruswick also reported that their activities have led to much positive feedback from students, who enjoyed their interactive and creative approach to teaching.[15] Google+ is another innovative product that many information professionals may find helpful. Kathy Fredrick describes Google+ as "Google's answer to Facebook."[16] Google+ allows for the sharing of announcements, pictures, and videos, and offers blogging and a chat feature much like Facebook, but unlike that social networking site, Google+

goes further by offering its users free video conference services for up to ten people via its hangout feature. The hangout feature allows for library users to take part in virtual workshops, small library instruction sessions, or a one-on-one research consultation. This dynamic resource has potential to enhance instruction and learning through its gathering, sharing, and use as a teaching and research tool.

PROFESSIONAL COMPETENCIES

The RUSA Task Force on Professional Competencies defines a laundry list of competencies a reference librarian should possess. These professional competencies fall broadly into five main categories, of which, we will discuss the first four:

1. Access
2. Knowledge Base
3. Marketing/Awareness/Informing
4. Collaboration

Each of these competency categories has its own subset of more specific competencies that capable reference librarians should use in the discharge of their responsibilities. These professional competencies cover the entire range of duties a reference librarian is expected to perform, from serving patrons to managing resources and staff.

During the last two decades, there has been a dramatic change in the delivery of reference and user services. In a world once dominated by imposing tomes full of tiny print, the digital technologies that have taken over have changed not only the way we access information, but also the roles and responsibilities of the reference librarians who curate these materials.

> As the reference environment changed in the 1990s, the roles of reference librarians also changed from conservators, collectors, and resource counselors. At present, reference librarians have become information counselors, mediators between users and materials, and educators in response to availability of technology and the need for greater expertise in assisting students and faculty both within and outside the library walls. [17]

Access

A reference librarian has the primary role of providing patrons (students/faculty/staff) with access to information resources that meet their needs. With the profusion of resources available to us in the twenty-first century, reference librarians need to know more about our own collections than ever before. According to RUSA, this means

> understanding information needs and information behavior of primary users and developing the skills to effectively meet those information needs. Access includes competencies related to coping with user information overload, recognizing the importance of user time and convenience, and removing barriers to service. Access competencies include the ability to identify documents through a knowledge of bibliography and indexing, the ability to identify and provide solutions that minimize cognitive and physical barriers to access, and the ability to assess for individual users materials that will provide the appropriate level of linguistic and conceptual access. [18]

In other words, our patrons/users have such an overwhelming array of sources to choose from that they will need help in determining what resources will be useful, and then we will provide them with both guidance to those resources and the most relevant information. Responsive reference librarians should have the necessary communication skills to determine the details of a patron's information needs, and analyze the available sources to recommend the one most appropriate for the patron's interest and content level. Reference librarians think critically during reference transactions, and possess the ability to analyze, on the fly, what the patron is telling them, and apply their analysis to finding the best resources to answer the patron's question. The ability to think critically about what resources are applicable is dependent on the librarian's second major professional competency: knowledge base.

Knowledge Base

It is incumbent upon reference librarians to have knowledge, both broad and deep, of the resources at their disposal. They must also have enough breadth of knowledge to determine what a patron really needs. Patrons often perceive that librarians have the ability to conjure up answers to simple and complex questions, seemingly from thin air. However, in the best interest of librarians and their patrons, this misperception should not continue because

> when a librarian, through a good reference interview or years of experience, understands what a patron needs even better than that person knows or can articulate, and can immediately find whatever information is needed, an impressed patron's awe might well become exaggerated, as in turn, might the librarian's self image. [19]

Today, the sheer vastness of resources available has changed the role that the reference librarian should play. The best reference librarians don't simply produce answers as if by magic, but actually engage and teach patrons how they may best find those answers on their own. Though a reference librarian must possess extraordinary knowledge of the resources in order to answer a patron's questions, it's no longer simply enough for the librarian to know where to find things. Reference librarians must become teachers and instructors. They must learn to empower students, faculty, and the general public, to use the resources as the librarian uses them. They must engage library users, and teach them how to answer their own questions. In order to change public perceptions of what librarians do, and to draw more people into the library to learn how to find information, the reference librarian must engage in the third competency.

Marketing/Awareness/Informing

Information literacy has generated a lot of buzz in the library profession, evidenced by the profusion of articles written on the topic. For example, in the database *Library Literature & Information Science Full Text* (H. W. Wilson), there were 3,331 articles with "information literacy" in the title or abstract and the database *Library and Information Science Abstracts* (ProQuest) had 4,941 titles at the time of the search. This is a topic near and dear to the hearts of instruction librarians, most of whom are also reference librarians. The problem that reference librarians face when trying to improve the information literacy of their students centers around actually getting them into the library for instruction and assistance.

Many reference librarians struggle to make the extent of library services known to their community. As expressed by the librarians at Northwest Vista College (NVC) in Texas, "Many instructors and students have told us they were not aware that the college had a library."[20] In addition to not knowing that the college had a library, the staff at NVC also said that "some faculty members who knew of the library's existence were not familiar with what our library had to offer."[21] The staff of the NVC library speculate that the changing nature of the services libraries provide has led to a disconnect between what people know about library services and what is really true about library services.

If librarians seek to instill productive information-seeking behaviors in students, to increase their ability to find relevant articles, to parse the articles, and to derive usable information and conclusions from them, then they must strive to reach out to as many of the students on a campus as possible. And according to Reeves et al.,

> In order for an information literacy effort to succeed, librarians must have the support and respect of the teaching faculty. Faculty who are knowledgeable about the information resources available through the library, and aware that the library provides instruction, are much more likely to send their classes for instruction.[22]

NVC's faculty outreach program consisted of three elements: (1) getting librarians out of the library and into direct contact with faculty members, (2) enabling free-flowing communication between librarians and the surrounding academic community, and (3) drawing faculty into the library, which they accomplished through a series of afternoon workshops held in the library that sought to demonstrate various multidisciplinary databases to those faculty. The librarians also gave the faculty a general overview of library services. They held the workshops beginning in January during the faculty's in-service week so as to not conflict with their class schedules.

Reeves et al. note that in order to be successful, these outreach programs must remain ongoing. More importantly though, the communication and collaboration skills of the librarians help keep the faculty interested in continuing to learn about library services, and to convince them of the value of the services available to their students. Perhaps one of the biggest stumbling blocks to the acceptance of librarians as teachers on the same level as faculty is the fact that the most visible services rendered by the library—circulation and interlibrary loan—are essentially clerical. This misperception masks the actual academic nature of reference and instruction services. Collaborating with faculty on research projects may be one way for reference librarians to demonstrate their knowledge and skills. This brings us to the fourth of the competencies RUSA defines for reference librarians: collaboration.

Collaboration

Nancy E. Bodner et al. say that one of the goals of collaboration is that "a librarian develops and maintains partnerships beyond the library and the profession to strengthen services to users."[23] The teaching faculty of the universities and colleges where reference librarians work serve as a critical group to develop and maintain such partnerships. This goal is tied to three separate strategies, all of which can be applied to members of the faculty as easily as to anyone else:

1. Identifies partners who have knowledge and expertise of value to the library's users.
2. Communicates effectively with partners to ensure mutual understanding of goals, objectives, and values.
3. Forms partnerships to improve existing systems and to develop new products and services.[24]

In an academic library setting, the partners who know and value the library's services are most likely to be found among the faculty and student body. Identifying these partnerships and opportunities to collaborate creates an environment that fosters interaction and creativity between librarians and faculty for student success.

Secondly, the reference librarian should use the collaboration to clearly communicate what services the library may provide for the faculty and the students. With every successful interaction with faculty, include a gentle push to share the positive experience with their colleagues and spread the word about the benefits they received from working with the library. Market research tells us that for every person who has had a good experience, ten will express they had a bad one. Thus, the librarian should encourage the sharing of favorable experiences in order to best promote the library's services.

Finally, the reference librarian should take advantage of that good working relationship to find out what areas of service need improvement, and what changes would be most useful to that particular faculty member and his/her colleagues. "The reference department of the twenty-first century library has to provide services, which are constantly being shaped by changes in the information environment and the expectations of patrons of this fast-paced era."[25]

PERSONAL COMPETENCIES

In addition to possessing professional competencies, librarians need to demonstrate their mastery of personal competencies. The establishment of these personal competencies will ensure the success of librarians within an organization and in the field of librarianship. Elizabeth J. Wood, Rush Miller, and Amy Knapp describe personal competencies as "interpersonal skills (e.g., effective communication) and the ability to contribute to teams and to the organization as a whole."[26] Personal competencies include the abilities to develop and engage in (1) relationships (creating and maintaining partnerships), (2) judgment and decision making (critical thinking), and (3) interpersonal skills (interacting with various constituencies).[27] These personal competencies enable librarians to work with patrons and fellow librarians and help promote a positive, professional environment.

The fifth section of the *Core Competencies*, titled "Reference and User Services,"[28] enumerates the basic skills librarians need upon graduation. The following competencies in that section exemplify personal competencies:

- 5C: "The methods used to interact, successfully with individuals of all ages and groups to provide consultation, mediation, and guidance in their use of recorded knowledge and information";
- 5E: "The principles and methods of advocacy used to reach specific audiences to promote and explain concepts and services";

- 5F: "The principles of assessment and response to diversity in user needs, user communications, and user preferences";
- 5G: "The principles and methods used to assess the impact of current and emerging situations or circumstances on the design and implementation of appropriate services or resource development."[29]

In his book *Working with Emotional Intelligence*, Daniel Goleman hints strongly at the importance of achieving personal competencies as he describes essential skills needed in a professional workplace.[30] Goleman expresses the importance of a variety of traits employees need to create a positive and successful work environment, such as "character," "personality," "soft skills," and "competence."[31] Goleman states, "There is at last a more precise understanding of these human talents, and a new name for them: 'emotional intelligence.'"[32] In terms of this chapter, many personal competency traits of reference librarians mirror what Goleman describes as emotional intelligence: personal and social abilities.

According to Goleman, personal competencies form the basis of emotional intelligence.[33] Moreover, he describes a competence as "a personal trait or set of habits that leads to more effective or superior job performance—an ability that adds clear economic value to the efforts of a person on the job."[34] Libraries are important for today's economy. Typically, evaluators of academic libraries link the quality of service to the actual librarians themselves rather than the products offered.[35] This service delivery supported by librarian expertise serves as an important value.[36] Therefore, librarians who demonstrate a high aptitude for emotional intelligence tend to have their expertise [or personal competence] evaluated positively.[37] By providing a value to the communities they serve, libraries exemplify "value as results," which "focuses on how library service helps people to change in some way." This value does not have a financial benefit, but "rather the value of information is its contribution to making improvements in users."[38]

Due to the current culture of assessment, academic librarians have to prove the value of the academic libraries that serve their institutions. When librarians provide the best possible service, they demonstrate high emotional intelligence or excellence in personal competencies for a reference and user services librarian. Therefore, when librarians perform with competence and confidence, those assessing these libraries may view the library as a valuable commodity for the institution and community. Librarians have long been viewed as potential change agents. Laura Saunders states that "reference librarians will need to move beyond management functions to leadership, whereby they build relationships and create visions to move followers toward action for change."[39] Thus, reference librarians have an opportunity to boost their image and value in the twenty-first century by making timely and decisive changes.

Saunders conducted a study asking reference librarians and hiring managers to reveal the particular knowledge, skills, and competencies they deem valuable in reference services.[40] Participants in the study had to select competencies they felt were essential for reference librarians to possess in the following categories: general, technology, and personal/interpersonal.[41] The top five competencies chosen by the respondents include the following: verbal communication skills, listening, approachability, comfort with instruction, and adaptability/flexibility.[42] Consequently, the competencies Saunders found in her study relate directly to emotional intelligence via service orientation. Goleman defines *service orientation* as "anticipating, recognizing, and meeting customers' needs."[43]

In order to meet the needs of diverse customers, librarians must possess the competency of being able to work with diverse groups. The Association of College and Research Libraries (ACRL) had similar sentiments; its Racial and Ethnic Diversity Committee created the *Diversity Standards: Cultural Competency for Academic Librarians (2012)*. The diversity standards' guidelines were based on the National Association of Social Workers' definition of *cultural competence*: "A congruent set of behaviors, attitudes, and policies that enable a person or a group to work effectively in cross-cultural situations."[44] Currently, eleven standards exist that highlight how academic librarians may demonstrate cultural competency. For instance, Standard 1: Cultural Awareness of Self and Others exemplifies emotional intelligence through cultural competency, as it requires librarians to have an awareness of and sensitivity to diversity when engaging with customers.

Librarians that provide excellent service and knowledge exemplify how emotional intelligence impacts the library work environment and demonstrates cultural competency. The ALA Core Competences of Librarianship, under section 5, "Reference and User Services," 5A and 5B, states librarians should "provide access to relevant and accurate recorded knowledge and information to individuals of all ages and groups (5A) and retrieve, evaluate, and synthesize information from diverse sources for use by individuals of all ages and groups."[45] These standards put into perspective the importance of reference librarians possessing the competence to interact with diverse populations.

Librarians strive to introduce patrons to new resources and nontraditional methods of learning. These resources include print and electronic resources, social media services, and statistical and assessment services. They also seek to build personal relationships with the people and organizations in the communities they serve. The level of personal competence (emotional intelligence) that librarians possess will determine the quality of service they give to their patrons. Research has shown that librarians who have high personal competence have more success in working with their patrons in furthering their critical thinking and information-literacy skills.

Richard Paul and Linda Elder define *critical thinking* as "the art of analyzing and evaluating thinking with a view to improve it."[46] Reference librarians help their patrons develop critical thinking skills by showing how the information sources and services available to them intertwine. Moreover, through showing their patrons this interconnected relationship, they illustrate how information sources and services impact their research, lives, and communities. Thus, reference librarians encourage their patrons to "carefully analyze information sources and services."[47] In conclusion, reference librarians successfully provide service to their patrons through the incorporation of high personal competence and the introduction of the latest resources to use when conducting research.

CONCLUSION AND RECOMMENDATIONS

The twenty-first-century reference librarian requires technical, professional, and personal competencies. Moreover, librarians should assess themselves on how they practice these competencies in their day-to-day work on an annual or semiannual basis. Librarians may perform self-assessments through official evaluations, self-evaluations, or peer-to-peer constructive feedback. Now, more than ever, the "successful reference interview would be enhanced if librarians would cultivate emotional intelligence," and build personal and professional partnerships that will lead to future success for the library and its users.[48] Furthermore, librarians who demonstrate and apply all of these competencies help develop and promote new learning, effective information-seeking behaviors in their patrons, and beneficial relationships inside the library and surrounding academic community.

In order to accomplish the library's overall mission of facilitating the academic pursuits of students and faculty at their school, reference librarians must put these competencies into practice every day on the job. Continuous technological learning, professional education, and interpersonal skills development serve to enhance librarians' interactions with their users. The application of these competencies benefits the library, students, faculty, and ultimately the academic community they serve by positioning librarians to play an integral role in supporting the research agenda of their faculty and fulfilling the mission of their institution. When students, faculty, and the administration recognize the added value of the library's ability to provide a pipeline to the resources, information, and technology they need, everyone has the tools and opportunity for greater success.

NOTES

1. American Library Association, "Core Competences of Librarianship," American Library Association, 2009, accessed September 30, 2013, www.ala.org/educationcareers/careers/corecomp/corecompetences.

2. Intel, "Moore's Law Inspires Intel Innovation," accessed September 30, 2013, www.intel.com/content/www/us/en/silicon-innovations/moores-law-technology.html.

3. Elizabeth J. Wood, Rush Miller, and Amy Knapp, *Beyond Survival: Managing Academic Libraries in Transition* (Westport, CT: Libraries Unlimited, 2007), 82.

4. Ibid.

5. Laura Saunders, "Identifying Core Reference Competencies from an Employers' Perspective: Implications for Instruction," *College & Research Libraries* 73, no. 4 (2012), accessed October 14, 2013, www.nclive.org/cgi-bin/nclsm?url=%22http://search.ebscohost.com/login.aspx?direct=true&db=a9h&AN=77936928&site=ehost-live%22.

6. RUSA Task Force on Professional Competencies, "Professional Competencies for Reference and User Services Librarian," *Reference & User Services Quarterly* 42, no. 2 (2003): 290–95.

7. American Library Association, "Core Competencies."

8. Ibid.

9. RUSA Task Force, "Professional Competencies."

10. Ibid.

11. John H. Heinrichs and Jeen-Su Lim, "Emerging Requirements of Computer Related Competencies for Librarians," *Library & Information Science Research* 31, no. 2 (2009), accessed September 10, 2013, 10.1016/j.lisr.2008.11.001.

12. Diane Neal, "The Library School's Role in Preparing New Librarians for Working with Technology," in *Core Technology Competencies for Librarians and Library Staff: A LITA Guide*, ed. Susan M. Thompson (New York: Neal-Schuman, 2009), 52.

13. Youngok Choi and Edie Rasmussen, "What Qualifications and Skills are Important for Digital Librarian Positions in Academic Libraries? A Job Advertisement Analysis," *Journal of Academic Librarianship* 35, no. 5 (2009): 465.

14. Ilka Datig and Claire Ruswick, "Four Quick Flips," *College & Research Libraries News* 74, no. 5 (2013), accessed September 9, 2013, http://crln.acrl.org/content/74/5/249.full.pdf+html.

15. Ibid.

16. Kathy Fredrick, "Google . . . Plus, " *School Library Monthly* 29, no. 6 (2013): 23, accessed December 13, 2013, www.nclive.org/cgi-bin/nclsm?url=%22http://search.ebscohost.com/login.aspx?direct=true&db=a9h&AN=86739775&site=ehost-live%22.

17. Mary M. Nofsinger, "Training and Retraining Reference Professionals," *The Reference Librarian* 60, no. 64 (2008): 11.

18. Nancy E. Bodner, Muzette Z Diefenthal, Nancy Huling, and Kathleen M. Kluegel, "Professional Competencies for Reference and User Services Librarians," American Library Association, September 29, 2008, accessed December 11, 2013, www.ala.org/rusa/resources/guidelines/professional.

19. Beth Posner, "Know-It-All Librarians," *The Reference Librarian* 37, no. 78 (2003): 115.

20. Linda Reeves et al., "Faculty Outreach," *The Reference Librarian* 39, no. 82 (2003): 58.

21. Ibid.

22. Ibid., 61.

23. Bodner et al., "Professional Competencies for Reference and User Services Librarians."

24. Ibid.

25. Justin O. Osa, "Managing the 21st Century Reference Department," *The Reference Librarian* 39, no. 81 (2003): 35.

26. Wood, Miller, and Knapp, *Beyond Survival*, 82.

27. Ibid.

28. American Library Association, "Core Competencies."

29. Ibid.

30. Daniel Goleman, *Working with Emotional Intelligence* (New York: Bantam Books, 2006), 4.
31. Ibid.
32. Ibid.
33. Ibid., 17.
34. Ibid., 16.
35. Megan Oakleaf, ed., *Value of Academic Libraries: A Comprehensive Research Review and Report* (Chicago: Association of College and Research Libraries, 2010), 23.
36. Ibid.
37. Ibid.
38. Ibid., 23–24.
39. Laura Saunders, "Identifying Core Reference Competencies from Employers' Perspective: Implications for Instruction," *College & Research Libraries* 73, no. 4 (2012): 392, accessed October 14, 2013, http://crl.acrl.org/content/73/4/390.full.pdf+html.
40. Ibid., 390.
41. Ibid., 395.
42. Ibid., 398.
43. Daniel Goleman, *Working with Emotional Intelligence*, 151.
44. ACRL Racial and Ethnic Diversity Committee, "Diversity Standards: Cultural Competency for Academic Librarians," *College & Research Library News* 73, no. 9 (2012): 551, accessed December 16, 2013, http://crln.acrl.org/content/73/9/551.full.pdf+html.
45. American Library Association, "Core Competencies," 3.
46. Richard Paul and Linda Elder, *The Miniature Guide to Critical Thinking: Concepts and Tools* (Dillon Beach, CA: Foundation for Critical Thinking, 2008), 4.
47. Bodner et al., "Professional Competencies for Reference and User Services Librarians."
48. Marshall Eidson, "Using 'Emotional Intelligence' in the Reference Interview," *Colorado Libraries* 26, no. 2 (2000): 8.

BIBLIOGRAPHY

ACRL Racial and Ethnic Diversity Committee. "Diversity Standards: Cultural Competency for Academic Librarians." *College & Research Library News* 73, no. 9 (2012): 551–61. Accessed December 16, 2013. http://crln.acrl.org/content/73/9/551.full.pdf+html.

American Library Association. "Core Competences of Librarianship." Accessed September 30, 2013. www.ala.org/educationcareers/careers/corecomp/corecompetences.

Bodner, Nancy E., Muzette Z. Diefenthal, Nancy Huling, and Kathleen M. Kluegel. "Professional Competencies for Reference and User Services Librarians." American Library Association. September 29, 2008. Accessed December 11, 2013. www.ala.org/rusa/resources/guidelines/professional.

Choi, Youngok, and Edie Rasmussen. "What Qualifications and Skills are Important for Digital Librarian Positions in Academic Libraries? A Job Advertisement Analysis." *Journal of Academic Librarianship* 35, no. 5 (2009): 457–67.

Datig, Ilka. "Four Quick Flips." *College & Research Libraries News* 74, no. 5 (2013): 249–57. Accessed September 9, 2013. http://crl.acrl.org/content/74/5/249.full.pdf+html.

Eidson, Marshall. "Using 'Emotional Intelligence' in the Reference Interview." *Colorado Libraries* 26, no. 2 (2000): 8–10.

Frederick, Kathy. "Google . . . Plus." *School Library Monthly* 29, no. 6 (2013): 23–25. Accessed December 13, 2013. www.nclive.org/cgi-bin/nclsm?url=%22http://search.ebscohost.com/login.aspx?direct=true&db=a9h&AN=86739775&site=ehost-live%22.

Goleman, Daniel. *Working with Emotional Intelligence.* New York: Bantam Books, 2006.

Heinrichs, John H., and Jeen-Su Lim. "Emerging Requirements of Computer Related Competencies for Librarians." *Library & Information Science Research* 31, no. 2 (2009): 101–6. Accessed September 10, 2013. 10.1016/j.lisr.2008.11.001.

Intel. "Moore's Law Inspires Intel Innovation." Accessed September 30, 2013. www.intel.com/content/www/us/en/silicon-innovations/moores-law-technology.html.

Neal, Diane. "The Library School's Role in Preparing New Librarians for Working with Technology." In *Core Technology Competencies for Librarians and Library Staff: A LITA Guide,* edited by Susan M. Thompson, 41–70. New York: Neal-Schuman Publishers, 2009.

Nofsinger, Mary M. "Training and Retraining Reference Professionals." *The Reference Librarian* 30, no. 64 (1999): 9–19. Accessed December 1, 2013. 10.1300/J120v30n64_02.

Oakleaf, Megan, ed. *Value of Academic Libraries: A Comprehensive Research Review and Report.* Chicago: Association of College and Research Libraries, 2010.

Osa, Justin O. "Managing the 21st Century Reference Department." *The Reference Librarian* 39, no. 81 (2003): 35–50. Accessed December 1, 2013. 10.1300/J120v39n81_04.

Paul, Richard, and Linda Elder. *The Miniature Guide to Critical Thinking: Concepts and Tools.* Dillon Beach, CA: Foundation for Critical Thinking, 2008.

Posner, Beth. "Know-It-All Librarians." *The Reference Librarian* 37, no. 78 (2003): 111–29. Accessed December 2, 2013. 10.1300/J120v37n78_08.

Reeves, Linda, Catherine Nishimuta, Judy McMillan, and Christine Godin. "Faculty Outreach." *The Reference Librarian* 39, no. 82 (2003): 57–62. Accessed December 2, 2013. 10.1300/J120v39n82_05.

RUSA Task Force on Professional Competencies, "Professional Competencies for Reference and User Services Librarian," *Reference & User Services Quarterly* 42, no. 2 (2003): 290–95.

Saunders, Laura. "Identifying Core Reference Competencies from Employers' Perspective: Implications for Instruction." *College & Research Libraries* 73, no. 4 (2012): 390–404. Accessed October 14, 2013. http://crl.acrl.org/content/73/4/390.full.pdf+html.

Wood, Elizabeth J., Rush Miller, and Amy Knapp. *Beyond Survival: Managing Academic Libraries in Transition.* Westport, CT: Libraries Unlimited, 2007.

Chapter Thirteen

Professional Competencies for the Virtual Reference Librarian

Digital Literacy, Soft Skills, and Customer Service

Christine Tobias

To be a reference librarian requires a specialized set of professional competencies. Traditionally, the competencies taught in library and information science programs include the ability to conduct an effective reference interview, familiarity with print and electronic reference sources in different subject areas, and efficient web searching and navigation skills. However, the evolution of technology has prompted academic libraries, as well as public libraries, to expand the provision of reference services in the digital environment to incorporate virtual reference (VR), such as web chat and instant messaging. While the purpose of reference remains the same, the venue of VR by its nature requires the additional competencies of digital literacy, soft skills, and customer service. Librarians not only must be able to use a computer effectively but also must be familiar with mobile tools and technologies, and understand how to find, create, and share content appropriately. Furthermore, the librarian must exhibit soft skills, also referred to as people skills or emotional intelligence, to adapt face-to-face conversational elements into each online session. To contribute to the success of the library's VR service, the librarian must value customer service, striving to develop positive interactions so that every patron is a happy customer who will use the service again. While the professional competencies required in traditional reference services continue to be relevant and necessary, adaptation to the digital environment requires the acquisition of these new competencies.

DIGITAL LITERACY

In the broadest sense, *digital literacy* refers to one's knowledge of and ability to utilize a range of technology for finding and evaluating information, producing and sharing original content, and connecting and collaborating with others.[1] In the context of VR, *digital literacy* refers to the librarian's ability to use a variety of technological tools, including but not limited to a computer, to engage with patrons in the provision of reference service. For librarians, communication with patrons in VR most often incorporates web chat, instant messaging (IM), e-mail, and text messaging, and librarians who are digitally literate will effectively translate face-to-face conversational elements into online communication for a successful transaction.

To provide VR, it is necessary for librarians to understand how to utilize the appropriate technology and software to conduct successful reference transactions. The Reference and User Services Association (RUSA) *Guidelines for Behavioral Performance of Reference and Information Service Providers* do not mention digital literacy specifically and do not extensively address expectations for librarians beyond the application of technology.[2] However, as a professional competency for librarians, digital literacy is important since it addresses the need to communicate differently in VR sessions than in traditional reference services by being attentive, making decisions quickly, and understanding standard language and grammar practices of IM. Additionally, digital literacy includes communicative multitasking, in which the librarian exchanges communication with more than one patron in simultaneous sessions, successfully manages to move between sessions while keeping the exchanges organized, and keeps the communication going in a productive and efficient manner.

Establishing comfort with online communication is dependent on several factors. The most basic skill required of a librarian in VR is the ability to use a computer and proficiency with a keyboard and mouse. In the early adoption of VR, it was often emphasized that the librarian would need to type quickly.[3] It was feared that slower typists would have trouble keeping the patron's attention long enough to answer the question.[4] However, as VR has become an innovative form of practice in libraries, the profession has taken notice that digital literacy is multifaceted. Not only is keyboarding proficiency necessary, but it is also essential for librarians to understand communication etiquette for chat and IM transactions.[5]

Communication and behavior in VR is different and more complex than in physical, face-to-face interactions. For example, the nonverbal cues present in interactions at the traditional reference desk are lacking in VR. Without the presence of visual and audio cues, particularly tone of voice, gestures, and body language, the librarian must learn how to communicate strictly in textual terms.[6] In VR, writing and spelling skills are highlighted, but the language used resembles spoken word more than written word. Furthermore, librarians engaged in IM not only become speakers and listeners, as is done in face-to-face conversation, but also perform as readers and writers who depend on context and negotiate meaning. In other words, *digital literacy* implies that the librarian understands writing as the equivalent of talking, and reading as the equivalent of listening in VR transactions.[7]

Another aspect of digital literacy for librarians is the understanding that chat and IM are interactive, engaging, and fast-paced modes of communication,[8] and the standard rules of grammar do not always apply.[9] This difference between spoken and online communication necessitates an adjustment from the librarian. Since VR transactions are generally fast-paced, time is valuable and does not allow the privilege of constructing grammatically perfect sentences with accurate spelling and punctuation. "Silence is indistinguishable from absence,"[10] so to avoid lulls in communication, the librarian must refrain from composing long messages.[11] Since long missives are an obstacle to maintaining the faster pace of conversation and it can be difficult to read multiple lines of text, it is appropriate for the librarian to *talk* in short sentences or use only a few words at a time.

Additionally, some rules of conversation, such as recognition of turn-taking, are different in VR, especially in real-time interaction of chat or IM.[12] It is not always easy to discern when one person is finished composing dialogue, often resulting in crossed messages.[13] While writing, spelling, and grammar skills are traditionally held in high esteem by reference librarians, the new generation of librarians will understand that grammar has an alternate form in VR. Users of chat and IM may use misspellings of words as shorthand such as OK, K (ok), kewl (cool), or use abbreviations such as BRB (be right back), BTW (by the way), ATM (at the moment), or IDK (I don't know).[14]

Digital literacy for librarians also encompasses the ability to successfully engage in communicative multitasking, which means having to communicate simultaneously with multiple patrons.[15] Communicative multitasking "requires participants to pay attention, keep various channels of communication and topics straight and to keep different chats going in a sensible manner."[16] This multitasking ability in VR is essential as it helps librarians understand users' behaviors and expectations. Since college students and younger users of technology are adept at running multiple web sessions or other programs while browsing the Internet,[17] it is safe to assume that they may expect the same level of skill from librarians. The traditional reference desk model engages one patron with a librarian, conducting one transaction at a time. In VR, however, particularly in chat and IM, a librarian may be required to conduct transactions with several patrons simultaneously, which can be stressful and challenging. Thus, librarians must be able to move smoothly from one session to the other.[18]

SOFT SKILLS

Additionally, the use of soft skills is an essential component for the effective transfer of traditional reference skills into the digital environment. Soft skills are interpersonal skills demonstrating a person's ability to communicate effectively and build relationships with others in one-on-one interactions. This skill set includes listening and responding in a receptive way, enhancing communication and promoting problem solving and conflict resolution. [19] As a professional competency in VR, soft skills refer to the librarian's ability to understand people and manage communication during the session as a social interaction. [20] In order to conduct the reference interview without the contextual cues present in traditional in-person reference services, such as body language and tone of voice, librarians apply soft skills through active listening, conversing in a pleasant and polite tone, and applying subtle niceties to enhance the transaction on a personal level.

Ideally, a good reference librarian has a specific set of personality traits, such as service orientation, patience, approachability, and respect. Soft skills are essential for librarians not only as a means for understanding the patron, but also for increasing positive affect, or pleasant feelings, leading to a successful transaction. [21] In VR, patrons must state their inquiries or requests for information using only written text. Active listening, using writing as the equivalent to talking and reading as the equivalent of listening, provides the librarian the opportunity to sense underlying concerns, emotional overtones, and other understated or unclear issues. [22] This helps draw the librarian's attention to the reference interview, [23] and the use of soft skills, particularly courtesy and empathy, in interactions with those who have difficulty expressing themselves in writing will enhance the experience.

Without the visual and audio cues present in face-to-face conversation, an unwelcoming tone or a curt, abrupt response from the librarian can be easily read as unfriendliness or an unwillingness to help, resulting in an unsatisfactory experience and an unhappy patron. [24] For this reason, librarians will need to use word expression to exhibit what is normally conveyed unconsciously through gesture or physical action in face-to-face communication. A polite, engaging tone can be established through choice of words, expressions, or phrasing; sarcasm, disrespect, or condescension should always be avoided. For example, asking the patron, "Why don't you try looking in the catalog?," can be off-putting, while saying, "I'm wondering if you have looked in the catalog yet," has a much softer tone to it. Also, the librarian should use an appropriate level of formality and pace, taking cues from the patron, to match the timing and conversational tone accordingly to exhibit service orientation. [25] Through the application of soft skills, the librarian shows sensitivity and sets the tone of the conversation, establishing the level of formality and expressing personal interest in the patron's question.

Soft skills in VR also include the use of professional judgment from the librarian to determine appropriate clarification questions and responses based on the conversation up to that point, adapting to the communication style displayed by the patron.[26] Careful consideration of the content and tone observed during the interaction and the ability to remain open to new cues is essential.[27] By working comments into the dialogue, the librarian engages with the patron, showing that she is listening and actively working on answering the question. Frequently acknowledging the patron's responses with phrases such as "I see" or "I understand," and emphasizing with comments such as "That is a tough question," "Sorry this is taking so long," or "Wow, this database is being slow today" helps establish the librarian as an active listener with a positive service orientation.[28] If appropriate, a sense of humor relieves stress, puts patrons at ease, and establishes rapport.[29] Explanations of gestures can help convey nonverbal cues, providing additional depth of meaning to the interaction by describing the librarian's feelings or actions.[30] Emoticons, graphical images used to represent facial expressions, will also help transmit the intended meaning and add a social element to the librarian's written messages.[31]

VR occurs in real time just as service at the traditional reference desk does, so it is important for the librarian to determine if the patron is in a hurry or if there is no time constraint. Often, college students tend to be pressed for time, so the librarian should use soft skills to read the necessary cues and determine the patron's expectations about receiving an answer versus receiving instruction.[32] While chat and IM generally tend to be active and fast-paced, there may be cases where the patron seems detached, unresponsive, or distant. This often occurs when interacting with college students who may be multitasking (e.g., checking Facebook or sending a text message) while waiting to hear how they can search for a book in the library catalog. In such a situation, it is important for the librarian to practice patience while waiting for a response from the patron.

CUSTOMER SERVICE

The third professional competency necessary for librarians in VR is customer service. Closely related to soft skills, customer service plays a huge role in determining the value and success of reference services through application of standard business practices. Customer service can be defined as the library's ability to meet the needs and expectations of patrons[33] and is accomplished not only by helping patrons find what they want, but also by doing so in a way that makes them feel good about the transaction.[34] The librarians with the strongest propensity for customer service are those who truly value VR as a service point and are thus willing to make every effort to satisfy patrons' requests. As mentioned earlier when discussing soft skills, these librarians have a strong public-service attitude and are comfortable conducting reference transactions in the digital environment. They are committed to continuous learning and are motivated to improve and enhance their reference service skills.[35]

Librarians should strive for excellence and display top-notch customer service skills in VR from the start to the end of each and every session through an engaging, pleasant personality. Building rapport is essential for a successful transaction. A common error of librarians is immediately searching for an answer without greeting the patron, leaving the patron to think that no one is helping her.[36] Setting the tone by offering a personal greeting will provide a clear interest and a willingness to help to the patron.[37] The initial communication the patron receives should be some type of welcome message, such as a simple, friendly "Hello!" followed by an acknowledgment or clarification of the question.[38] The librarian can show approachability by making introductions to the patron and working the patron's name into the conversation. For example, a greeting script such as "Hi John! I'm Christine, a librarian at your college. I can help you find your book" builds more rapport than "What book do you need?" This type of disclosure creates a personable touch and builds rapport to sustain a high level of engagement throughout the transaction.[39]

During hectic and busy times in VR, the librarian will need to make a disciplined effort to concentrate despite the variety of distractions in order to provide undivided attention to each patron.[40] Incoming chat or IM sessions should be picked up as soon as possible, and patrons who are waiting in the queue should be acknowledged immediately. Communicating with new patrons, letting them know that the service is busy and that there are other patrons currently being helped ahead of them, gives reassurance that they are not being ignored, and confirms that the VR service is open and staffed with helpful librarians.[41]

Another aspect of customer service is spending quality time with each patron and providing sufficient time to explore each question. As a service point, VR enhances the reference interview process because patrons must state their question using their own vocabulary, which reveals their level of understanding to the librarian.[42] Reference interviews in VR will take longer than at physical service points, such as the reference desk, because it may take several turns in the conversation for the librarian to clarify the question by paraphrasing.[43] With the absence of contextual cues, patience and diligence are essential as the librarian may spend more time eliciting information and creating a dialogue to clarify the patron's information needs and make sure the patron's question is understood.[44]

VR offers the opportunity to engage the patron in the process of finding information. The librarian can, with the patron's permission, depending on the amount of time available, talk the patron through the process. The librarian should continually communicate the progress in finding an answer and give an estimate of the time needed to do so. Giving continual feedback to the patron as information is located establishes engagement and helps the patron feel that the librarian cares enough to spend time with them. When providing an answer, the response from the librarian should be clear, easy to read, and free of library jargon. Furthermore, the patron should be asked if he is interested in how the answer was found.[45] In terms of customer service, this creates a learning opportunity and enhances the value of the library, increasing the likelihood that the patron will be a repeat customer.

To promote customer service in VR, the librarian must be a problem solver, using different approaches to seek a solution, and be willing to go above and beyond to find the appropriate information for the patron. For example, if the information sought is not readily available on the appropriate website, the librarian should take the extra effort to make a phone call to obtain the information for the patron. "Persistence, dedication, and commitment connote the ability to stick with something in the face of difficulties or obstacles. The librarian who is sure that he/she can effect [sic] a satisfactory outcome is more likely to stay with the task and explore alternative solutions to help the user."[46] Furthermore, the librarian must be flexible in using various means to deliver information. While VR is a valuable research service point, there are some inquiries or questions for which chat or IM is not the appropriate means for delivering information. If the question deserves a lengthy or complex answer, delivery by phone or e-mail may be more appropriate.[47] It is an essential customer service skill for the VR librarian to recognize when the question should be referred to a subject specialist or another department, or can be more effectively answered through e-mail,[48] in person, or by phone.

Evaluating the level of customer satisfaction in VR is important. Before ending the session, the librarian should always ask the patron if the information given is relevant, if it actually answers the question, and if the patron has any additional questions.[49] The librarian should also request an evaluation of the service provided and the experience[50] either through seeking feedback or encouraging the patron to fill out an exit survey. Good customer service requires expression of appreciation, so the patron should always be thanked for using the reference service and should be encouraged to use it again.

CONCLUSION

The skill sets required of reference librarians have always included conducting an effective reference interview, having familiarity with print and electronic reference sources in different subject areas, and searching and navigating the web efficiently. However, the evolution of reference services in public and academic libraries incorporates VR, using various modes of online communication, such as web chat and instant messaging, as a service point. While the traditional skills for reference librarians will continue to be necessary, VR requires specialized professional competencies in addition to those historically taught in library and information science programs. These competencies include digital literacy, soft skills, and customer service.

Professional guidelines for reference librarians generally address the need for digital literacy, especially in terms of computer-mediated communication and related technological skills. However, future revisions of these guidelines must consider a direct inclusion of behavioral competencies and standard business principles, focusing particularly on soft skills and customer service. Additionally, library and information science programs should adjust curricula to train new librarians in these specialized competencies, and library administrators must show a commitment to professional development and prioritize staffing VR with those librarians who have finessed these skill sets. With the ubiquity of information and the evolving need to provide reference services in the digital environment, it is becoming increasingly important for librarians to develop positive relationships with patrons by adding a personal touch and giving excellent service. These recommendations, if followed, will help libraries sustain value and relevancy in the digital environment.

NOTES

1. "Enhancing Digital Literacy," New York City Department of Education, accessed December 17, 2013, http://schools.nyc.gov/community/innovation/ConnectedFoundations/EDL/default.htm.

2. "Guidelines for Behavioral Performance of Reference and Information Service Providers," Reference and User Services Association, American Library Association, accessed November 1, 2013, www.ala.org/rusa/resources/guidelines/guidelinesbehavioral.

3. Michelle Fiander, e-mail to Digital Reference Services Yahoo Group mailing list, December   15,   2001,   http://groups.yahoo.com/neo/groups/dig_ref/conversations/topics/4623?var=1.

4. Jana Smith Ronan, *Chat Reference: A Guide to Live Virtual Reference Service* (Westport, CT: Libraries Unlimited, 2003), 93–94.

5. Buff Hirko and Mary Bucher Ross, *Virtual Reference Training : The Complete Guide to Providing Anytime, Anywhere Answers* (Chicago: American Library Association, 2004), 10–11.

6. Ronan, *Chat Reference*, 144.

7. Beth L. Hewett and Russell J. Hewett, "Instant Messaging (IM) Literacy," in *Handbook of Research on Virtual Workplaces and the New Nature of Business Practices*, ed. Pavel Zemliansky et al. (New York: Information Science Reference, 2008), 457.

8. Ronan, *Chat Reference*, 146.

9. Hirko and Ross, *Virtual Reference Training*, 12.

10. Ronan, *Chat Reference*, 152.

11. Ibid., 147.

12. Hewitt and Hewett, "Instant Messaging (IM) Literacy," 462.

13. Ronan, *Chat Reference*, 147.
14. Ibid.
15. Hewett and Hewett, "Instant Messaging (IM) Literacy," 462.
16. Ronan, *Chat Reference*, 94.
17. Hewett and Hewett, "Instant Messaging (IM) Literacy," 462.
18. Richard Bopp and Linda Smith, *Reference and Information Services: An Introduction* (Denver, CO: ABC-CLIO, LLC, 2011), 77.
19. Maxine Kamin, *Soft Skills Revolution: A Guide to Connecting with Compassion for Trainers, Teams, and Leaders* (San Francisco: John Wiley & Sons, 2013), 12.
20. Peter Capelli and Shinjae Won, "Soft Skills," in *Sociology of Work: An Encyclopedia,* ed. Vicki Smith (Thousand Oaks, CA: SAGE, 2013), 813, http://dx.doi.org./10.4135/9781452276199.n287.
21. Alicia Grandey, James Diefendorff, and Deborah E. Rupp, eds., *Emotional Labor in the 21st Century: Diverse Perspectives on the Psychology of Emotion Regulation at Work* (New York: Routledge, 2013), 70.
22. Hirko and Ross, *Virtual Reference Training*, 12.
23. Ronan, *Chat Reference*, 154.
24. Hirko and Ross, *Virtual Reference Training*, 11.
25. Ronan, *Chat Reference*, 149, 153.
26. Bopp and Smith, *Reference and Information Services*, 76.
27. Ibid., 77.
28. Ibid., 153.
29. Ibid., 77.
30. Ronan, *Chat Reference*, 147.
31. Eugene F. Provenzo et al., *Multiliteracies: Beyond Text and the Written Word* (Charlotte, NC: Information Age, 2011), 22.
32. Ronan, *Chat Reference*, 156–57.
33. Hong Miao and Mia Wong Bassham, "Embracing Customer Service in Libraries," *Library Management* 28, no. 1/2 (2007): 54, doi: 10.1108/01435120710723545.
34. Kiran Kaur and Diljit Singh, "Customer Service for Academic Library Users on the Web," *The Electronic Library* 29, no. 6 (2011): 738, doi: 10.1108/02640471111187971.
35. Hirko and Ross, *Virtual Reference Training*, 11.
36. Ronan, *Chat Reference*, 152.
37. Hirko and Ross, *Virtual Reference Training*, 13.
38. Ronan, *Chat Reference*, 152.
39. Ibid.
40. Bopp and Smith, *Reference and Information Services*, 76.
41. Ibid., 80.
42. Ronan, *Chat Reference*, 152.
43. Ibid., 78.
44. Hirko and Ross, *Virtual Reference Training*, 13.
45. Ibid., 80.
46. Bopp and Smith, *Reference and Information Services*, 76.
47. Hirko and Ross, *Virtual Reference Training*, 12.
48. Ibid., 83.
49. Ibid., 84.
50. Ibid., 13.

BIBLIOGRAPHY

Bopp, Richard, and Linda Smith. *Reference and Information Services: An Introduction.* Denver, CO: ABC-CLIO, LLC, 2011.
Cappelli, Peter, and Shinjae Won. "Soft Skills." In *Sociology of Work: An Encyclopedia*, ed. Vicki Smith, 813–14. Thousand Oaks, CA: SAGE, 2013. http://dx.doi.org./10.4135/9781452276199.n287.

"Enhancing Digital Literacy." New York City Department of Education. Accessed December 17, 2013. http://schools.nyc.gov/community/innovation/connectedFoundations/EDL/default.htm.

Grandey, Alicia, James Diefendorff, and Deborah E. Rupp, eds. *Emotional Labor in the 21st Century: Diverse Perspectives on the Psychology of Emotion Regulation at Work.* New York: Routledge, 2013.

"Guidelines for Behavioral Performance of Reference and Information Service Providers." Reference and User Services Association (RUSA). May 28, 2013. www.ala.org/rusa/resources/guidelines/guidelinesbehavioral.

Hewitt, Beth L., and Russell J. Hewett. "Instant Messaging (IM) in the Workplace." In *Handbook of Research on Virtual Workplaces and the New Nature of Business Practices*, edited by Pavel Zemliansky et al., 455–72. New York: Information Science Reference, 2008.

Hirko, Buff, and Mary Bucher Ross. *Virtual Reference Training: The Complete Guide to Providing Anytime, Anywhere Answers.* Chicago: American Library Association, 2004.

Kamin, Maxine. *Soft Skills Revolution: A Guide to Connecting with Compassion for Trainers, Teams, and Leaders.* San Francisco: John Wiley & Sons, 2013.

Kaur, Kiran, and Diljit Singh. "Customer Service for Academic Library Users on the Web." *The Electronic Library* 29, no. 6 (2011): 737–50. doi: 10.1108/02640471111187971.

Miao, Hong, and Mia Wang Bassham. "Embracing Customer Service in Libraries." *Library Management* 28, no. 1/2 (2007): 53–61. doi: 10.1108/01435120710723545.

Provenzo, Eugene F., Amanda Goodwin, Miriam Lipsky, and Sheree Sharpe, eds. *Multiliteracies: Beyond Text and the Written Word.* Charlotte, NC: Information Age, 2011.

Ronan, Jana Smith. *Chat Reference: A Guide to Live Virtual Reference Services.* Westport, CT: Libraries Unlimited, 2003.

Chapter Fourteen

Mediating for Digital Primary Source Research

Expanding Reference Services

Peggy Keeran

In contemplating how web-based technologies have broadened the types of research questions reference librarians encounter in consultations with faculty and students, research for digital primary source materials stands out. With the amount of primary source material that has been and will be digitized, and the ability of researchers to create their own digital collections either by scanning microfilm or by creating images of documents in physical archives using digital cameras, how has technology expanded the boundaries of reference services to encompass this area of research, and how will it continue to do so in the future? In this chapter, I will consider the implications for professional competencies of reference librarians.

Digital collections provide researchers with access to a wealth of primary source materials unimaginable just twenty years ago, permitting historic documents and objects to be discovered and accessed from afar. Because of the prevalence of digital commercially and freely available collections and finding aids, research in and access to primary sources, which was once chiefly the purview of special collection curators and archivists, has pushed the boundaries of what services can be offered by reference librarians. In this chapter I will discuss how web-based and other technologies have allowed reference librarians in the humanities to play a greater role in this arena. I will turn to the literature to explore the opportunities and challenges digital collections of primary sources present and then give concrete examples, based on my experiences at the University of Denver Libraries, how these issues manifest themselves in reference consultations, in order to articulate ways in which humanities reference services have been expanded. Primary sources are here defined as items created at the time of an event or during a lifetime, era, or period that afford the foundation for, insight into, or context of the patron's research project; these can include documents like organizational or personal papers and manuscripts, monographs, serials, data, objects, and more. A digital image of a primary source may variably be referred to as a scan, facsimile, or surrogate.

The University of Denver Libraries serve a student population that is roughly half undergraduate and half graduate. As the arts and humanities reference librarian, my liaison responsibilities encompass art and art history, English, foreign languages, history, philosophy, religious and Judaic studies, and performing arts. Although still dependent on microfilm for some access to surrogates, we have worked to replace as much as possible with digital versions. We hold an abundance of primarily American and British commercial primary source databases useful to researchers in the humanities, such as books, newspapers, periodicals, images, sound, manuscripts, ephemera, government documents, census records, city directories, and statistics. As do many institutions, we acquire MARC records to load into the library catalog whenever possible in order to enable items to be discovered within the digital collections, and we add or harvest records into our library catalog for items in freely available collections such as *Making of America* and *HathiTrust*. We belong to the Center for Research Libraries, which holds both digital and microform collections. Our reference model is comprised of a Research Center desk staffed by graduate students and hour-long consultations scheduled with reference librarians in the Research Center itself. This model allows our librarians to delve into topics that require or would be enhanced by primary sources.

THE EVOLVING DIGITAL PRIMARY SOURCE LANDSCAPE

Before the web, reference librarians' involvement in accessing primary sources varied, depending on the materials being sought. They played a minor role in helping faculty and students access primary source materials that would have been located in physical archives, such as organizational or personal papers. For libraries with robust special collections and archives, patrons would be directed to those departments for potentially relevant papers. For communities with more modest holdings, reference librarians helped patrons locate scholarly editions or print/microform facsimiles, if available. If the location of desired documents was unknown, humanities librarians helped to identify collections and institutions by using directories such as the *National Union Catalog of Manuscript Collections* (*NUCMC*) or Lee Ash and William G. Miller's *Subject Collections: A Guide to Special*

Book Collections and Subject Emphases as Reported by University, College, Public, and Special Libraries and Museums in the United States and Canada. They would consult biographical sources or search prefaces to scholarly works to discover if any archivists, librarians, or holdings of specific institutions were acknowledged, and they would search for specialized guides to resources within disciplines. But, once possible resources and locations of physical primary sources had been identified, and contact information ascertained, the role of the reference librarian was virtually over.

On the other hand, research involving books, newspapers, and magazines were within the responsibilities of reference librarians, and digital collections of these types of publications may appear to have made researchers much more independent (but I will argue otherwise later). Whereas in the past, patrons depended on librarians and interlibrary loan to locate and borrow materials not locally owned, online catalogs, union catalogs, and ultimately *WorldCat* made local, regional, and national library holdings easier to search and items simpler to request. Prior to the web, librarians could provide remote access to rare books by purchasing microform collections, such as the *Early English Books* I and II (*EEBI* and *EEBII*), microform collections started in the 1930s and based on the extensive bibliographies, commonly called the *Short Title Catalog* (*STC*), of books published in England and its colonies between 1475 and 1700; the bibliographic volumes covering 1475–1640 were compiled by A. W. Pollard and G. R. Redgrave, and the subsequent *STC* covering 1641–1700 compiled by Donald Wing. The U.S. versions of these bibliographies are commonly referred to by their compilers (Evans and Shaw-Shoemaker), and cover the years 1640–1820. Access to these massive microform collections entailed consulting complex printed guides, which often required consultation with a librarian for interpretation of entries in order to view the collection.

Prior to the web, most academic libraries generally held few newspapers and their accompanying indexes, and access was typically via microform. At the University of Denver, we had indexes to and microform for the *New York Times*, *Wall Street Journal*, *Times of London*, and *Denver Post*. We could identify microfilm of other newspapers to be borrowed via interlibrary loan, but these often lacked indexes. Since the advent of the web, digital versions of full-text searchable newspapers, back to the seventeenth century and from around the world, are being produced, both commercially and freely available. Since the work done by William Frederick Poole in compiling *Poole's Index to Periodical Literature* in the late nineteenth century and the H. W. Wilson indexes launched at the turn of the twentieth century, periodicals, on the other hand, have been much more widely indexed, including scholarly, popular, and trade publications. Sadly, the once-innovative *Poole's* and Wilson periodical guides seem archaic in the web-based world of today, for even the electronic versions are bound by the limited original information and access points (citations organized by subject).

Microfilming projects, which provided librarians and researchers with surrogate access to original content, have actually been much more successfully migrated to the online environment, for the images can be digitized and the text OCR'd for full-text search capability. *Early English Books Online* (combining *EEBI* and *EEBII*), Evans's *Early American Imprints*, and Shaw Shoemaker, along with microfilm collections such as *British Periodicals* and *American Periodicals* have been (mostly) successfully migrated from film to digital format, and are viewable, if not entirely searchable, via web-based interfaces. (The qualifier *mostly* will be addressed below, in reference to the Spedding article.) The careful bibliographic work done by the compilers Pollard and Redgrave, Wing, Evans, and Shaw-Shoemaker have contributed to the quality of the searchable metadata describing each item.

However, not all microform collections have been digitized, and not all libraries can afford to purchase the plethora of commercial databases containing rare books, periodicals, newspapers, and other types of primary source materials. Microform readers were (and for those institutions without digital microform scanners, continue to be) difficult to use, and printouts problematic. Some microform collections were only available in a format no longer supported by technologies available to libraries, thus preventing access. In recent years, this seemingly dated form of access has been transformed by technology. Digital microform scanners, which can project almost any type of microform onto a computer screen, allow researchers to scan and create their own digital collections of primary source materials from microforms. Whereas in the past, only portions of newspaper pages could be printed at a time, new technologies permit whole pages to be scanned, and then software used to zoom in to specific parts of a page. These digital scanners are much more flexible in terms of the size of microform that can be viewed; in the past, it was difficult for music researchers in the United States to view scores that were filmed in European libraries, due to the differences in standards for creating microfilm facsimiles, but these types of obstacles have become less frustrating.

LITERATURE REVIEW: PRIMARY SOURCE RESEARCH IN THE DIGITAL AGE

There has been little mention about the role of reference librarians in researching digital primary source materials, and how this has broadened our areas of expertise, possibly because this skill has creeped in as more and more digital content became available. Turning to archivists, the profession that consistently offers reference services for primary source materials as part of their daily responsibilities, may provide guidance for approaching this type of query more systematically. Mary Jo Pugh explains that there are three important intellectual aspects of reference service in the archives: facilitating research, undertaking research, and educating users.[1] Because knowledge of one's archives is crucial for ensuring effective access, archivists must conduct research on their own collections. Most finding aids are standardized, but archives frequently have some that are not, and that lack of consistency requires mediation. Although each query, whether in person or remotely, is directly related to the collections, the questions vary widely. Many patrons have never visited an archive, so education, frequently on an individual basis, is necessary. As the archivist is the most knowledgeable person about a specific archive, the interactions between archivist and researcher require continual communication throughout the course of the project. The web, of course, is broadening the audience for archives as it is bringing more remote users to the archive through online finding aids and digital content, but the essential reference practices of archivists may identify ways for reference librarians to respond to queries for digital primary sources.

In the literature, scholars and librarians write about their experiences with digital primary source materials. Their insights about opportunities and challenges are useful for reference librarians, because we understand and can address the problems articulated. We have a repertoire of skill sets that can be broadened to mediate the needs of all levels of researchers who are navigating the digital landscape of primary sources. Each of the selected readings offered here is by authors who understand the foundational background and contexts of their area of interest, which is vital as they explain how the online environment can affect their research. Other technological factors discussed that either enhance or undermine success include: intended audiences of websites; diversity of search engines and organization; metadata; quality of images, OCR'd text, and transcriptions (PDF versus HTML); and comprehensiveness of the collection.

Nina Lager Vestberg, a professor of visual studies, analyzes and evaluates the methods used to make accessible two British photography collections: the Warburg Library and the Conway Library at the Courtauld Institute of Art.[2] Each institution had its own practices for organizing the physical photography collections. When the institutions began to create databases of digital versions of their collections, the Warburg designed its database for iconographers who are knowledgeable about their topic, while the Conway Library was designed by web developers more knowledgeable about the range of visitors, from art historians to the general public. The Warburg simply made a digital version of their analog collection for an audience of iconographers, while the Conway chose to make their interface more user friendly and more accessible to the general public. Although reference librarians familiarize themselves with different search interfaces and the scope of specific databases, when conducting research into a digital archive such as the Warburg Library, the importance of knowing the background of the institution and the development of the database informs how best to search its contents. Vestberg's example of searching for *arrows* as a keyword, in order to find images of St. Sebastian, the martyr shot to death with arrows, illustrates the limits of the metadata assigned and the narrowness of the intended audience, for this search does not successfully retrieve the images sought, although they are contained in the database. But she also acknowledges that searching for the essential components of an image has always been a dilemma, one that "is unlikely ever to be completely resolved, whether by technology or hermeneutics, because in the final analysis what activates meaning in any given image, as in any given archive, is the work of looking, searching and finding."[3] As a result of the decisions made about the organization, browsing is an essential strategy for searching the Warburg database, but the very nature of images makes any technical discovery solution unlikely—a continuing challenge for reference librarians and researchers alike.

Alexander Maxwell, a professor of history, offers feedback from a historian and a heavy user of digital content, comparing access to and quality of the digital collections of freely available content from a variety of libraries and institutions from around the world.[4] He notes frustrations with clunky interfaces and images that are slow to load and difficult to view in greater detail, and he considers the excellence of the *Google Books* search interface to be the standard to be achieved by all. He describes the importance of browsing for historians, even online, but is still concerned when content is only searchable using traditional categorization, which he believes is a barrier to the content. "Unprecedented technological advances can bring the unique materials of research libraries to new audiences, yet the dramatic pace of technological change may turn traditional expertise into a liability"[5] (which was also noted earlier in the discussions about *Poole's* and Wilson indexes). Maxwell's broad survey of the sites he visits regularly illustrates the wealth of information available, and sometimes found in unlikely places, such as his serendipitous discovery of an 1821 scan of *Wiburgs Mancherley* (a German-language magazine published in Vyborg, now in Russia), a title not found in *WorldCat* but unexpectedly found in Finland's *Historical Newspaper Library*.

Surveying both free and commercial resources available for the long eighteenth century (identified by the author as encompassing the English Restoration, the Enlightenment, and the Romantic era, roughly 1660–1830), Dr. Paddy Bullard, a senior lecturer in English, evaluates various types of tools and collections, and the challenges and opportunities they offer for researching primary source materials[6]: the *English Short Title Catalog*, which incorporates the *STC* mentioned above, and which he speculates could become "a hub for digitized content" for this era[7]; aggregators that allow cross-searching a range of sites to subject-specific databases (*The British Book Trade Index*); projects that bring together dispersed documents (*Newton Project*); and commercial databases (*British Periodicals, Eighteenth Century Collections Online*). Although both types of projects are valued by researchers, Bullard recommends to digital creators that "publicly funded academic projects must acquire the pragmatism and ambitiousness of scale that commercial developers have always shown [and that] commercial developers must adapt themselves more generously to the principles of scholarly openness and accuracy."[8] Patrick Spedding, also a lecturer in English, describes his frustrations with searching *Eighteenth Century Collections Online* (*ECCO*) for a particular word—*condom*—employing fuzzy searching to catch the variant spellings throughout the century.[9] Even using the Boolean *not* to eliminate nonrelevant references to the Bishop of Condom and fuzzy searching to catch alternative spellings, he wasn't successful at locating texts. When the term would have been used in the sense Spedding desired, printers would often substitute the word with a euphemism or even a series of dashes, which further frustrated his goal, for search engines have "no way of searching for such meaning-laden dashes."[10] In this case, the ability to browse texts easily and efficiently is crucial as well. Both Bullard and Spedding voiced concern with the lack of transparency by commercial publishers about the ways text is converted to optical character recognition (OCR) and searched, admittedly more of a problem for eighteenth-century scholars than for those conducting research during later eras when fonts were more standardized and easier for the technology to decipher. Because of Google's willingness to share the OCR'd text as well as the digital image, Spedding is able to illustrate why the OCR in *Google Books* causes a search to fail within a specific text, which is helpful to other eighteenth-century researchers. Spedding also questions if OCR can really be effective when the digital content is actually generated from microfilm, as is the case with *ECCO*, thus removing it twice from the original. Bullard praises careful transcription of facsimiles, where both versions are presented, while Maxwell also raises questions about transcribed, HTML text, rather than digital images, because the text is "mediated and unreliable."[11] Reference librarians are not able to solve these problems themselves, but we can communicate such concerns to commercial vendors, and we can take such issues into account when working with patrons using digital primary sources.

Two selected publications by librarians are helpful for understanding specific strengths of *Google Books* and *HathiTrust*. Eamon P. Duffy writes of the value the Library of Congress subject headings add to *HathiTrust* by allowing much more targeted searching for primary sources than is possible in most full-text databases.[12] Duffy compares keyword versus subject versus combined searches to illustrate how the subject headings help retrieve more relevant primary texts written between 1800 and 1914 for the topic "Peruvian guano mines." He laments the fact that participating institutions don't necessarily include subject headings as a matter of course when uploading records, and he recommends they be encouraged to do so in order to benefit researchers. Dália Leonardo describes her research process and presents an annotated bibliography of early modern era, secular, visually rich, foreign-language books that have been digitized and made available in *Google Books*.[13] Leonardo concludes that *Google Books* is an invaluable resource for primary source research, for it "offers unprecedented access to works in the public domain in a variety of languages and fields of study,"[14] and she incorporates this resource into her instruction and individual research consultations as a means of discovering primary sources.

In their study to determine what it takes to be a good reference librarian today, Trina J. Magi and Patricia E. Mardeusz determine eight categories of necessary skills, knowledge, and experience, including "knowledge about reference sources and their effective use."[15] In this category they describe a consultation for primary source materials, in which the patron did not want to pay for access to particular parole board transactions involving the Charles Bronson murders: "After consulting both bibliographic tools and free Web resources, together with Google and YouTube, the librarian ultimately located through WorldCat a documentary film that contained parole hearing testimony."[16] Perhaps librarians should explore opportunities for purchasing access to required digital primary sources in such cases.

Reference librarians have long developed skills to search both deeply and broadly for relevant resources on topics, and these skills are precisely what enable us to expand our reach to include research for and within digital primary source materials. We understand the scope and limitations of databases; have knowledge of the breadth and types of free and commercial databases available; develop, hone, and maintain the skills necessary for searching across a variety of platforms; and evaluate the quality of resources. Leveraging our expertise, we conduct effective reference interviews to solicit keywords and use controlled vocabulary to execute a range of strategies in order to locate documents. In other words, we are uniquely poised to provide substantive, mediated reference service into the world of digital primary sources, in the way that archivists and special collections librarians offer assistance to their patrons to delve deeply into the physical archives. With the complexity of research for primary source materials, longer consultations rather than short reference desk interactions are essential.

FACILITATING PRIMARY SOURCE RESEARCH IN THE DIGITAL AGE

Although mediated research for primary sources in the digital age will probably not reach the intense levels of continual interactions with patrons throughout the research process as occurs in the physical archives, or the depth of knowledge individual archivists have for their collections, the reference librarian can appropriate some of the components of reference service as practiced by archivists: facilitating research, undertaking research, and educating users.

Educating Ourselves

As mentioned above, the University of Denver Libraries offer a wealth of digital content to their community, and load or harvest MARC records for freely available online materials. It is difficult for the reference librarians at our institution, let alone the faculty and students, to remember everything that is available to us commercially; including freely available resources beyond those in our catalog into the mix can be even more overwhelming. But not all digital collections have MARC records to the level that would reveal individual parts of collections. For example, we have records for the main components of *ProQuest History Vault*, but not for the individual collections of the personal and organizational papers. In a mediated consultation with a graduate student who was conducting primary source research on the Civil Rights movement and who wanted to use the letters and papers of Bayard Rustin, I overlooked the fact that some of Rustin's papers, physically located in the Library of Congress, are digitally available in *History Vault*; the records in the library catalog were insufficient, for in the words of archivists, we have collection-level records, not item-level records. It isn't always enough to know just the scope of the resource; it is necessary for reference librarians to conduct research on our own digital primary source collections in order to know the contents at a much deeper level. In addition, it becomes our responsibility to educate ourselves on how to search for freely available digital collections and navigate institutional websites and databases, so that, if faced with a query the local collections can't satisfy, we can turn to the external digital world.

Mediating Research and User Education

Academic reference librarians are largely tasked with educating our patrons in the research process in order to create generations of lifelong learners, so, even when facilitating primary source inquiries, teaching the researcher is part of the process. Research inquiries for primary source materials are highly individualized, and may require surrogates that are available through commercial or freely available digital collections, or that might be published as scholarly editions or available as facsimiles in microform. If no surrogate is available, then a visit to the physical archives themselves could be required. Although some researchers have experience with archival research, many patrons perhaps have not delved into digital primary source databases and may not understand what they will or won't find, how to search effectively and navigate to or view documents, or even understand what it is that they are finding. The reference librarian consultation with any level of user experience becomes part mediation and part education. This involves communicating in order to provide verbal guidance about our own thought processes as we work together through the problem, so the patron understands why we are taking the various routes to find materials. Working closely together, the reference librarian and researcher can brainstorm what types of primary sources will be required for a project, determine if the local commercial databases might contain relevant documents, and identify institutions that may have special collections or archives of interest as well as collaborative projects in which digital collections have been created. Generating a list of keywords must include not only today's terminology and subject headings but also the words and phrases used during the time being explored, even if the words are considered offensive or archaic today, or if no standard word or phrase existed. For example, according to the *Oxford English Dictionary*, *silk road* came into being sometime early in the twentieth century (although a search on *silk road* and *silk route* in *Google Books*, limited to the nineteenth century, did retrieve some earlier references), so a scholar working on that topic in an era prior to the creation of the phrase will have to determine what words to search instead. It is therefore clear that the consultation also requires discussions about the limitations of keyword searching. Commercial databases developed by major publishers such as Gale, ProQuest, and Adam Matthew may have search interfaces that are familiar to researchers, but because the content for each primary source database can be so unique, it is best if search engine interfaces are discussed in the consultation in terms of the primary source materials offered and a variety of search strategies employed.

I argue here that digital collections have not necessarily made researchers completely independent. In searching *British Periodicals* for articles written by a specific Victorian literary critic, the familiar ProQuest interface lulled a faculty researcher into thinking a straightforward author search should work, but it didn't. She knew the topic discussed in the articles and she knew the publications, but couldn't find what she needed. This is when the reference interview is vital, in order to tease out background information about events and people. In this case, background information about publishing practices at the time and about the subject being researched is essential, in order to understand the effectiveness of typical searching. If searching by author, which publications, if any, offered signed articles? Although *British Periodicals* does incorporate the *Wellesley Index to Victorian Periodicals, 1824–1900* author attributions, those only account for a portion of the journals in this database, and anonymous articles were the norm rather than the exception. (An aside: if searching *British Periodicals* as part of the entire *C19: The Nineteenth Century Index [C19]* for an author, it is important to realize that *Poole's* uses initials for authors' first names; as mentioned above, *Poole's*, although innovative at the time, is bound by the limited information captured at that time, so both the full name and the surname with initial must be searched in *C19* to find references in *British Periodicals* as well as *Poole's*.) If the articles can't be found through a direct approach, then other strategies come into play. Does the patron know what topics the individual wrote about and/or in which periodicals he was published and/or during which years? If so, that knowledge can direct the next steps. If not, traditional reference tools can be consulted. Does a bibliography to the author's writings exist? Is there a biography about the author, perhaps in the *Oxford Dictionary of National Biography*, that might indicate in which journals he published? Once more information about the background and context is established, alternative strategies can be employed, such as searching for any articles in *British Periodicals* that are identified in an author-centered bibliography, or searching or browsing a particular periodical for articles. It is here that a weakness of *British Periodicals* emerges: although citations for articles within an issue of a journal can be displayed, there is no way to actually browse an issue page by page, which is frustrating for researchers who have to or prefer to employ this type of strategy.

There are a variety of strategies for searching primary source materials that are part of open-access projects. Generally, locating a specific institution is a good first step. Reference librarians use standard reference tools, such as OCLC's *WorldCat* and its freely available *ArchiveGrid*, to search for archives in the United States and around the world, and then, once identified, to search the websites for specific institutions for digital collections. But standard research tools such as those from OCLC are not comprehensive, and they don't necessarily search for various types of primary source materials, such as images or freely available digital collections. If searching for primary source materials from other countries, finding national websites is helpful for discovering digitizing projects for a country's primary source materials, from sound to images to newspapers to the letters and papers of prominent historical figures. Together, the reference librarian and researcher can identify potential institutions that might offer digital content, such as national libraries and archives. For example, digital surrogates of newspapers, objects, maps, video, images, and more are available via the Bibliothèque Nationale de France's *Gallica*, which also allows searching for digital content available through other French institutions. *Gallica* would be worth searching with students in need of digital surrogates of ephemera for a French course on World War I, or for maps of pre- and post-Haussmann Paris. Many countries have their own instance of Google. During a consultation with a student, a search in images.google.com for details of the nineteenth-century statue of Giordano Bruno by Ettore Ferrari, located in Campo di Fiori in Rome, was not fruitful, but a search on *statua di Giordano Bruno* in the images section of the Italian google.it found not just images of the sculpture itself, but details for every section of the sculpture. These are just two sample strategies for extending searches beyond traditional reference tools and the limits of Google.

RECOMMENDATIONS

As well as acknowledging how reference librarian skill sets ideally benefit researchers seeking primary source materials, how can we can broadcast information about our expertise and collections? In addition to leveraging the librarians' reference skills to expand services to encompass primary sources, some potential recommendations that emerge from the discussion above are:

Determine the needs for primary sources at your institution, and communicate how the reference librarians can facilitate research to the faculty:

1. Identify courses that would benefit from incorporating primary source materials.
2. Identify commercial databases the library holds that contain potentially useful primary sources.
3. Create research guides to commercial and freely available websites of primary source materials that support the curriculum.
4. Collaborate with the archivist or special collections curator at your institution to educate patrons about both physical and digital primary source materials and ways to use them in research.
5. Determine if and how in-depth consultations can be incorporated in a sustainable way into reference services.

Ensure digital primary source collections and their parts can be found in the library catalog or via other library discovery tools:

1. Load MARC records.
2. If no individual MARC records are available, then, if possible, tag the records with keywords that will retrieve items within the collections.

Explore ways to provide access to primary source materials not held by the library:

1. If commercial databases are too expensive, consider purchasing a microform scanner for your patrons, so that existing microform versions of desired content can be digitized by the researcher.
2. If there is potential to purchase or subscribe to a database that would benefit a specific patron's primary source needs, request a trial in order to work with the patron, which is an excellent way to learn the strengths and weaknesses of a resource.
3. If desired documents are behind a pay wall, develop strategies for providing access to the researcher, such as creating a fund to pay for such documents.
4. Develop strategies for discovering freely available content via Google and other web search engines, national libraries and archives, and collaborative open access projects.
5. If no print, microform, or digital versions of the materials exist, identify locations where the materials (may) reside, and explore the website for that institution or organization for finding aids and contact information. (Would negotiating with the other institution, to either create digital surrogates or even borrow the physical materials, be possible?)

CONCLUSION

In her survey of the literature on the future of mediated reference in the archives in the unmediated web environment, Sigrid McCausland notes: "Online access to finding aids and to records themselves has been a reality since the 1990s, but archival reference practice seems to have shifted slightly and slowly rather than significantly."[17] In the case of reference librarians, we do not appear to have recognized that there has been a change for us, and that our service responsibilities have broadened to include in-depth research into digital primary sources. By acknowledging the shift, there is much we can contribute by engaging with researchers to identify, locate, and use digital primary source materials.

NOTES

1. Mary Jo Pugh, *Providing Reference Services for Archives & Manuscripts* (Chicago: Society of American Archivists, 2005), 24–27.
2. Nina Lager Vestberg, "Ordering, Searching, Finding," *Journal of Visual Culture* 12 (2013): 472–89.

3. Ibid., 484.
4. Alexander Maxwell, "Digital Archives and History Research: Feedback from an End-User," *Library Review* 59, no. 1 (2010): 24–39.
5. Ibid., 33.
6. Paddy Bullard, "Digital Humanities and Electronic Resources in the Long Eighteenth Century," *Literature Compass* 10, no. 10 (2013): 748–60.
7. Ibid., 750.
8. Ibid., 756.
9. Patrick Spedding, "'The New Machine': Discovering the Limits of ECCO," *Eighteenth-Century Studies* 44, no. 4 (2011): 437–53.
10. Ibid., 445.
11. Maxwell, "Digital Archives and History Research," 27.
12. Eamon P. Duffy, "Searching HathiTrust: Old Concepts in a New Context," *Partnership: The Canadian Journal of Library and Information Practice and Research* 8, no. 1 (2013): 1–13.
13. Dália Leonardo, "Google Books: Primary Sources in the Public Domain," *Collection Building* 31, no. 3 (2012): 103–7.
14. Ibid., 103.
15. Trina J. Magi and Patricia E. Mardeusz, "What Students Need from Reference Librarians: Exploring the Complexity of the Individual Consultation," *C&RL News* 74, no. 6 (June 2013): 288–91.
16. Ibid., 289.
17. Sigrid McCausland, "A Future without Mediation: Online Access, Archivists, and the Future of Archival Research," *Australian Academic & Research Libraries* 42, no. 4 (2011): 312.

BIBLIOGRAPHY

Bullard, Paddy. "Digital Humanities and Electronic Resources in the Long Eighteenth Century." *Literature Compass* 10, no. 10 (2013): 748–60.
Duffy, Eamon P. "Searching HathiTrust: Old Concepts in a New Context." *Partnership: The Canadian Journal of Library and Information Practice and Research* 8, no. 1 (2013): 1–13.
Leonardo, Dália. "Google Books: Primary Sources in the Public Domain." *Collection Building* 31, no. 3 (2012): 103–7.
Magi, Trina J., and Patricia E. Mardeusz. "What Students Need from Reference Librarians: Exploring the Complexity of the Individual Consultation." *C&RL News* 74, no. 6 (June 2013): 288–91.
Maxwell, Alexander. "Digital Archives and History Research: Feedback from an End-User." *Library Review* 59, no. 1 (2010): 24–39.
McCausland, Sigrid. "A Future without Mediation: Online Access, Archivists, and the Future of Archival Research." *Australian Academic & Research Libraries* 42, no. 4 (2011): 309–19.
Pugh, Mary Jo. *Providing Reference Services for Archives & Manuscripts.* Chicago: Society of American Archivists, 2005.
Spedding, Patrick. "'The New Machine': Discovering the Limits of ECCO." *Eighteenth-Century Studies* 44, no. 4 (2011): 437–53.
Vestberg, Nina Lager. "Ordering, Searching, Finding." *Journal of Visual Culture* 12 (2013): 472–89.

Index

About the Contributors

Consuella Askew is currently associate dean for Public Services at Florida International University Libraries. Throughout her twenty years as a librarian and administrator, she has worked in a variety of library environments: school, academic, and public. She also spent several years working with the Associate of Research Libraries LibQUAL+ program. She received her MLIS from the University of North Carolina at Greensboro and her EdD in Higher Education from Florida International University.

Eileen K. Bosch is an associate professor and library instruction coordinator at Bowling Green State University (BGSU), where she provides library instruction and reference services in Spanish and Portuguese. She also coordinates library programs for international students. She has published and presented at several national and international conferences on topics related to diversity and mentoring, international students, and library services to minorities. Eileen has previously worked at California State University, Long Beach, as an Associate Librarian. She holds a MLIS degree from Kent State University and a Master Degree in Education from Bowling Green State University.

Kawanna Bright is the head of Information and Research Services at the Florida International University, Green Library. She is a 2003 graduate of the University of Washington, iSchool. Kawanna has previously held positions as a Minority Resident Librarian (UTK), an Instructional Services Librarian (UTK and NCSU), and as a head of Information Services and Student Engagement (UTSA). She is a former president (2010–2011) of the American Library Association Library Instruction Roundtable. Kawanna's research interests include reference and information services, information literacy and library instruction, leadership and management issues, and diversity in libraries.

Matthew P. Ciszek is an associate librarian at the Penn State University Libraries and the head of the Lartz Memorial Library at Penn State Shenango. Matt has been a librarian for over fifteen years and has worked in library automation, access services, and library management for various library vendors and academic libraries. His research interests include LGBT issues in academic libraries, diversity in higher education, marketing and promotion in libraries, library leadership and administration, and collection development and assessment.

Danielle M. Colbert-Lewis, MLIS, reference librarian at the James E. Shepard Memorial Library at North Carolina Central University, holds an MLIS degree from the University of Pittsburgh, an MAEd degree in Education Leadership and Policy Studies from Virginia Tech, and a BA degree in Anthropology from the University of Virginia. As a reference librarian, Ms. Colbert-Lewis instructs classes for diverse populations of students, faculty, and staff. Her research interests cover mentoring new librarians, trends in libraries, legal issues in librarianship, and higher education.

Kathleen Collins is the coordinator of reference services for the Odegaard Undergraduate Library at the University of Washington, where she is currently working to integrate research help services and writing tutoring in the Odegaard Writing and Research Center. In her spare work time she serves as UW Seattle's sociology subject librarian, selects materials for the children's and young-adult literature collections, co-chairs the libraries' citation tools team, and has just joined the libraries' assessment committee. Reach Kathleen at collinsk@uw.edu.

Angela Courtney is the head of the Arts and Humanities Department and the Reference Services Department at the Indiana University Bloomington Libraries. She is also the librarian for English literature and theater. She is coeditor of the *Victorian Women Writers Project*, the author of *Literary Research and the Era of American Nationalism and Romanticism*, and coauthor of *Literary Research and the Literatures of Australia and New Zealand* and *Literary Research and Postcolonial Literatures in English* in the Scarecrow Press series: Literary Research: Strategies and Sources. She edited the *Dictionary of Literary Biography: 19th-Century British Dramatists* volume.

Michael Courtney is the outreach and engagement librarian and the librarian for online learning at Indiana University Bloomington. Michael is also an adjunct faculty member in the Department of Information and Library Science, School of Informatics and Computing, Indiana University. He has written about transformations in academic reference librarianship as well as the impact of discovery systems on student learning. Michael is currently researching outdoor picture gardens in mid-twentieth-century Western Australia.

Lori Driver is the interim head of government documents at Florida International University Libraries. She received a BA in Business Management with a concentration in Human Resources from American Intercontinental University in 2006, and a Master of Library and Information Science from the University of South Florida in 2009. Upon completion of her MLIS, Lori accepted the position as the government documents librarian and most recently, interim department head of government documents. Along with being the government documents librarian, Lori is also the political science liaison to the university's School of International and Public Affairs.

Ellie Dworak serves as reference services coordinator at Albertsons Library, Boise State University, where she manages the library's LibAnswers service alongside other in-person and online reference projects. Recent initiatives include guiding reference staff in developing a shared set of best practices for reference service with assessment strategies; analyzing and coding LibQual+ data to identify larger trends as well as unit- and service-level reports; and mining LibAnswers statistics and query records to identify improvements. Ellie is fascinated by the shifting space where information and users meet, and on optimizing that experience without sacrificing the rich complexity of the information/knowledge universe.

Li Fu is the head of Access and Outreach Services and faculty librarian in University of San Diego. She is an outreach librarian for nonacademic units on/off campus. She holds MLIS and MA degrees and has completed doctoral courses in Organizational Leadership. She has published two book chapters in *Academic Libraries in the United States for the 21st Century: Theories and Practice*: chapter 11, "Web Technologies in Libraries," and chapter 12, "Library Systems"; and a journal article in the *Information Technology Outreach* in the UIC Library. She has also presented at various national/international conferences. You can reach her at lif@sandiego.edu.

Merinda Kaye Hensley is the instructional services librarian and assistant professor at the University of Illinois at Urbana-Champaign. She is also the co-coordinator of the Scholarly Commons, a library unit that serves the emerging research and technology needs of scholars in data services, digital humanities, digitization, and scholarly communication. She served as a member of ACRL's Student Learning and Information Literacy Committee and the Information Literacy Standards Revision Task Force. She earned her Bachelor of Arts in Political Science from the University of Arizona and a Master of Science in Library Science from the University of Illinois at Urbana-Champaign. Find her online at www.library.illinois.edu/people/bios/mhensle1.

Peggy Keeran is the arts and humanities reference librarian and holds the rank of professor on the University of Denver Libraries faculty. She is the coeditor for Scarecrow Press's Literary Research: Strategies and Sources and coauthor of three of the series' volumes: *British Romantic Era, British Renaissance and Early Modern Era*, and *British Eighteenth Century*. She is also coeditor of the second edition of *Research within the Disciplines: Foundations for Reference and Library Instruction*. She has an MLIS in Library Science and an MA in Art History from the University of California, Berkeley.

Corinne Laverty, PhD, is head of the education library, teaching and learning specialist at Queen's University Library, and educator-in-residence at the Centre for Teaching and Learning at Queen's University. Her research interests focus on the development and assessment of information literacy in higher education in face-to-face, blended, and online courses. She provides support for faculty and librarians on the design of effective research assignments, systematic development of information literacy skills, and inquiry-based learning assessment. In her role as education librarian, she creates resource-based learning experiences for teacher candidates and mentors students in graduate education studies.

Elizabeth A. Lee, PhD, is associate professor of language and literacy, faculty of education, Queen's University, Canada. Her research interests are information literacy, school libraries, adolescent literacy, and graphic novels. In 2009 she was co-investigator for the Ontario Library Association's research study of Exemplary School Libraries in Ontario. Her current research focus is information literacy at the tertiary and post-graduate level that includes an international collaboration with colleagues in Hong Kong and Singapore. She teaches graduate and teacher education courses in cognition, reading, children's literature, adolescent literacy, and language arts.

Melanie Maksin is the librarian for political science, international affairs, public policy, and government information at Yale University. In addition to her subject-specialist responsibilities, she also coordinates liaison program outreach to graduate students across the Yale libraries and leads the Reference, Instruction, and Outreach Committee. She holds a BA in history from Swarthmore College and an MLIS from the University of Pittsburgh, and in

2011 she participated in ACRL's Information Literacy Immersion Program (Teacher Track). Melanie has presented on and written about instruction and outreach strategies related to government information and other primary sources.

Valeria E. Molteni is an assistant professor at the MLK Library, San José State University. She has a licensure in librarianship and documentation from the National University of Mar del Plata, Argentina, and a MSIS from UT Austin. She has published and presented at national and international conferences on scientometrics, bibliometrics, evaluation of higher education systems, and services for minorities and international students in academic libraries. In the United States, she worked at the Benson Collection at University of Texas, Austin; and her previous position was as the Multicultural and Outreach Librarian at the University Library, CSU Dominguez Hills.

Carrie Moore is the head of information and research services/assistant professor at Albertsons Library, Boise State University. Carrie received her MLS in 2002 from Emporia State University. She focuses on instruction, reference, and outreach services in her position. Her projects range from designing library curriculum that is uniformly taught to every first- and second-year student to working with faculty on new mobile learning initiatives. She is actively working on projects to incorporate mobile devices into library instruction sessions.

David J. Rachlin, MLIS, reference librarian at the James E. Shepard Memorial Library at North Carolina Central University, holds an MLIS degree from the University of North Carolina–Greensboro and a BA degree in History from Rutgers University. As a reference librarian, Mr. Rachlin instructs library users on research strategies, best demonstrated practices for information seeking, and the nuances of academic database searching. Mr. Rachlin's research interests cover information literacy, best practices of librarianship, bridging the digital gap for students of underrepresented cultural and economic backgrounds, and copyright issues in secondary and postsecondary education.

Deb Raftus is the University of Washington Libraries' liaison to the French and Italian Studies, Spanish and Portuguese Studies, and the Latin American and Caribbean Studies programs in Seattle, Washington. She also mentors and supervises future librarians (current MLIS students) in reference and instruction services. Deb has presented and written about reference services, digital humanities, international acquisitions, and research assignment design. Deb holds a BA and an MA in French, and she's currently tackling Spanish. Find her online at: http://guides.lib.washington.edu/draftus.

Jamillah Scott-Branch is the head reference librarian at North Carolina Central University in Durham, NC. In this role, she manages the library's instruction and outreach initiatives as well as interlibrary loan, and is responsible for identifying emerging technologies that can be incorporated into library services. Previously, she served as the Technology and Media Services Librarian at Elizabeth City State University in Elizabeth City, NC. She holds a Master in Library Science from North Carolina Central University.

Christine Tobias is a user experience and reference librarian at Michigan State University Libraries, where she has served as the virtual reference (VR) manager since 2008. She is also the quality-control manager for Research Help Now, a cooperative VR service for academic libraries in Michigan. Christine is currently serving as the co-chair for the Reference Services Section (RSS) VR Tutorial Subcommittee for the American Library Association (ALA) and has made presentations on a variety of reference topics at state and national conferences, most recently at the Reference Research Forum at the ALA Annual Conference 2013.

Zara Wilkinson is a reference librarian at the Camden campus of Rutgers University. At Rutgers-Camden, she is liaison to the Departments of English, Fine Arts, Philosophy, and Religion. In addition to reference and bibliographic instruction, Zara participates in a number of outreach activities, including roving reference in the residence halls and the library's robust social media presence. Zara received her MLIS from the University of Pittsburgh in 2010. She has also earned a BA in English Literature from the University of Pittsburgh and an MA in English Literature from West Chester University.